Mysticism

in

Christianity

Contents: What is Mysticism; The Mystical Element in the Gospel and Epistles; The Montanists, The Gnostics, and the Alexandrines; Neo-Platonism; The Influence of Neo-Platonism in Christianity; Three Types of Medieval Mysticism; The German Mystics of the Middle Ages; English, Italian, Spanish, and French Mystics; Post Reformation Mysticism in England; Puritan Mystics; Jacob Boehme and William Law; Modern Mysticism; Bibliography, Index.

W.K. Fleming

ISBN 1-56459-577-3

EDITOR'S GENERAL PREFACE

IN no branch of human knowledge has there been a more lively increase of the spirit of research during the past few years than in the study of Theology.

Many points of doctrine have been passing afresh through the crucible; "re-statement" is a popular cry and, in some directions, a real requirement of the age; the additions to our actual materials, both as regards ancient manuscripts and archaeological discoveries, have never before been so great as in recent years; linguistic knowledge has advanced with the fuller possibilities provided by the constant addition of more data for comparative study; cuneiform inscriptions have been deciphered, and forgotten peoples, records, and even tongues, revealed anew as the outcome of diligent, skilful and devoted study.

Scholars have specialized to so great an extent that many conclusions are less speculative than they were, while many more aids are thus available for arriving at a general judgment; and, in some directions at least, the time for drawing such general conclusions, and so making practical use of such specialized research, seems to have come, or to be close at hand.

Many people, therefore, including the large mass of the parochial clergy and students, desire to have in an accessible form a review of the results of this flood of new light on many topics that are of living and vital interest to the Faith; and, at the same time, "practical" questions—by which is really denoted merely the application of faith to life and to the needs of the day—have certainly lost none of their interest, but rather loom larger than ever if the Church is adequately to fulfil her Mission.

It thus seems an appropriate time for the issue of a new series of theological works, which shall aim at presenting *a general survey* of the present position of thought and knowledge in various branches of the wide field which is included in the study of divinity.

▼

The Library of Historic Theology is designed to supply such a series, written by men of known reputation as thinkers and scholars, teachers and divines, who are, one and all, firm upholders of the Faith.

It will not deal merely with doctrinal subjects, though prominence will be given to these; but great importance will be attached also to history—the sure foundation of all progressive knowledge—and even the more strictly doctrinal subjects will be largely dealt with from this point of view, a point of view the value of which in regard to the "practical" subjects is too obvious to need emphasis.

It would be clearly outside the scope of this series to deal with individual books of the Bible or of later Christian writings, with the lives of individuals, or with merely minor (and often highly controversial) points of Church governance, except in so far as these come into the general review of the situation. This detailed study, invaluable as it is, is already abundant in many series of commentaries, texts, biographies, dictionaries and monographs, and would overload far too heavily such a series as the present.

The Editor desires it to be distinctly understood that the various contributors to the series have no responsibility whatsoever for the conclusions or particular views expressed in any volumes other than their own, and that he himself has not felt that it comes within the scope of an editor's work, in a series of this kind, to interfere with the personal views of the writers. He must, therefore, leave to them their full responsibility for their own conclusions.

Shades of opinion and differences of judgment must exist, if thought is not to be at a standstill—petrified into an unproductive fossil; but while neither the Editor nor all their readers can be expected to agree with every point of view in the details of the discussions in all these volumes, he is convinced that the great principles which lie behind every volume are such as must conduce to the strengthening of the Faith and to the glory of God.

That this may be so is the one desire of Editor and contributors alike.

W. C. P.

LONDON 1911.

PREFACE

THE object of the following pages is to provide an introduction to the study of mystical thought as it has developed itself within the confines of the Christian Faith. Interest in Mysticism has in recent times become so pronounced and wide-spread that it is hoped that, even amongst the various and excellent works which have appeared in response to that interest, room may perhaps be found for an attempt to present the subject in its historical sequence, and in such a form as may best meet the wants of the general reader. My grateful thanks are due to the Dean of St. Paul's, by whose kind permission I am enabled to quote, amongst the definitions of Mysticism given, several of those which he has collected in Appendix A of his "Christian Mysticism", as well as to avail myself generally of the help afforded by his invaluable works on the subject; and, amongst other works consulted, I wish to express my special indebtedness to Baron von Hügel's "Mystical Elements in Religion", Professor Rufus Jones' "Studies in Mystical Religion", Miss Underhill's "Mysticism", and Fr. Sharpe's recent book, "Mysticism: Its True Nature and Value".

W. K. FLEMING.

January, 1913.

CONTENTS

ix

x   ·   CONTENTS

MYSTICISM IN CHRISTIANITY

CHAPTER I

What is Mysticism?

NOT many years ago some apology would have been needed for an attempt to sketch the history and development of the spiritual experience and doctrines of Mysticism in the life of Christianity. Of late years, however, the sound of the word Mysticism has been much in the air. After long neglect, scarcely broken by the appearance of Vaughan's cross-grained, but well-informed and useful "Hours with the Mystics," interest in them and their teaching has re-awakened with a vengeance. Dean Inge's invaluable Bampton Lectures, which at present may be said to constitute the necessary text-book on the subject, Miss Underhill's copious and intimate work "Mysticism," and Baron von Hügel's commentary on the life of St. Catherine of Genoa, have been accompanied by a long series of lesser books, good, bad, and indifferent, dealing with special aspects of the same theme, or working it out through its biographical features. This sudden output of mystical books is a striking phenomenon, if we look on it in the light of supply answering demand. It indicates a certain state of the public mind, a desire—rather restless and incoherent, it is true, but still a desire—for the essential truths of life and the mysteries that underlie its surface. It shews in some degree a reaction from materialism and such vogues as the gospel of "push." Of course the character of the supply is often far less satisfactory than the fact of the demand. All is not Mysticism that professes the name. But the true variety—what in Germany would be called " der Mystik ", as apart from " Mysticismus "—is well able to take care of itself and of its secret, even though its reputation may be injured by people who go by hearsay, or who mistake for it its degradations of emotionalism or fanaticism.

The truth is that the name Mysticism itself does need apology. It has labelled many things, and not all of them are good. The subject stands sorely in need of something like the German distinctions. " Isms " too often are noxious ; most are suspicious. They usually imply either the stiffening and stereotyping of some principle of life and conduct into a mechanical system, or its cheapening and debasement to lesser ends and uses. Or they suggest the sound of a " fad ". We find as a fact three accusations quite commonly brought against Mysticism, which correspond loosely to the disadvantages that attach to " isms " in general. These accusations are that Mysticism deals in unsafe and presumptuous speculation ; or that it encourages a sort of extravagant, unhealthy, hysterical self-hypnotism ; or that it is merely quasi-spiritual feeling, vague, dreamy and unpractical.

Perhaps we shall best begin by dealing with the last of these charges, for it will bring us to close quarters with our subject. That which is vague and dreamy is not usually susceptible of precise definition. Yet Mysticism has enjoyed and suffered—both are true—a large number of definitions. If we collect and examine some of these, it may be possible to construct a notion of what Mysticism is not, and what it is, and so to answer the other two objections.

Ewald says, " Mystical theology " . . . . " is the craving to be united again with God." Pfleiderer : " Mysticism is the immediate feeling of the unity of the self with God . . . the endeavour to fix the immediateness of the life in God as such, as abstracted from all intervening helps and channels whatsoever." Lasson : " It is the assertion of an intuition which transcends the temporal categories of the understanding. . . . Mysticism is not content with symbolic knowledge, and aspires to see the Absolute by pure spiritual apprehension." He adds, " Nothing can be more perverse than to accuse Mysticism of vagueness. Its danger is rather an overvaluing of reason and knowledge." We may take two French definitions, the first latently hostile, as is shewn by one question-begging term, the second weak through its tendency, common with French thinkers, to connect Mysticism with outward physical phenomena, but each in its way important. " Mysticism ", writes Victor Cousin, " is the pretension to know God without intermediary, and, so to speak, face to face. For Mysticism, whatever is between God and us hides Him from us." Ribet says, " It is a supernatural drawing of the soul towards God in which the soul is passive, resulting in an inward illumination and caress ; these supersede thought, surpass all human effort, and are able to have over the body an influence (retentissement) marvellous and irresistible." Coming to thinkers in our own midst, we find Professor Seth Pringle-Pattison writing, " The thought most intensely present to the mystic is that of a supreme, all pervading and indwelling Power, in Whom all things are one " [and] " the possibility of direct intercourse with this Being of beings ; . . God ceases to be an object, and becomes an experience." Professor Caird declares Mysticism to be " religion in its most concentrated and exclusive form ; it is the attitude of the mind in which all other relations are swallowed up in the relation of the

soul to God." [1]   The poet, Coventry Patmore, declares,
" What the world calls Mysticism is the science of ultimates
. . . the science of self-evident reality, which cannot. be
' reasoned about ' because it is the object of pure reason or
perception. The Babe . . . at its mother's breast and
the Lover . . . are the types and princes of mystics ".[2]
Valuable as coming from one who would not readily be suspected of sympathy with the mystical experience is Jowett's
definition.   " By mysticism we mean not the extravagance
of an erring fancy, but the concentration of reason in feeling,
the enthusiastic love of the Good, the True, the One."
Charles Kingsley introduces us to a considerable phase or
department of mysticism in one of his letters : " The great
Mysticism is the belief which is becoming every day stronger
with me that all symmetrical natural objects are types of
some spiritual truth or existence . . . all day glimpses of
that other world, floating motes from that inner transcendental life, have been floating over me . . . The earth is
the next greatest fact to that of God's existence ". This
approaches to ¦Récéjac's, " Mysticism is the tendency to
approach the Absolute morally, and by means of symbols ",
though the latter method can never be more than a tempera-
mental phase of Mysticism.

We cannot leave the field of definition, very partially
explored though not without a selective purpose, without
noticing Professor James' famous " four marks, which,
when an experience has them, may justify us in calling it
mystical ".[3] These are (1) Ineffability. The experience
cannot be imparted or transferred to another. Again to
quote Patmore, " By this you may know vision ; that it
is not what you expected, or even what you could have

[1] The above definitions are quoted from the interesting collection
cited by Dean Inge: *Christian Mysticism, Appendix A.*
[2] *The Rod, the Root, and the Flower,* p. 39.
[3] *Varieties of Religious Experience,* p. 380.

imagined : and that it is never repeated ". (2) Noetic quality.
" Mystical states are states of knowledge . . . and inarticu-
late as they remain, carry with them as a rule a curious sense
of authority for after-time ". To these he adds as lesser,
though usual, marks, (3) Transiency ; even memory can but
imperfectly reproduce such states, though when they recur
they are recognized—a vividly accurate bit of diagnosis ;
and (4) Passivity : the subject feels as if in the grasp of a
superior power. It is curious that Miss Underhill, in her
remarkable work on Mysticism, finds it necessary to raise
objections to these four " marks " of Professor James,[1]
which, although they do not constitute a complete analysis
of the mystical consciousness, are nevertheless authentic
characteristics so far as they go. It is surely needless,
for instance, for her to protest that " true mysticism
is active and practical, not passive and theoretical ". Every
true mystic would assert it to be both ; there is no contradiction between Professor James' " passivity " and the
working out—as its direct result, indeed,—of the most
practically beneficent of lives. As he says himself, " Mystical
states . . . modify the inner life ", and by consequence the
outer also, and so the history of the mystics is very largely
the history of practical workers and reformers. Then
again, Miss Underhill's statement that the mystic is in no
way concerned with the visible universe—" the mystic
brushes aside that universe even in its most supernormal
manifestations "[2]—would seem to be wholly beside the
mark The place that Symbolism has held in the system of
certain mystics, from St. John downwards, and the peculiar
snare of Mysticism, the temptation to Pantheism, are sufficient to disprove it. But Miss Underhill in her own final
analysis of the word echoes one important definition of
Mysticism already noticed, " it is the art of establishing

[1] E. Underhill : *Mysticism*, p. 96.   [2] *Ib.*

man's conscious relations with the Absolute " ; [1] she lays an
entirely right emphasis on it as " that organic process which
involves the perfect consummation of the Love of God " ;
and she adds one element of mysticism which may fairly be
claimed as its *differentia*, but which as debatable matter
must be discussed further on ; " the living union with the
One " is a process " entailing . . . the liberation of a new,
or rather latent, form of consciousness, which imposes on
the self the condition which is sometimes inaccurately called
' ecstasy ', but is better named the Unitive State ". [2]

It is fair to remember, in passing, that Mysticism has
been adversely defined as well, even by those who are under
none of the ordinary misapprehensions as to the meaning
of the term. Professor Seth Pringle-Pattison considers
Mysticism to be haunted by the peril of Pantheism, and to
issue naturally in Quietism. Victor Cousin criticises it as
substituting)' ecstasy for reason, rapture for philosophy ".
Harnack's dictum that " Mysticism is rationalism applied
to a sphere above reason " is probably well known, and
equally well known should be Dean Inge's comment that
the words " rationalism " and " reason " in the sentence
should be transposed. Again, Hermann and the Ritschlian
school in general are bitter against the mystics, and dis-
count internal experience of the Christ compared with the
Christ-picture presented to the mind by the Gospel-history.
That there is some ground for suspicion of the attitude adopted
by some mystics towards the historic Christ, and even with

---

[1] But it is singular again that in the same paragraph this writer
should assert that " mysticism is not a philosophy ". It is certainly
very much more than a philosophy, for, as Queen Christina of
Sweden observed, " Philosophy neither changes nor corrects a
man " ; but a philosophy, all the same, it cannot escape being.
Cf. Dean Inge, paraphrasing Van Hartmann (*Christian Mysticism*,
p. 337), " the relation of the individual to the Absolute, an essential
theme of philosophy, can only be mystically apprehended ".

[2] Underhill : *Mysticism*, p. 96.

regard to the Christ-fact itself, will be seen later. R. A. Vaughan, in his curious but indispensable book, snarls at the very thing that attracts him, as "that form of error which mistakes for Divine manifestation the operations of a merely human faculty". James Hinton tells us that Mysticism is "an assertion of a means of knowing that must not be tried by ordinary rules of evidence ; the claiming of authority for our own impressions". As for Vaughan, he somewhat lessened the force of his hostile verdict by recording, in a kind of fascinated fashion, all the operations of that "merely human faculty" whose nature by the way he never explains, and Hinton's words sound very like a claim on the part of the colour-blind to judge of the properties of red and green, a claim at least oblivious of the poet's words, "Nothing worthy proving can be proven, nor yet disproven".[1]

Now the definitions given will at least help us to dismiss from our minds the notion that Mysticism is a something nebulous and vague. Not that a mere number of definitions would do that of themselves. They might be mutually destructive by contradicting each other ; and we cannot fail to have noticed certain divergences of opinion even in those we have reviewed. But there is a striking repetition or agreement of ideas on certain points, and it is fair to construct out of these one or two important results as to the question : What is Mysticism ? First, we are enabled to dismiss wrong perceptions on the subject. (1) Mysticism is not equivalent to Symbolism merely, though certain mystics have employed Symbolic methods of teaching ; still less has it anything to do with Allegory. Bunyan was both a mystic and an allegorist, but his mysticism is deducible from the "Grace Abounding" rather than from the "Pilgrim's Progress". (2) Mysticism has nothing whatever to do with occult pursuits, magic and the like, although the

[1] Tennyson : *The Ancient Sage.*

successors of the great Plotinus, it is true, and others in later times, lost their way, and floundered into this particular morass. (3) Nor has it any connexion with miracle-working and the like ; for this mistake modern Roman Catholic hagiographies are largely responsible. (4) Although mystics have frequently had visions, and " vision " is a word of frequent and warrantable vogue amongst them, Mysticism is not the dreaming of dreams, not dreaminess at all in fact. The occurrence of visions was always assigned to a low place in the mystical scale of ascent, and was looked upon rather in the nature of an encouragement vouchsafed to beginners. Plotinus gave a definite sphere in his scale of spiritual advancement to the exercise of social and civic duties, and the German medieval mystic, Eckhart, ranked Martha above Mary on the mystical grade. Indeed, mystics have, more commonly than not, been known as very practical men and women.

Perhaps it is necessary to add one thing more. Some writers have so whittled away the significance of the term as to make it mean little, if anything, more than spirituality, of mind. But while every mystic is, at any rate potentially a spiritually minded person, every spiritually minded person is not by any means a mystic. What the some-thing more, or the something different may be, we must now try to discover.

I. The first important step we take by means of the word itself. For Mysticism has a close etymological connexion with the term " the Mysteries " applied to certain pagan initiations of the world of St. Paul's day. A mystic ($\mu\acute{\upsilon}\sigma\tau\eta\varsigma$) was one initiated into Divine things : he must keep his mouth shut ($\mu\acute{\upsilon}\epsilon\iota\nu$) about them, because the initiation was secret. Later, the idea came to be that his eyes were shut ; either, as the adjective $\mu\upsilon\sigma\tau\iota\kappa\grave{o}\varsigma$ implied, because the secret knowledge was discerned " as through a glass darkly ", and through symbols, or, in the Neo-Platonists' use of the expression, because, when rapt in contemplation, the eyes were closed to external things. The idea, as will be seen, passed over (bearing some false impressions in its transit) into the Christian Church ; indeed, our instinctive habit of closing the eyes in prayer quite definitely derives from it. A little mystical treatise of the fourteenth century, the *Theologia Germanica*, has a suggestive thought with regard to the two eyes with which nature has provided us. We are taught thereby, it tells us, that there are two sorts of vision, the outward and the spiritual. We, says the *Theologia*, have, as it were, to close one eye in order to focus clearly with the other, whichever kind of vision we choose ; only Christ could see all life, material and spiritual, whole and undistorted, with both eyes at once. To return to the Mysteries, which, through the Neo-Platonists and pseudo-Dionysius, exercised so marked an effect on the theology of the Medieval Church. There was one note common to all of them—Eleusinian, Bacchic, or Mithraic. They professed always to give an Experience, actual knowledge, actual power, actual life. Hence mystical doctrines, in their turn, are never merely speculative, in the ordinary sense of the word, even if they lead on to speculation.[1] In its essence Mysticism is experimental. It is, says Professor Rufus Jones, " religion in its most acute, intense, and living stage ".[2] " The mystic is a thorough-going empiricist ".[3] Every true mystic would say, " We speak that we do know : we testify to that we have seen ". It is an Experience all through, varying with the individual mystic, but having certain broad notes of teaching and of consent.

[1] " ' Speculative ' or Dogmatic Theology is like the theory of optics . . . mystical theology is the sight itself, with all that it involves of exercise and training. Speculative theology is a science ; mystical theology is an art." A. B. Sharpe : *Mysticism : Its True Nature and Value*, p. 7.

[2] *Studies in Mystical Religion*, p. 15.

[3] Josiah Royce : *The World and the Individual*, vol. i. p. 81.

An Experience of what ?

II. The mystic is athirst for God : is it too bold in this connexion to use the late Dr. Moberly's expression, in his " Atonement and Personality " and to say that he is " in love with God " ?   It is God who " ceases to be an object and becomes an experience ".   " Awareness of relation with God " is that to which he awakes ; " direct and intimate consciousness of the Divine Presence " that in which he dwells. But then he believes that this keen attraction, this God-fascination could never be his except by God's own enabling him to feel it.[1] " We love Him ", as St. John says, " because He first loved us ".   It is, from one point of view, on which all mystics from St. Bernard to Coventry Patmore have insisted, a love-mystery,—God's love to the soul, the soul's to God.   It is " in His light that we see light ", or, as Eckhart phrases it in a wonderful sentence, " The eye with which I see God is the same as that with which God sees me ".   Our love to God is part and proof of God's love to us.   " Theologia mystica ", as both Gerson and Bonaventura agree, " est animi extensio in Deum per amoris desiderium ".[2]

III. Therefore, because he is in love with the Divine, Immediacy of Communion is the mystic's longing.   " Mystical theology craves to be united again with God ", " to know God without intermediary and, as it were, face to face ".   That is natural ; the lover cannot bear anything to come betwixt himself and the beloved.   Like Browning's Johannes Agricola, " For I intend to get to God ; For 'tis to God I speed so fast, For in God's breast, my own abode, I

---

[1] Cf. Ottley's *Rule of Faith and Hope* (Library of Historic Theology), p. 214. " Mysticism is optimistic because it implies confidence in the infinite willingness of God to bestow what man is essentially capable of receiving ".

[2] " Mystical theology is the mental approach to God through the desire of love ".

lay my spirit down at last ". It is only right to say that this longing for immediate contact with the Divine had and has its dangers. It closely resembles at times the Asiatic passion for absorption, and faintly suggests not seldom the image of the moth and the candle-flame. Some of the Christian mystics, again, are found confessing to the temptation to " get past " the Cross, and, leaving Christ on one side, to reach the Father. Julian of Norwich is amongst these ; the counteracting fact is that there would have been no Christian Mysticism—and the Christian Faith is the surest and most natural home of Mysticism—had this temptation not been always and strenuously resisted, and the Mystical Way of discipline, purgative and practical, evolved and tested as the true and only safe approach to the communion so ardently desired. " Without holiness no man shall see the Lord ".

IV. But this longing for contact with the Absolute led directly to a repeated emphasis of belief in the One-ness of God, as the " supreme, all-pervading, and indwelling power," of " enthusiastic love of the Good, the True, the One ". This, of course, was no more than an affirmation of the central doctrine of the Christian Faith, but nevertheless it was an assertion of inestimable value for the untutored Europe of the Middle and early-Middle Ages. It was there, precisely, that this particular emphasis was needed. The West never had the instinct for the One—the Absolute—which, with all its exaggerations, has been the vital witness of the East, and its gift to the world, and which made Mohammedanism, in one aspect of its origin, a Christian sect in revolt against degradations of Christian belief.

V. To this root-conviction, its legacy from, and link with the East, the mystics added the corollary of belief in the unity of all existence in God, the belief that behind all apparent divergence, contradiction, or duality, lies a synthesis, a resolution at last. This made them glorious optimists ; God

is in all, and all is in God.   As St. Bonaventura says,
" His centre is everywhere, His circumference nowhere ".
This certainly led towards such a " higher Pantheism "
as that of Tennyson's, " The seas, the hills, and the plains,
Are not these, O soul, the vision of Him Who reigns ? " And
the mystics would have said " Yes ".   But when it came to
the further question, " Is not the vision He ? " they would
have stopped short, and answered " No ".   For Nature, or
the Universe, is not the circumference of God.   Yet Nature
is full of God, and points to God.   With Kingsley, as we saw,
it is " the next greatest fact to that of God's existence ".   With
other, and older mystics, it was even more :   Erigena spoke
of " the Word of God, Who is the Nature of all things ".
In such minds there could rest no doubt as to the importance
of symbols in the gradual manifestation of truth.   Wholly
congenial to the methods of the East in imparting knowledge,—and Mysticism, it may be again recalled, took its
rise in the East—where the secrets of wisdom are not scattered carelessly broad-cast for every profane eye to rest
upon, and every heedless foot to spurn, Symbolism had
passed over to the West.   It had all the authority of the
Great Teacher Himself, and of the Fourth Evangelist ; but
it was also nourished and stereotyped by the means of its
transit.   The writings of Dionysius the Areopagite, from which
Western Mysticism received its first inspiration, regarded
Christianity somewhat in the light of " a Platonic mysteriosophy ".   They were indeed, for the most part, Neo-
Platonist reasonings, " slightly sprinkled with water from a
Christian font ".[1]   All the same, they, and the phase of
thought which they inculcated, helped indirectly to prepare
the way for the great school of Nature-Mysticism, which,
after the shock of the Reformation had displaced the con-

---

[1] Prof. Rufus Jones : *Mystical Religion*, p. 110 ; cf. H. Workman :
Christian Thought to the Reformation, p. 153.

ventional religious landmarks of centuries, obtained, and in
modern poetry still retains, so large a sway.

VI. But in the systematized mystical theology of the
later Medieval Church the world in which God is primarily
reflected was the world of the human soul. Henry More,
the Cambridge Platonist, summing up both sides of the
problem, said, " Nullus in microcosmo spiritus, nullus in
macrocosmo Deus ". Human personality is, or is meant to
be, the clearest mirror of God. To use St. James' words, it
is that in which a man looking can see τὸ πρόσωπον τῆς
γενέσεως αὐτοῦ, " the face of his genesis, his true birth ".
For " grace ", says Ruysbroek, " works from within out-
wards "; until even " landscape is a state of the soul '.
" Closer is He than breathing, and nearer than hands and
feet ", or, a sa Provençal mystic of the seventeenth century,
Antoine Yvan, daringly put it, " Aux amoureux de Dieu
avec Dieu, puisque Dieu est en nous, comme le blanc au
linge et à la neige, et comme la douceur au sucre et au miel, et
comme le chaleur au feu, et plus proche de nous que nous,
et plus nous que nous ".[1]

To many—to Tauler, for example, and the Cambridge
Platonists of the seventeenth century—the soul was a
universe in miniature (a microcosmus) in which the spiritual
Christ is born and suffers, is crucified, and rises again, the
experience of which Longfellow in his " Golden Legend "
makes Luther the mouthpiece :—

> . . . " The spiritual agonies,
> The inward deaths, the inward hell,
> And the divine new births as well,
> That surely follow after these,
> As after Winter follows Spring ".

We have then before us the facts of the mystical love-search

---

[1] Henri Brémond : *La Provence Mystique au XVII⁰ Siècle*, p. 10.

after God, and of the twin methods of finding the object of that search, symbolically through the world of outward Nature, and experimentally in the world of human nature. The search itself is the evocation of the higher, inward self, the substitution of that higher self for the lower, and the merging or losing—which, in mystical paradox, would be the true realization—of the individuality in God. Perhaps this is the not unfitting place to indicate two, and very opposite, dangers which have always beset the path of mystical progress. Are upward steps ever without danger of some corresponding fall ?

The first of these perilous tendencies of Mysticism was, as has been already hinted, towards Pantheism. The sense, strong in so many mystics, of the Eternal, glimmering or shining everywhere through the veil of the finite, led on to the temptation to identify Nature with God. This identification, when it becomes absolute, is what is known as Pantheism, and, of course, provides a short cut to the realization of the Divine Oneness. Like all short cuts, it has its fascinations, but, not unlike many short cuts, it soon lands its travellers in difficulties. It leads them, indeed, into a bog, and this bog is the necessary confusion or blurring of the distinction between Good and Evil. How explain the indubitable evil or imperfection or flawiness in Nature without either saying that it is not evil, whereby the moral intuitions are outraged, or else lowering the whole conception of the Divine Purity? There is no escape for the logical Pantheist from this dilemma, for the apparent deliverance from it, the assertion, with Browning, that evil " is naught, is null, is silence implying sound ", is the surrender of the Pantheistic for the Panentheistic position, a recognition, so far as the verdicts on Nature of human consciousness or knowledge are concerned, of the inevitability of God's transcendence, that is to say, if the moral standard is to be preserved. By Pantheism pure and simple the standard of

Good for the individual must be compromised in the long run.

In turning to the other danger that haunted Mysticism, one, too, that affected it far more nearly, we come upon a curious instance of the motion of the intellectual see-saw. What saved Mysticism from Pantheism was the strong sense, shared by all the mystics, of God's transcendence of any and every symbol, however eloquent. Many of them loved and valued the symbolic, but always either as a means of expression, or as a schooling for beginners. They could not think that the symbol in itself was the goal of conception and ideal. They were sure that the Reality infinitely outmeasured and overpassed its richest symbols ; for, by the very virtue of the origin and derivation of the mystical cultus, they were " after the Absolute ", and it was Immediacy of Communion with the Divine, and not a mediated contact, that they yearned for. The service of mystical theology in this respect to the Western Church, ever prone to matter-of-fact definition and a rather self-satisfied logic, can scarcely be over-rated. But to many of the mystics it had its own peculiar perils, even while the service rendered was of permanent value, and gained its strength from an undoubted truth. From the so-called Dionysius the Areopagite down to the end of the Middle Ages we find in full vogue amongst mystical thinkers what is known as the Negative method of approach to God—the *Via Negativa*. It is the opposite pole of thought to Pantheism. Instead of piling up all the symbols within reach, it was felt so strongly that nothing could really express, or be worthy to express, God, that, with the object of reaching Him, the mind was deliberately stripped of every earthly likeness, or analogy, or symbol, of His Being. So St. Augustine taught. " We must not even call God ineffable ",[1] he says, or rather quotes, " since this is to make an

[1] *De Trin.* vii. 4, 7.

assertion about Him.   He is above every name that can
be named". "He is best adored in silence ; best known
by nescience ; best described by negatives ".[1]   Our own
Hooker echoes this.   "Our safest eloquence concerning Him
is our silence, when we confess without confession that His
glory is inexplicable, His greatness above our capacity and
reach ".   So by abstraction,—by saying that God is *not*
this or that, or the other quality because so infinitely
beyond them—there was reached as the term of the soul's
adventure what amongst the mystics was known as " the
Divine darkness", "the vacant ground", "the waste
place" of the Godhead.   Exaggeration was easy in this
direction, and many such mystical phrases sound repellent to Western ears, or merely indicative of the exhaustion
of the intellect or the emotions.   But again it must be
remembered that the East was the source of the mystical
experience, and that the vehicle whereby the transit of
mystical philosophy was made from East to West was the
Greek language, with its almost endless possibilities of refinement on refinement of abstraction ; and, lastly, that
both the Greek proto-mystics and their nearest imitators, the
German school of the thirteenth century, were trying to
express in terms what, as we saw in Professor James' " four
marks", is really an ineffable experience.   But it is of
practical interest to note that from this school of thought
arose its corollary in action, Asceticism ; and very naturally.
If, to get to God, the mind must be stripped of every concept and every imagination, it was right, surely, also to
strip the body of all that could satisfy, enrich, ease, and
perhaps thereby delude.   All the comforts and the intellectual joys of life were capable of being viewed, *sub specie
aeternitatis,* as veils that hid or distorted the vision of God.
   But Mysticism, touching at times the two extremes of

[1] See Rufus Jones : *Mystical Religion,* p. 95 note.

Pantheism and Negativism, never abode long by either of them. Its early insistence on Experience and its early alliance with the Platonic school of Philosophy came to the rescue. Its experience must be spiritual; its philosophy—and Mysticism cannot help being a philosophy—involved the use and indeed the exaltation of Reason, and the admission of the Emotions as its bondservants, in the apprehension of God. Then the curious fact of world-history, the fact that the Church has travelled always Westwards, with a result of constant reinforcement to the Faith from the practical Western genius to be up and doing, to define and to act, helped Western Mysticism to live a life, intellectual and practical, whose high and gracious sanity is of the atmosphere of the Holy Gospels themselves. To name most of the European medieval mystics is to name men and women of fruitful and self-sacrificing Christian life and activity.

If we now return to the mystical thought of man in his relationship with God, we shall be able to summarize it briefly as follows, and then turn to what became a component and distinctive part of strictly Christian Mysticism—the systematization of the mystical life. The soul, in mystical thought, has the power of sight in spiritual things, as the body's eyes have in things natural. But to be able to see God, man must partake himself of something God-like. It is in His light that we see light. This is as we should expect. Human vision has to be trained to its work. It is the person who knows something of Art, has taken pains to study Art, has in fact something of the artist in him, who can truly see a picture in a way that the ignoramus or the casual sight-seer cannot. It is the musician who can best hear music. Even so, "blessed are the pure in heart, for they shall see God". "We shall be like Him, for we shall see Him as He is"—and that sight is impossible without likeness. Selfishness, anger, sensuality, are disqualifications for the heavenly vision. "Man must clean his mirror if

God is to be reflected in it ". Now there is, the mystics
taught, a ground of potential likeness to God in everyone.
Some likened it to a seed that could be tended, some to a
spark that could be fanned to a flame. The Germans of the
fourteenth century talked much of this " Fünkelein ", or
little spark at the apex, as they pictured it, of the soul.
The question was, how to tend the seed to its growth, how
to fan the spark to a flame. So we come to the Mystic's
scheme of the inner life.

VII. Mystics in general taught the *scala perfectionis*,
the ladder of perfection. This has three rungs or grades.

(*a*) Purgative : which includes contrition, confession,
hearty amendment, and also, which is interesting, the social
and civic virtues. The great non-Christian mystic, Plotinus,
insisted on these, as representing, he said, the Divine qualities of order and limitation. " The true mystic ", says
Ewald, " never withdraws himself from the business of
life, no, not even from the smallest business ". We may say
that this " grade " is the Christian life as commonly lived
out by good practical people. This part of the " scala "
also includes " ascesis," which, looked on simply and sensibly
as " training " in the Pauline sense, has always held a
place in the Christian scheme, or, for the matter of that, in
the lives of all who are in earnest over their profession or
business.

(*b*) The second stage is the Illuminative. The outward duties
have now become natural and habitual, and the struggle is
transferred to the inner life. The " warfare and pilgrimage "
stage of experience is sensibly entered upon ; the soul often
experiences a marked diminution of spiritual comforts,
" accidie " has to be met and conquered, dryness, coldness,
and what St. John of the Cross termed the " Dark Night of
the Soul " encountered and won through. God, in fact,
has now to be chosen and loved for Himself, not for blessings,
helps, or visions that proceed from Him. Sometimes that

strange, penetrating aphorism of Spinoza seems to come true,
" Whoso loves God must not expect to be loved by Him in
return ". Yet through this hard school the soul is learning
to choose the highest good for its own sake. It learns that
" we do not enter the Path because it is pleasant, but because
it is the only Path ".

(c) The third and highest rung of the " scala " is the
Unitive stage. The soul is joined to God, and like the loved
disciple lies in His breast. Irenaeus, Athanasius, Clement,
Origen, Augustine all quite commonly use and press the idea
of identification with God as the goal of the spiritual life,
nay, they use the, to our modern ears, startling phrase deificari, θεοποίεσθαι, without hesitation. Indeed, Harnack
says, " After Theophilus, Irenaeus, Hippolytus, and Origen,
the idea of deification is found in all the Fathers of the ancient
Church, and that in a primary position . . . as also in
Cyril, Sophronius, and late Greek and Russian theologians." [1]
It is impossible to enter here upon this branch of the subject
at length ; it must suffice to point out that the modern
conception of " personality " has altered materially from
the limited interpretation put on the word in ancient times ;
and that the Greek θεός was a far lower and vaguer term
than the Western " deus," so that θεοποίεσθαι is misleading
if regarded as anything but an approximate equivalent of
" deificari ". The main concept of θεός amongst the Greeks
was the quality of freedom from the doom of mortality. A
Divine Being is one " who only hath immortality ". This
sort of deification—the imparting of immortality—was,
says Harnack, " the idea of salvation taught in the Mysteries ",
(that is, in the Pagan Mysteries) and the thought was caught
up and carried into Christianity. Christ " brought life and
immortality to light through the Gospel ". Clement of
Alexandria, not an exact thinker, but one whose mind re-

---

[1] Quoted by Inge : *Christian Mysticism*, Appendix C. p. 358.

sponded with vivid reactions to ideas " in the air " of his day, connects the two notions. τὸ μὴ φθείρεσθαι—to be imperishable—is to share in Divinity.[1] The later mystics of thirteenth and fourteenth century Germany appropriated the idea, only with a difference. In earlier days, this share in the Divine Nature was a gift acquired as the higher ethical stage, or imparted from without ; in later days, it was a development of that which was uncreated and godlike in the original constitution of man's nature.[2]

But in any case, as the Divine Being is infinite, so the Unitive stage is an infinite process, though begun in time, and occasionally realized by temporal foretastes or glimpses.

VIII. The last sentence brings us in conclusion to the consideration of perhaps the most vexed question—certainly a subject more pregnant of misunderstanding than any other—in connexion with the mystical life and temperament, the experience of the Ecstasy. Yet it is a subject that cannot be passed over, a question that must be discussed, inasmuch as the experience itself, or at any rate the capacity for the experience, constitutes the very *differentia* of Mysticism. What, then, was the Ecstasy ? It was a state of inward sensation or knowledge, for both descriptions are true, that supervened at times during the third stage of the Scala, if one may separate the stages in this rather mechanical way ; of course they often had interaction. It was a foretaste here of the perfect Union only fully to be entered upon hereafter—a touch of eternity manifesting itself in time. Even in the lives of the greatest mystics it was a rare experience ; Plotinus is described as having had it thrice ; St. Paul, as far as we can judge from his own

---

[1] *Strom.* v. 10. 63.

[2] It is important to remember that, in both East and West, the apparent dangers of this doctrine were safeguarded against by belief in the Divinity of Christ, " the only (uniquely) begotten son of God,".

account in 2 Corinthians, once. But, unhappily, the word "ecstasy"—literally, a standing outside of oneself—has been so diverted from its original use that many people have little or no idea as to what the actual "ecstasy", or "rapture" was, or is. It has been confused with the seeing of visions, or the hearing of "locutions", and it has been ascribed to all sorts of abnormal pathological conditions, involuntary or self-induced. First, let us note that there is nothing "ecstatic" (in the ordinary sense of the adjective) about the experience. It is neither vision-seeing, nor clairaudience. Indeed it possesses in the highest degree the "four marks" whereby Professor James distinguished Mysticism itself; it cannot be described afterwards (like a vision or dream); it conveys to the subject the sense of an absolute certitude of knowledge; it is transient; and it is not self-induced, but involuntary—a "rapture" in fact. The subject has the sense of being seized upon, as St. Teresa described the experience, or filled or possessed by a Power other than the self, although intimately at one with the self. Fr. Sharpe, in his admirable treatise, "Mysticism; Its True Nature and Value," [1] likens the ecstasy, in the subject's passivity ("we can do nothing on our part", says St. Teresa), in its essential indescribability, and in its legacy of certitude, to ordinary sensation. "Sensation is incapable of being defined or proved; the one thing that we know about it is that it occurs. Whatever the conditions may be and whether there is an adequate cause present or not, the one indubitable fact in sensation is the certainty of the experience. . . . This is precisely the case of the mystic". What may be added is that the sensation, whenever or however produced, is that of contact with the Absolute; and again, that the true access or invitation to the experience is the love-fascination of which we have already spoken. Thought has its place and value, but love is the primary cause. "Plotinus the

[1] *Op. cit.* ch. iii.

ecstatie is sure, whatever Plotinus the metaphysician may think, that the union with God is a union of hearts ; that ' by love He may be gotten and holden, but by thought never.' He, no less than the medieval contemplatives, is convinced, to quote his own words, that the Vision is only for the desirous ; for him who has that ' loving passion ' which ' causes the lover to rest in the object of his love '." [1]

It has been urged that the ecstasy or trance-experience, with all its four marks,—or something closely analogous to it—may be induced by artificial means. Professor James, in his " Varieties of Religious Experience ", gives several examples of such. Certain forms of narcotics, methods of breathing, or ways of self-hypnotization, are productive of effects closely resembling the mystical experience.[2] As instances of the latter we may mention Jacob Behmen's discovery that the trance state could be induced by steadfast gazing at a bright metal disc, or the beam of light coming through a keyhole, and Tennyson's curious experience [3] of what followed the constant repetition of his own name, with its accompaniment of an accentuated consciousness of individual personality. The latter merits further consideration, but in any case, short cuts or attempted short cuts to the goal of the mystical life no more disprove the reality of the attainment of that goal, than the occasional achievements of " Dutch courage " disprove the reality of genuine fortitude, the fitful brilliance now and then imparted to the brain by semi-intoxication refutes the existence

[1] E. Underhill : *Mysticism*, p. 445. cf. Plotinus. *Enneads* vi. 9. " The soul, therefore, when in a condition conformable to Nature, loves God, wishing to be united to Him . . . this, therefore is the life of God and of divine and happy men . . . a flight of the alone to the Alone ".

[2] In his treatise *De Canonisatione*, Pope Benedict XIV. notes various conditions, natural or arising from disease, which may produce seemingly mystical experiences.

[3] Cf. *The Ancient Sage*. And see Memoir, by his Son, vol. i. p. 320.

of what we call "genius," or the dubious methods and results of the spiritualistic séance affect one way or the other the Christian's faith in the Resurrection, and his hope in the life of the world to come.

To return : the Ecstasy is experience on the spiritual plane analogous to bodily sensation, and, like sensation, essentially indescribable. The soul feels that it is caught up, rapt, into immediate apprehension or touch of a world that is not ours, or of which ours is but the shadow, a world in which God is all, and all is in God. No imagery, no form, is to be recalled afterwards. In this sense it is that Noack describes Mysticism itself as " formless speculation ". To quote Dr. Inge's definition of the Ecstasy, " (It) begins when thought ceases, *to our consciousness*, to proceed from ourselves. It differs from dreaming because the subject is awake. It differs from hallucination because there is no organic disturbance : it is, or claims to be, a temporary enhancement, not a partial disintegration, of the mental faculties. Lastly, it differs from poetical inspiration, because the imagination is passive ".[1] We are not without modern and detailed instances of the experience thus analyzed. We have already glanced at Tennyson's account of his inducement of the trance by the repetition of his own name, but a better and more authentic description of it, apparently uninduced, is to be found in the " In Memoriam", canto xcv, when he

—" came on That which is, and caught
The deep pulsations of the world "—

more authentic, because, apparently unwittingly, he describes as precedent conditions of the state the very conditions indicated by Plotinus himself—the feeling of stillness borne in upon the soul, and the soul's apartness from all human distractions.[2] He tells of the " calm that let

[1] Inge : *Christian Mysticism*, p. 14.
[2] *Infra*, pp. 257–8.

the tapers burn, unwavering ", and how " in the house light after light went out, and I was all alone ". The other great instance of the trance-state is Wordsworth's

> " serene and blessed mood
> In which the breath of this corporeal frame,
> And even the motion of our human blood
> Almost suspended, we are laid asleep
> In body, and become a living soul
> And see into the life of things ".[1]

And there are glimpses of the same experience in Browning, Coventry Patmore, and in the almost Nature-worship of T. E. Brown, especially in the last-named's " Epistola ad Dakyns ". But they can all be brought under the great twin characteristics of the experiences of Wordsworth and of Tennyson—which are indeed the two main modes of mystical approach to God—namely, the conception of the Divine as immanent in the world of Nature, or the sense of individuality rendered abnormally acute and finding itself suddenly dissolved into the sense of an infinitely wider and all-embracing Personality.

We may say, in any case, that the mystical temperament is marked out either by the capacity for this experience, or at any rate, by the capacity to understand and in some way respond to the thought of it. This would suggest that the true mystic is compact of the nature of the seer and the nature of the spiritual man. For the man of ordinary spiritual goodness is by no means necessarily a mystic, nor is the visionary, or the " psychic " person, by virtue of that quality alone, a mystic ; but combine the two, personal holiness and, for want of a better term, the touch on the unseen, and there are the makings of a mystical saint. " First ", as Archbishop Benson was wont to translate the Pauline phrase, " first the psychic, then the spiritual ".

It is in consequence of its intense belief in and desire for

[1] *Tintern Abbey*. And see *infra*, p. 255.

immediate touch and communion with God, that Mysticism has always been a living force. The mystics would not take things at second-hand. Life is life, and must be known as energizing power ; Love must be actually felt as love. Mysticism is not indigenous to Christianity ; indeed, it may be said that to its presence, its yearning for the truth, its insistence on reality, other forms of faith have invariably owed the vitality they had or have ; nevertheless, it is true, that in Christianity Mysticism found its fittest home, its best discipline, and its freest and most congenial range of vision and of endeavour.

CHAPTER II

The Mystical Element in the Gospels and Epistles

" MAN", said Jacobi, " is a yonder-sided animal".
Whatever brings him to authentic sight or touch,
even for a moment, of this " otherness " in his being gives
him for that moment the mystic's outlook on things. Such
partial glimpses, afforded by Nature, or Art, or Thought,
are common, and often appear to have little to do with
Religion as such. The momentary clue is, in fact, mostly
not followed up, else a different conclusion might be arrived at. But, in any case, the mystical instinct or temperament is found elsewhere than in Christianity. The
sense of " an experience deeper than science, more certain
than demonstration ", " when we possess ourselves as one
with the whole " [1] may be induced by the study of metaphysics, or by such thoughts as the " million-millionth of
a grain, which cleft and cleft again for evermore, and ever
vanishing, never vanishes ", or by the pursuit of beauty, or
by some shattering cry like Mohammed's, " There is no
God but God ". It has been indeed at the core of every
religion worthy of the name, for, as we have seen, it implied
and insisted on first-hand experience. But we can expect,
and we shall not be disappointed, to find the mystical element
at its highest and best within its natural home, Christianity,

[1] S. T. Coleridge: *The Friend*, Essay xi.

and that from the very outset. True, it received a vast reinforcement, later, from Greek sources, indeed, Christian Mysticism, viewed as a system of life and philosophy, can but trace its parentage thence. But, interesting as this is historically, it would be disconcerting to the mystic and dishonouring to the Christian Faith, so immense and far-reaching was that imported Greek influence, were we obliged to stop there. It would mean that Christianity, in part, was not master of its own soul; that what persecution had failed to accomplish by force had been accomplished by subtler means, and that the purity of the faith, proof against direct attack, had been moulded and leavened at last by that very Pagan mentality which had done, almost ostentatiously, without the Christ offered for its acceptance. Christian Mysticism looks back further than Dionysius the Areopagite, and to sources higher than even the marvellous thought of Plotinus, for its own warrant and its true principles. It looks back indeed to the New Testament; it claims as two of its chief prophets, St. Paul and St. John, and it owns as its Master and Inspirer, the Lord Jesus Christ. It does not claim that the Epistles of St. Paul and the Johannine writings are mystical treatises and nothing else, any more than it would assert that Christ was a Mystic merely and made appeal only to mystics.[1] The aim of Christianity is catholic; it is meant to embrace human nature as a whole and not a specialized function of it. There are, and always have been, many devout Christians who would not own to the mystical temperament: but there are, it may be added, many more to whom doctrines

---

[1] " Christ ", says the late Canon Moberly, " is the true mystic. . . . . He alone has realized all that mysticism and mystics have aimed at ". But he uses the term mysticism in a general sense as " the realization of human personality as characterized by and consummated in the indwelling reality of the spirit of Christ, which is God "; *Atonement and Personality*, p. 312.

strictly mystical in their nature are dear, or who profess
them as part of their Christian belief, but who would not
recognize such a name for them.

Traces of such doctrines, traits of mystical teaching
and experience, are not wanting, to begin with, in the
Synoptic accounts of our Lord's life, themselves by no means
in intention mystical documents. The temptations in the
wilderness, for example, whether facts, or symbolic sum-
maries of a life-experience, are intensely mystical in their
range of meaning, order, and suggestiveness. The account
of the Transfiguration, with its significant and glorified
witnesses, is another instance in point, and the ἀγαλλίασις
of Luke x. 21, with its mysterious accompanying utterances, resembles, if we may say so with all reverence, the
mystical Rapture or Ecstasy. It is remarkable also that
Christ should have chosen as His nearest companions men to
whom the vision-state was familiar. This fact has been
blurred to the ordinary Bible-student by the habit of regarding the Apostles and early saints as men in some ways
wholly differentiated from ourselves, accepting their experiences as true but refusing to allow those experiences any
relation with human nature, even sanctified human nature
as we know it. But to the student of psychology at the
present day these experiences are of the highest interest,
and the events narrated in the Synoptic gospels and the Acts
warrant the supposition that Christ must have set deliberate value on the " visionary " gift in those who companied
with Him most closely, or served Him best. Peter, James,
John, and Paul all possessed it pre-eminently, at least at
the outset of their ministry, if we judge by their own accounts, or the writings of their companions.[1] But from

---

[1] St. Peter is usually regarded as a non-mystic, a plain, practical
man of strong human predilections and sympathies. It is sufficient
to remember that he witnessed the Transfiguration, that the beginnings of Gentile conversion owe themselves to his strange trance

the teaching of Christ set down by the Synoptists without preconceived arrangement or " tendency " it is also possible to deduce the mystical warrant. There is the Experience that runs all through it—an experience unique indeed and beyond definition, but still an experience towards which the Christian fellowship is beckoned—of immediate communion with God. There is the intense realization of a hidden but vital union between the Christ and His society, and that to all time : " where two or three are gathered together in My Name, there am I in the midst of them ". There is the finding of God in the child-like heart—the kingdom of heaven in their innocent faces ; there is the great maxim of the Sermon on the Mount as to the Divine vision, " blessed are the pure in heart, for they shall see God ". There are the crucial laws of gain through loss and of life through death which lie at the root of mystical ethics. And there is the mystical say-ing, " The Kingdom of God is within you ", which is repeated with a remarkable amplification in a logion of the Oxyrhyn-cus Papyri, " and whosoever knoweth himself shall find it ". A logion still better known beautifies and hallows the least and meanest manual labour ; " Raise the stone, and thou shalt find Me ; cleave the wood, and there am I ".

We pass now from the Lord to His disciples, and although everywhere in the New Testament writing sayings essentially mystical confront us from time to time—in the Epistles of St. James and St. Peter, for example—two names will always be appealed to by mystics as lending warrant and illustration to their doctrines, the names of St. Paul and of St. John. The Pauline Epistles and the Johannine writings, indeed, contain in germ and suggestion a vast portion of that body of mystical theology afterwards to be system-

on the housetop, and that the account of his escape from prison mentions his familiarity with such experiences. " He wist not that it was true, but thought he saw a vision ".

atized by the exact mind of the Western Church ; and then to be again desystematized by the thought of post-Reformation Englishmen, never so willingly unlogical as when in touch with religion. It will be well to consider St. Paul first. There is this advantage in doing so, that we know St. Paul not only from his writings, but from his biography, and chiefest by certain autobiographical reminiscences, which, from the mystical point of view, are of the highest importance.

This " prince of all true Christian mystics " [1] has a gospel, which he boldly terms " my gospel ", and asserts to have come to him through revelation, and not by means of men ; he has been brought " to know the wisdom of God in a mystery ". The whole tenour of his life has been changed by the vision that he saw on the road to Damascus. This vision some have identified with the experience of the " man in Christ " narrated in 2 Cor. xii., but probably erroneously. For although infinitely more momentous than other visions which, as an experience, he shared in the earlier stages of his " life in Christ " with his fellow Apostle, St. Peter, the narrations of Acts ix. and 2 Cor. xii. can hardly refer to the same event, if but for the reason that the experience on the way to Damascus was capable of description, both as regards what was seen, and what was heard, whereas the experience of the " rapture " to the " third heaven " was not. The former in fact, in mystical phraseology, was vision, the latter ecstasy.

It may be well to attempt to sum up the special points with regard to which Mysticism gains its inspiration and direction from St. Paul, " who, in his mystical outbursts and in the systematic parts of his doctrine . . . gives us the earliest, one of the deepest, and to this hour by far the most influential, among the at all detailed experiences

[1] W. Major Scott : *Aspects of Christian Mysticism*, p. 14.

and schemes . . . as to the relations of the human soul with God ". [1]

(1) In the first place, there is the early insistence, as we have noted, on visions, which, although not possessing the first of Professor James' four marks of mystical experience, Ineffability, have all the other three—Transiency, Noetic Quality (they convey new knowledge) with Authoritativeness (" I was not disobedient to the heavenly Vision ") and Passivity. There are several instances in which important activities of St. Paul are stimulated or strengthened by visions, that is, by something definitely seen and heard in the trance state. His first visit to Europe is inspired by such a vision or dream ; his impulse to " witness in Rome " comes from a vision of the Lord ⁄and a direct commission from Him (Acts xxiii. 11) ; he is bidden to leave Jerusalem on his first visit to the temple after his conversion, while he was " in a trance " (Acts xxii. 17), he is consoled against danger in Corinth, in Jerusalem, and on board ship in the storm, the last time by " an angel of God " (Acts xxvii. 23). In fact, it is scarcely realized how large a part these psychic experiences had in moulding the life and labours of the great Apostle.

(2) By the first and most startling of these visions Paul is brought to Christ, yet not, and most emphatically not, to the knowledge of the Christ of the Gospel history. He did not at first, he tells the Galatians, deem it necessary to gather historical evidence with regard to the Lord's ministry, death, or resurrection. " I conferred not with flesh and blood ", he says, and even when he did meet Christ's life-companions, Peter and John, they " added nothing " to him, or to his internal conviction. A certain modification of this attitude of bare dependence on personal revelation is discernible at the end of the First Epistle to

---

[1] Fr. von Hügel : *The Mystical Element of Religion*, vol. ii. p. 320.

the Corinthians. Here he does cite proofs of the Resurrection in order to meet the objections of gainsayers. But in 2 Corinthians, he is back again, with even stronger emphasis, at his former position, " Though we have known Christ after the flesh, yet henceforth know we Him no longer ". St. Paul, in fact, will have knowledge of Christ, not as a man, but as Man ; and yet even that scarcely sums up his Christology. It is a cosmic Christ that he preaches, a Christ pre-existent as God, or as " in the form of God ",[1] a Christ in Whom, through Whom, and for Whom all things were created,[2] a Christ in Whom all things " hold together ",[3] and Who is therefore, in that sense and not merely historically, eyes to the blind, ears to the deaf, the principle of the senses themselves ; moreover, a Christ Who is in some way coeval with the time-series, Who is, till the completion of that, " all and in all ",[4] and Who is the actual nature of man, as such. For " the measure of the stature of the fullness of Christ " is the goal of completed manhood.[5] All this He is for man, not by virtue of certain historical events enacted by a historical person at a given date, though these have their vast significance as being the representation on the world stage of an eternal Process, but by virtue of His interaction as spirit, in and through ourselves. " Now the Lord is that Spirit ". St. Paul discourages for all time the attempt of some later mystics to " get past " Christ to the " vacant ground " of the undifferentiated Godhead. He points us instead to the " fullness of Christ " as the medium by and through which the Godhead makes possible and practical communion with man's nature. " As the air is the element in which man moves, and yet again the element of life which is present within the man : so the Pneuma-Christ is for St. Paul both the ocean of the Divine

---

[1] Phil. ii. 6.   [2] Col. i. 15-17.   [3] Col. i. 17. Rev. Vers.
[4] Col. iii. 11.   [5] Eph. iv. 13.

Being, into which the Christian is plunged, and a stream which, derived from that ocean, is specially introduced within his individual life." [1] This brings us to a third and most distinctive phase of all mystical teaching, which also derives from St. Paul.

(3) " I live, yet not I, but Christ liveth in me." This is the great Pauline watchword of the spiritual life. It must be an internal, experimental process. From the outset it was so. Even when describing for the Galatians the vision near Damascus which elsewhere he pictures in objective terms, he puts aside everything that was outward —the light, the voice—in favour of the interior change which these but symbolized. " When it pleased the Father to reveal His Son *in* me." " In me ", after all, and not " to me ". In fact, with St. Paul, the individual Christian must experience personally as a life process the redemptive work of Christ. The victory over death and sin was achieved *for* us ; but it must also be achieved *in* us. The soul, in fact, is the microcosm in which a universal law is to be carried out. " My little children, of whom I travail in birth again, until Christ be formed in you ".[2] That is the beginning of the process. " Buried with Him by baptism into death ".[3] That is the continuation. " Raised together with Christ ", " walk in newness of life " : [3] " if ye then be risen with Christ, seek those things that are above ",[4] these are further steps towards such an identification of being that at last " to live is Christ ",[5] " Christ, Who is our life ".[6] How fruitful this doctrine was, and how, more than anything else, it served to save Mysticism from a vague craving for absorption into the Absolute, we shall see later. Here it is sufficient to note its prominence and

[1] H. T. Holtzmann : *Lehrbuch der N.T. Theologie*, vol. ii. pp. 79–80, quoted in von Hügel.
[2] Gal. iv. 17.   [3] Rom. vi. 4.   [4] Col. iii. 1.
[5] Phil. i. 21.   [6] Col. iii. 4.

persistency in the Pauline thought. Bethlehem, Calvary, the Resurrection and Ascension are to be re-enacted within the compass of the human soul.

(4) A fourth characteristic of Pauline mysticism is the sanction he gives, in one or two celebrated passages (Rom. vii. 1–4 ; Eph. v. 23–32), to the teaching regarding Christ and the Church which represents their relationship as that of a Bridegroom to His bride. This analogy receives, of course, additional warrant from the Old Testament, where the Jewish Church is so spoken of (Isa. liv. 5 ; Jer. iii. 14) ; from some parables and expressions of our Lord ; and from one or two passages in the Apocalypse. It was caught up, however, with much eagerness by the Church, and the idea so developed and particularized, that it became one of the most familiar expressions of mystical devotion. There were very few Greek fathers who did not make use of it ; Tertullian is found suggesting that " if the soul is the bride, the flesh is the dowry " [1] of Christ, and Dionysius in justification of mystical raptures quotes Ignatius' phrase, " My love has been crucified ". But, on the whole, the expression was confined on the one hand to the love of Christ *for the Church*, and this, even in St. Bernard's homilies on the Song of Solomon ; and secondly, to the love *of Christ*. The first conception was altered to that of the love of Christ for the individual soul, mainly by the mystics of the cloister,[2] and then gradually, in more recent times. perhaps in part owing to the renewed influence of Eastern imagery and thought, the specific figure of the Christ seems to have receded into the background and we hear of " Divine touches ", " real but purely spiritual sensations, by which the soul feels the intimate presence of God, and tastes Him with great delight ". It is interesting to compare in this

[1] *De Resurrectione*, 63.

[2] Cf. esp. Richard of St. Victor : *De Quatuor Gradibus Violentae Charitatis*.

respect the poetry of Crashaw in the seventeenth century and of Coventry Patmore in the nineteenth, both of them devout Catholic Christians ; the former takes the humanity of our Lord, under every possible aspect, as the object of his love ; with the latter, whose message is almost exclusively that of human marriage as the ultimate symbol of the intercourse between the soul and its Divine Lover, that Lover is always God, viewed, as it were, *haud sub conditione.*

(5) It is through the intimate personal notes of 2 Corinthians, that we learn of St. Paul's experience, at least once, of the highest psychological phase of Mysticism, the Ecstasy. Once more it is necessary to recall the differences that separate the Ecstasy from mere vision. The latter is of the lowest, the former occurs during the highest stages of the mystic life. Visions may occur often, the Ecstasy is one of the rarest of experiences. So much was said by way of attempted definition of the Ecstasy in the Introductory chapter that perhaps all that is needed here is to remind ourselves of one important distinction besides. The vision or trance, which includes something seen and something heard, can be exactly described ; the Ecstasy is so far a glimpse or audition of another sphere or dimension of being that its experience is quite indescribable in the language of this. Now we have several records of visions in St. Paul's life, one only of the Ecstasy. The former, as we have noticed, are fairly frequent in the Acts, bodily forms are seen, and voices with articulate messages of warning or encouragement heard ; and all are capable of the fullest description. There is but one psychic experience, (the one of all which left the deepest impress on the Apostle's soul and even some permanent mark, it would seem, on his physical being), which is for him wholly ineffable afterwards. This experience—of the " man in Christ " of 2 Corinthians xii.—through the halting words that seek to express it, corresponds so curiously to the " notes " of

the supreme mystical state as summarized in a more scientific age, that it is worth while to make a comparison. First, all Professor James' " marks " of the mystical experience are there, Transiency, Passivity, (" whether in the body or out of the body I cannot tell "), Noetic and Authoritative Quality, and last, Ineffability, (words were heard which " it is not lawful (possible) to utter "). But there is more besides. There is the sense of a veritable Rapture, —the subject " is caught " ; the sense of a heightened consciousness—he is " caught up " to a sphere of being above his own, symbolized by the " third heaven " ; and it is, in the double emphasis laid on " in the body, or out of the body, I cannot tell," an ἐκστάσις in the true meaning of the term. That the record of such an experience should occur in an Epistle indubitably and characteristically St. Paul's makes it all the more noticeable.

In the Johannine writings [1] another great body of mystical teaching is met with. It presents strong contrasts with that of St. Paul. To many minds it has a far greater attraction than that of St. Paul : in fact, the Fourth Gospel has been named " the charter of Mysticism ". To the age, again—an age, after all, of giants—for whose difficulties the study of Browning suggested satisfying solutions, the Johannine message was really the last word and the most conclusive on Christianity ; witness " The Death in the Desert ", and the conclusion of Bishop Blougram ; and to a certain, and very high, type of intellect it is so still. Yet, viewed as a mystical presentation or commentary on the Faith, it cannot be said to possess a universal appeal. It is with the greatest diffidence that we should trench on such debatable ground : but one or two points stand out clearly on any examination of the Johannine Gospel and Epistles.

[1] It is, perhaps, necessary to say that this term is not here intended to include the Apocalypse.

That they give, by their own method, the fullest warrant for a mystical apprehension of Christianity is beyond question : but it is equally beyond question that the apprehension is a highly specialized one. It is at least disputable whether we know anything as to the author's life ; but his " record " is at any rate by far the latest in its appearance. It is, in fact, absolutely invaluable as, and chiefly as, the impression left by the Christian Faith on a mind of the next century after Christ, and fully awake to the influence of the next century. It is Christianity entering on a new world, a new inheritance, and proving itself capable of absorbing what was best in the circumstances of current thought and feeling around it, and of fulfilling their noblest aspirations. This, perhaps, is the explanation of the fleeting adoption in the prologues of the Gospel and the First Epistle of the Logos-doctrine. For, although it would be unsafe to say that the Johannine Logos-doctrine is derived from that of Philo,[1] yet here we have the remarkable coincidence of two writers, both Jews, both strongly bent on bringing in the authority of Moses [2] for their philosophies, the one to reconcile Moses and Plato, the other, Moses and Christ, and both defining the Logos as God (with Philo, " the second God "), the " only and beloved Son of God," by Whose agency the worlds were made. With both He is the Bread of God, the Convincer of sin ; connected with Him are the ideas of Intercessor and Comforter ; He is the eternal Image of the Father, and, with Philo, we, unfit for direct sonship of God, may yet regard ourselves as sons

[1] It has been urged that the dates of the authors approximate too closely. Still, Philo was a contemporary of St. Paul, and the Logos-doctrine was certainly, as we say, " in the air," at the time of the Fourth Gospel, however early we place it. A stronger argument is the fact that Philo's work exercised little influence on the philosophy of the Second Century.

[2] See Inge : *Christian Mysticism*, p. 83. Cf. John i. 17, 45 ; ii. 14 ; v. 45, 47 ; vi. 32 ; vii. 19, 22, 23 ; ix. 29, 30.

of the Logos. Such resemblances can hardly be a long chain of chance coincidences. Where the separation of thought comes, and comes decisively, is that the author of the Johannine writings adds personality to his conception of the Logos and identifies Him, as Philo never attempted to do, with the Messiah, in set terms.[1] But then he claims emphatically, in both Epistle and Gospel, to have been an eye-witness of a life lived on earth, that died and rose again : unlike St. Paul, he knows " Christ after the flesh ", and insists on that knowledge as the very cornerstone of the Faith.[2]

What, then, are the contributions of St. John to the mystical element in religion ? We may say, perhaps, three. (1) The first, that by this very insistence on a historical revelation in time, he counterpoises the strong mystical tendency in succeeding ages to regard the Gospel story as a kind of drama merely, correspondent to a more vital reality, to what William Law called " the whole process of Christ ", His birth, death, resurrection, within the soul. In another sense Mr. A. E. Waite declares the same evacuation of the historical Incarnation, when he says, " The mystery of the Passion and of the Lamb slain from the foundation of the world is one of the mysteries of the unseen. The true Golgotha and Calvary are not of this world ". Emphatically the Fourth Evangelist declares that they are, that the Word of God was seen, heard, handled. Yet he views what he holds as historical under so mystical an aspect, that it would be right to say that for him all life is sacramental ; above all, the Life of lives. It is not as evidence chiefly that he puts down what he remembers of Christ's doings and sayings. The words are valued above the " works ", and the former cannot be heard, nor the latter seen, aright, unless first the soul has experienced

[1] John i. 41 ; iv. 25, 26. [2] 1 John iv. 3.

a process of illumination. The consequence is that he puts a strong emphasis on all that is transacted in human life. Things are important in themselves, but more important yet because they symbolize something beyond them. He will have nothing of the "overthrow of that warrantable, though more external, frame of Christianity", which Henry More lamented. The physical and the spiritual which God has put together for us here are not to be sundered. A spiritual revelation of God is impossible for him without its physical counterpart, an Incarnation, nor can he tolerate a Christianity which lays no stress on the earthly ministry of the Lord. He views life whole.

(2) The Johannine writings give a sanction, and, if we will study them carefully, a true guidance, to the use of Symbolism in the expression of mystical thought. It is necessary in the first place, to be sure what a true Symbolism implies. For while we find a writer like Récéjac announcing it as the very esssence of Mysticism,—Mysticism being in his view " the tendency to approach the Absolute, morally, by means of symbols "—we find others ready to deny that it has anything to do with Mysticism, whilst many would set it down as Allegorism, or at least be by no means clear as to the distinction between the two. The distinction is, broadly, this : Symbolism is teaching based on what is already fact ; Allegorism is teaching conveyed by some effort of the imagination. According to the intellect and inspiration of the allegorist, so is the worth and wealth of his message. Allegorism, therefore, in the hands of the Divine Master Himself, or in the hands of a gifted seer, like John Bunyan, has conveyed imperishable truths. On the other hand, Allegorism may descend to be the plaything of a sort of gaudy, over-decorated Christian nursery. For be it noted that the very essence of the allegory is that it is a story, an invention ; we do not regard it as fact. That is true alike of the Parables of the Synoptic Gospels, and of

the "Pilgrim's Progress." It is easy to see how this would come to be a danger, in some ages of the Church, to a certain kind of ingenious religious fancy. The temptation arose to find hidden meanings and obscure parallels to Christian doctrine in the most straightforward and historical of Old Testament narratives. By a very swift transition these narratives became less important as narrative than as allegory, and since in the very nature of allegory was bound up the something of fancy rather than of fact, we soon find the allegorist commentators on the Old Testament stories denying their importance, or indeed necessary veracity, as history at all. As early as Clement of Alexandria and Origen this was so ; but apart from so extreme a development of the allegorical tendency, its significance to us is that, unhappily, such playing with Bible stories is still called by many people "mystical interpretation". Needless to say, there is nothing whatever mystical about it, though some of these far-fetched glosses have the merit of a curious though misdirected ingenuity.[1]

But what, then, is Symbolism ? Let us return to our distinction. Symbolism is founded on facts, and, what is more, on universal facts. "The true Mysticism", said R. S. Nettleship, "is the belief that everything, in being what it is, is symbolic of something more ". The Symbolist goes to Nature, and asks, with Milton,

> "What if earth
> Be but the shadow of heaven, and things therein
> Each to each other like, more than on earth is thought ? "

Already in the first age of the Church, St. Paul had given the hint. "The invisible things of God from the creation of the world are clearly seen, being understood by the things

---

[1] The Notes of Dr. Neale's translations of medieval hymns give many instances of the kind referred to : see also his Commentary on the Psalms.

that are made,"[1] but he scarcely developed the thought.
It is St. John who takes it up, and makes of the great enduring powers of Nature, her methods of illumination, of
life, of nourishment, of cleansing, the precise modes through
and by which the manifestation of the Incarnate Word is
gradually effected and perfected, at once on the stage of the
world's history and also in the souls of men.[2] His symbolism
is symbolism in the true sense of the term.   There is nothing
arbitrary or forced in it.   For in the original connotation
of the word a "symbol" did actually convey, on a lower
plane, that which it represented on a higher.   A true
symbol always is, in some sense, that which it symbolizes.
We shall see the meaning of this statement if we consider
the symbols of which the Fourth Evangelist makes con-
spicuous use in his Gospel.   Thus the light of the sun does
enlighten the bodily steps and invigorate the bodily life
of men, while it also stands as symbol of that Eternal Light
of the soul which is his inward guide and monitor.   Bread
does support his physical strength, even while it is "not
by bread alone" that he lives, but by communion with
Him Who is the true Bread of Life sent down from heaven.
Water purifies and refreshes here, while yet it is true that
the accepted message of Jesus Christ is in man "a well of
water springing up into eternal life".   There are many
other symbols of the mission and office of the Son of God
in St. John, and in his use of them he shows more than
once that love of a divine paradox which is closely associated
with the mystical temperament, but is only after all the
effort to express, in language which must always be inadequate, the flashing of the many facets of the one diamond,
Truth.   Thus we have Christ shown to us as the Door, the

[1] Rom. i. 20.
[2] "These things highest and divinest which it is given us to see
and know express in some way all that which the supreme Nature
of God includes." Dion. Areop. *De Mystica Theologia*, 13.

Way and the Shepherd on the Way, the Truth and the Word that speaks it, the Water of Life and the Giver of the water, the Corn of Wheat and the Bread, the Enlightener and the Light, the Revealer and the Revealed.

(3) It is not merely through his use of Symbolism, however, that St. John is claimed as one of the prophets of Mysticism, but by the idea which underlies his symbolism. This idea, worked out gradually through the Gospel, insisted upon again and again in the Epistles, is that of unification between the believer and his Incarnate Lord. St. John, indeed, habitually dwells upon and illustrates the third and highest stage in the spiritual ascent. But the unifying process is gradual and progressive. It starts, as all growth starts, from a seed. Only once does St. John use this actual expression, but the expression and the train of thought to which it gave rise, were afterwards to become of vital importance in the history of Mysticism. " Whosoever is born of God " he writes[1] . . . " His seed is in him and he cannot sin because he is born of God." As Professor Rufus Jones has said, " It is a word which mystics have again and again adopted to express the implanting of the Divine Life within the human soul. It means that the principle by which a man lives unto God and resists the tendencies of the flesh is a Divine germ, something of God ' received ' into the soul, a new life principle which expands and becomes the Life of the person." [2] But the same idea is really innate in the " well of water springing up into everlasting life ", in the fruit-bearing of the Vine, in the life-producing gift of the Bread. It is remarkable that in St. John the very exercise of faith takes a new turn. It is in this Gospel that the phrase πιστεύειν εἰς becomes common. It is a virtue that extends itself, pro-

---

[1] 1 John iii. 9, cf. 1 Pet. i. 23, and cf. John xii. 24, for the idea.
[2] *Studies in Mystical Religion*, p. 17.

jects itself towards and into something. "Faith", with St. John, "begins with an experiment, and ends in an experience". The experience is that of self-dedication, the identification of the self with the life, aims, hope, "ascension" of Another. "We are *in* Him that is true" is the burden of the Epistle; "that we may be one" is the prayer of the 17th chapter of the Gospel. It is a gradual process; step by step must be taken, grace exchanged for ever fuller grace, and it is accompanied by strange and baffling experiences of sorrow, defeat, and pain. The Cross, with St. John, is a "lifting up", a stage in the upward journey to a fuller and Divine life. But that the life of absorption in the Christ is, not servitude, nor limitation, but a life of infinitely extended relations, "life that is life indeed" in its realities of interaction, service, helpfulness, is revealed by the wonderful symbol of the Vine and its branches. This is the climax of the Gospel's symbolism, as it is the summing up of its message: and it is significant that the picture of so actual a community of sympathy, interests, love as makes up the intense life of the society instead of the partial existence of the isolated self, should be represented as uttered by the lips of a historical Personage, a Friend speaking concerning fellowship with His friends.[1] This doctrine of the "unus Christus"—as St. Augustine describes the unification of Christ and His members—is, of course, to be found also in St. Paul, but under the less mystical figure of a body and its members, a body of which Christ is the Head. It is the absolute identification of the life of Christ with that of His disciples—the "ye in Me, and I in you"—which makes St. John the master of this school of mystical theology.

St. John and St. Paul are the two great mystical thinkers

[1] The question of the absolute historicity of the Johannine discourses does not, of course, meet us here. The point is that they were intentionally so represented by the writer.

of the New Testament ; but gleams and touches from that other world in which the after mystics habitually lived are met with in the pages of other writers.

St. Peter, who shares the Johannine conception as to the " incorruptible seed ", echoes the thought of both St. John and St. Paul as to the timelessness of the redemptive process ; it is an eternal life manifested indeed as born, dying, risen again in time, but its Idea, or Principle exists beyond any time-series. The Lamb of God was fore-ordained to this redemptive sacrifice " before the foundation of the world ", and the words are repeated in a more daring phrase yet by the writer of the Apocalypse, who speaks of the " Lamb slain from the foundation of the world ". Three lesser conceptions, dear to the hearts of mystics, are also found in the " Catholic " epistles and in the Apocalypse. One is the thought of the mirror, into which a man looks and finds, according to St. James, the face of his true self, τὸ πρόσωπον τῆς γενέσεως αὐτοῦ,[1] a variant in phrase, though scarcely in essential meaning, from St. Paul's " glory of the Lord " into which we, by looking, are changed. A second thought is that common both to St. Peter and the Epistle to the Hebrews, of this mortal life as an exile, a place of pilgrimage and yearning progress.[2] The comparison of life to a pilgrimage might be taken merely as a beautiful and natural way of picturing the toils and struggles of the way to heaven, especially amongst Eastern peoples to whom the practice of making pilgrimages was, as it is still, so familiar a method of piety. To the Jews, for example, with their annual journeyings to the great Paschal festival, the analogy would at once commend itself. Yet it is strange to trace the effects of the words in the Hebrews and St. Peter, compelling as they are in their wistful and sorrowing pathos, in the history of the Christian imagination. Not

[1] Jas. i. 23.
[2] Heb. xi. 13-16 ; xiii. 14 ; 1 Pet. i. 17 ; ii. 11.

only were they taken up in all practical seriousness by the
Medieval Church in the East and in the West, but, in the
form of the Crusades, they changed the history of Europe,
and in this country, the pilgrimage to one particular shrine
moulded part at least of our social life and intercourse.
In more modern days the idea still remained a favourite
one in hymns and devotional books, and the very word
" parish " is, by derivation, " the pilgrims' sojourning
place ". All this, after all, in passing. In Mysticism, above
and beside other interest, the conception of life as an exile
and a pilgrimage had this peculiar importance that it was
closely allied with the idea of the soul's emanation from,
quest after, and return to, " God Who is our home ".

This brings us to the last of the special ideas allied to
the mystic mood, which we find in the New Testament.
Jerusalem, the city-goal " whither the tribes go up ", suggested to Hebrew minds the picture of an ideal city " Jerusalem which is from above " as the term of the soul's
pilgrimage. It is in two specially Hebraic writings that the
idea makes its appearance and is insisted on—the Epistle
to the Hebrews and the Apocalypse. The father of all
faithful pilgrims, Abraham, " looked ", we are told, " for
a city which hath foundations, whose builder and maker
is God,". " Here we have no continuing city, but we seek
one to come." God has prepared for us " a city ", [1] and
this city is described for us with every detail of allegorical
beauty in the 21st and 22nd chapters of the Apocalypse.
Such a message came with vivid appeal to a world whose
three great representative nationalities, the religious,
the intellectual, and the imperial, looked each to a city-
centre, Jerusalem, Athens, and Rome ; but, whatever
be its continued persuasiveness elsewhere, it has never lost
its power of mingled strength and sweetness for English

---

[1] Heb. xi. 10, 16 ; xiii. 14.

ears. This is in part, no doubt, owing to the extraordinary force and charm of the English Authorized Version of the Apocalypse ; partly to the fact that in England all this imagery of pilgrimage and of a city as its goal received illustration and a lasting emphasis in the wonderful "Dream" of the Puritan tinker; partly, by the English veneration and cult of the home life, and the desire, in consequence, to think of death as a "going home", home in some safe place of meeting, of recognition, of ordered work and rest such as a City. Yet it is to be noticed that the poets, who are the mystics of our day, have seen their vision of a City too, but of a City more ethereal yet more enduring, lit by "the light that was never yet on land or sea". Tennyson sings :

> "I saw the spiritual city and all her spires
> And gateways in a glory like one pearl—
> No larger, tho' the goal of all the saints,"

And Francis Thompson can

> "dimly guess what Time in mists confounds ;
> Yet ever and anon a trumpet sounds
> From the hid battlements of Eternity ;
> Those shaken mists a space unsettle, then
> Round the half-glimpsèd turrets slowly wash again."

And Matthew Arnold, to whom also the vision came by the touch of a noble memory nobly sung, feels the ancient ache as of exile and the sure impulse of the age-long pilgrimage,

> "On to the bound of the waste,
> On the city of God".

CHAPTER III

The Montanists, the Gnostics, and the Alexandrines

CHRISTIANITY is a personal experience; it is also a religion professing a universal claim. On both these counts, the individual and the catholic, its note has had to be one of γνῶσις from the beginning; it must feel and know, and if it is to be the one exclusive faith, it must feel and know better and more fully than is possible with any other systems of belief, and must be able to sum up and fulfil all that is good and of promise in them. At least three great movements of thought in the early Church arose, in one shape or another, from this insistence on knowledge or experience, and, in part due to this very insistence, there are affinities to Mysticism in each. They also very plainly show the peculiar reactions that took place with regard to Christianity itself, from its necessary contact with the faiths and philosophies of the Eastern Roman Empire; and, in two instances at any rate, these reactions spelt danger to the Church.

Of these movements the first consideration is Montanism. Its ideas were, however, spiritual, not intellectual; it was certainly a reaction, in the minds of its supporters, yet a reaction due to no influence outside the Church, but from what they supposed to be a wrong trend of life within it. It will be convenient to consider it here, since its motive power was an insistence on knowledge, on a personal experience, and it is also not impossible that in certain psychic characteristics of the movement it borrowed part of its impulse from outside pagan mysteries.

Part, though, only. Montanus, its founder, who made his first appearance about 170, had been a priest of Cybele in his ante-Christian days. He was a Phrygian, and, preaching in the regions near Galatia, preached to a people naturally impressionable and excitable and very ready, from " the sibylline strain " in them, to receive his message. That message was, practically, " Back to primitive Christianity ! " We know, though we do not know the process, that during a hundred years of post-Apostolic life the Church had completed the system of its ministry, and that the three orders of that ministry, bishop, priest, and deacon, had practically assumed the functions, the authority, and the grades of service which they have ever since retained. But, to Montanus, the writings of the Apostles contained other elements of the Christian ministry and of the individual Christian's experience which he believed to be essential, and to be in danger, under a formal system, of passing out of remembrance. He sought to revive in himself the function of the " prophet " ; he announced the existence still of the prophetic " charismata " ; he refused to accept the view, already in vogue, that the Apostolic period was one of special light and inspiration, never to be expected again ; he laid stress on a progressive revelation to the Church, dwelling much on the promises of development contained in the last discourses of St. John's Gospel. In some ways the Montanists were representative of a spirit always latent and always needed in the Christian Church, the spirit of revolt against formalism and conventionalism ; in its emphasis on the importance of the individual experience of life, wholly so. Indeed, it gave saints and martyrs, Perpetua and Felicitas, to the Church Calendar, and one great genius, at least, Tertullian, to the roll of its apologists; at one time it very nearly gained recognition from the Bishop of Rome as a fully Catholic movement. But it was in the method whereby the individual's experience reached him that Montanus made the mistake, or rather laid the undue emphasis, which by its exaggerations stamped him and his followers as heretical. He had evidently himself experienced the Ecstasy,—perhaps his former life had rendered him especially susceptible to such psycho-spiritual states—and he found in the Pauline writings warrant for what he had felt; but he lifted his experience out of the realm of the exceptional to that of the normal. The reign or dispensation of the Holy Spirit had come, he taught, and the working of the Spirit would show itself in the complete supersession of human nature by the Spirit's indwelling. There would take place, not a gradual transformation " from glory to glory ", but nothing short of possession. " Man," he says—and the saying is that of a mystic who has travelled too far—" man is like a lyre, and the Holy Spirit plays on him like a plectrum; man sleeps, the Spirit is awake." The " immediacy " of Divine intercourse in this is attractive; but it is an immediacy that turns man into a mere medium or instrument, destroys personality as a condition of the intercourse itself, and so in turn would induce a nescience of the Personality of God. Whatever may have been the case, however, with Montanus, in his followers the Ecstasy soon sank into mere visionariness, and beautiful as are some of the visions, say, of St. Perpetua, so far is it from the fact that all human emotions or conditions are " put to sleep " during them, that her visions, like ordinary dreams, are full of human associations. With the later Montanists, the visions became " oracles ", and what was in inception partly a protest for spiritual freedom turned into a new, and severe, code of arbitrary laws.

(2) The importance of Gnosticism does not lie in anything

M.C.   E

that it had in common with Mysticism. Its only affinities
with the latter lay in the attempt which it made to solve
two problems which always confront the mystic, namely,
the relations of the Absolute to the world of matter, and
the existence of evil. But there the resemblance stops.
The " speculations " of the gnostic were speculations not
in the sense of some spiritual truth actually discerned, even
though " in a glass darkly ", but speculations in the normal
meaning of the word as we use it now—guesswork, and
often wild guesswork, of the imagination. It was indeed
γνῶσις " falsely so called ", for to our modern temper there
was nothing of " knowledge " about the theories of the
Syrian Saturninus, or of the Alexandrians Basilides and
Valentinus. All traces of authoritative intuition as well
as of the humility of the seeker after truth are absent from
the " metaphysics of wonderland " in which Valentinus
and his fellows indulged, a veritable " Pelagianism of the
intellect ", as Dorner has well phrased it. Moreover, the
hopeless dualism in which Gnosticism finally issued is quite
alien from the mystical instinct after a basic unity. For
all that, Gnosticism has a critical importance in the history
of thought and even of Christian mystical thought. The
religious intellect of the second century was powerfully
influenced by Platonism, and especially by one of Plato's
works, the *Timaeus*. The *Timaeus* teaches that God, being
essentially good, is withdrawn from the creation far into
some supreme heaven so as to avoid contact with matter
and its inherent evil. Now Gnosticism was really a parade
of " the ideas of Plato seen through the fog of an Egyptian
or Syrian mind." [1] All the, to us, uncouth jargon of a
lower God of creation, the Demiurge, the fantastic lists
of ever descending aeons with their partners and progenies,

---

[1] Bigg: *Christian Platonists*, p. 27. See for an excellent brief
sketch of the Gnostics Dr. Workman's *Christian Thought to the
Reformation*, pp. 31–39.

which the Gnostics used to bridge the baffling gulf between the Absolute and this universe, have an intense underlying significance. What may perhaps be faintly traced in one man's mind, in the case of Montanus, is here seen on an enormous scale and through the lapse of centuries, the clash and mingling of Christian and pagan systems of thought. If, as Dr. Workman says, " the first effect of the contact of Christianity with Hellenism was somewhat disastrous to the Church ", if " the meeting of the two streams led to a welter, in the whirlpools of which many were lost ", still something was gained. A foundation was laid—for even St. Paul uses in a favourable sense such terms of speculative Theism as *Gnosis* and *Pleroma*, and St. John brings his writings into relation with current outside thought—for nobler and more enduring movements of reconciliation to come. Gnosticism sought to harmonize with the Gospel all sorts and scraps of Hellenistic thought and of Eastern theosophy, to the latter of which ideas of emanations and unreal incarnations were not strange. Yet the very motive was of the utmost moment, though it cost the Church sore struggles with heresies bent on evacuating the Incarnation of all historical reality. For " Gnosticism, both within and without the Church, was an attempt to complete the reconciliation between speculative and revealed religion, by systematizing the symbols of transcendental mystical theosophy. The movement can only be understood as a premature and unsuccessful attempt to achieve what the school of Alexandria afterwards partially succeeded in doing."[1]

(3) So we come to the far more lasting and important phase of Christian thought known as Alexandrianism. Of Philo's work something has already been said. His thought was that of a true mystic ; his object that which became the passion of the next one or two centuries, the synthesis

[1] Inge : *Christian Mysticism*, p. 81.

of his religion and the best philosophy of his time. In his own case this meant reconciliation of Platonism and Judaism, and we have seen how interesting were the affinities of his Logos-doctrine—though we need not forget its points of difference—with those of the Fourth Evangelist. Still more important, perhaps, as reflecting a state of ethical opinion which was destined to grow and to influence deeply the Church, was his doctrine of the spiritual life. Only by the renunciation of the self can either virtue or knowledge be attained. Contemplation is exalted above the active virtues,—the soul must shun the whirlpool of life and not even touch it, it were better for it " to cut off its right hand "—and the highest vision of God is attained by the knowledge not of reason but of " clear certainty ". This is very like the authoritative intuition of the Ecstasy. But Philo's own influence on his times seems to have been smaller than might be expected. The unpopularity of the Jews and of their faith, to which certain passages in the Acts, the scorn poured upon them by satirists such as Juvenal, and various anti-Semitic riots up and down the Empire alike bear witness, may account for his work passing comparatively unnoticed. It is different when we come to the man who, 150 years later, set himself to do for Christianity what Philo had conceived it possible to do for Judaism. It is to St. Clement of Alexandria that the Church owed in large measure the priceless impulse to gather in, reconcile, assimilate to its own teaching what was truly durable and luminous in the vast treasuries of human thought around it, the impulse to move in the van, and not to lag with a dumb hostility in the rear, of intellectual progress. " The way of truth ", said Clement, " is one. But into it as into a perennial river streams flow from all sides." It was a bold undertaking this, the incorporation into the Faith of all that was best in the culture of the Hellenic world ; next to St. Paul's deliberate de-Judaizing of Christianity, the boldest work ever wrought for the Church. It set the example and opened the way for the after-entry of Neo-Platonism, for the work of St. Thomas Aquinas and the Schoolmen, for the Humanist efforts at the Reformation, unhappily unsuccessful with both warring parties, of Erasmus and the Oxford Reformers ; it is eloquent to the Church of the present day.[1] Dr. Hort's praise of the great Alexandrian father is well-deserved : " There is no one whose vision of what the faith of Jesus Christ was intended to do for mankind was so full or so true."[2]

Clement was born about 150, and by birth and training was probably an Athenian. Then he came to Alexandria and settled down to work in the great Christian catechetical school founded there in the latter half of the second century by Pantaenus, a man who illustrated well Clement's own maxim that " conduct follows knowledge as the shadow follows the body " by going in his old age as a missionary to India. Alexandria, then the second city in the Empire, was a place of which, even more emphatically than of Athens, might have been uttered St. Luke's description of the latter place at the time of Paul's visit. It had its famous University ; in its midst met and jostled every kind of current thought and speculation ; each " new thing " as it arose was eagerly discussed, as well as the problem of the " Unknown God ". For Alexandria was the link between East and West, and at this time the particular home of " three great tendencies then, as now, potent in shaping the thoughts of men, Egyptian symbolism with its esoteric beliefs and ancient priesthood, Jewish monotheism, and Greek science, philosophy and culture."[3] It was in the midst of such surroundings,

---

[1] Cf. Workman : *Christian Thought to the Reformation*, pp. 44 et seq.

[2] *Ante-Nicene Fathers*, p. 93.   [3] Workman : *op. cit.* p. 46.

where thought was free, and speculation rampant, that there flourished the invaluable Christian school, with its tuition of mathematics and sciences, of the Greek philosophies, and of the Old Testament Scriptures as preparatory to the higher knowledge of the Faith, and it was during his years of connexion with this school for catechumens and ordination candidates that Clement worked at note books,—" *Stromateis*," or " Clothes Bags," as he called them—on the True Philosophy, and at the " Pedagogue", his rationale of the Christian life and experience.

It is necessary to understand the circumstances of St. Clement's life and work in general, because they provide us with the key to the important contributions which he made to the body of mystical doctrine within the Church. It is curious how opinions differ as to Clement's personal claim to be a mystic. Thus Dr. Inge names him, along with Dionysius the Areopagite, a " founder of Christian Mysticism ", Dr. Bigg, in his " Christian Platonists of Alexandria ", calls him the father of all the Christian mystics, but no mystic himself, while Dr. Rufus Jones recognizes that " in high moods he hit upon elemental facts of universal religious experience ", but otherwise, rather than a mystic was, like Origen and Athanasius, a profound thinker, " interpreting Christianity to the Greek mind through the historical forms of Greek thought." [1] The truth is that he was no ecstatic, but a " cultivated, humane, and genial personality ", in thought discursive rather than deep, and extremely receptive to the ideas current in that mingled world in which he moved. But for that very reason his teaching in at least two directions marks an era in Christian thought. In his pre-Christian days he had been conversant with the various aspects and practices of Pagan religious systems. Prominent amongst

---

[1] *Studies in Mystical Religion*, p. 83.

these, the outstanding feature indeed of Hellenic religion of the time, was the cult of the Mysteries, themselves perhaps the survivals of some old-world kind of Nature-Mysticism. We may take the " public mysteries " of Eleusis, a place near Athens, as typical of the kind of rites observed. First of all, the " mystae ", who assembled at Athens, had to undergo a fast of several days, and then, after confessing the worst of their sins, were baptized either in the sea or in a salt lake on the road to Eleusis. This baptism washed away the guilt of former sins, and was followed by certain sacrifices and by the witnessing of Mystery-plays in which the truths to be communicated to the initiates were represented in shadow outline. The whole culminated in a sacramental meal partaken together by the initiates.

Now it is extremely easy to trace curious resemblances and coincidences between such ritual as this and external Christianity. To Clement of Alexandria first, and to a succession of theologians after him from the third to the fifth centuries, it became almost a passion " to transfer to the faith and practice of the Church almost every term which was associated with the Eleusinian mysteries and others like them." [1] A great sentence of his is probably well known, but it is so symptomatic of the medium through which he viewed Christianity that it may well be quoted here : " Oh truly sacred mysteries ! Oh stainless light ! My way is lit with torches and I survey the heavens and God. I am become holy while I am being initiated, and the Lord is my hierophant." '" Knowledge " with him " is more than faith." The Christian revelation is described as " the holy mysteries ", " the Divine secrets ", and of these " mysteries of the Word " Christ is the Teacher ;

---

[1] Inge : *Christian Mysticism*, Appendix B. *q.v.* for a full discussion of the subject.

we find within the Church, a reproduction of the two
grades of initiates at Eleusis there are the mere "*mystae*",
who only know the ordinary teaching of the Faith, and
there are the "*epopts*" (ἐπόπται), to whom the higher
wisdom of the true Gnostic has been vouchsafed. Just
as in the Greek mysteries, so in the Christian Faith, strict
secrecy is to be observed towards "the profane", the out-
sider. The lower stages of purifying discipline are τὰ
μικρὰ μυστήρια, "the little mysteries"; the highest spiritual plane is ἐποπτεία. So far as regards practice; and
the use of such mystery-terms in expounding Christian
doctrine was far more extended by Gregory of Nyssa,
Chrysostom and Athanasius. As regards inner doctrine,
there is one feature of the Mystery-religions which Clement
transported into the scheme of mystical theology in the
Church, and which owes itself directly to him. The main
object of initiation into the Mysteries was to obtain salvation, for the longing for salvation was especially prominent throughout the world of the first centuries of our
era. But in what did "salvation" consist? In the
gift—and this idea was common to Christians and Pagans
alike—of everlasting life. Now this everlasting life—
immortality—was a peculiar attribute of the gods. It
was conferred, the current thought ran, on any one who
participated in the mysteries, by revelation (*gnosis*), and
by the sacramental washing and eating, and it took effect
through a resultant purity of life. Now Clement not only
embraces the mystery-definition of salvation, but pushes
the thought further. The acquisition of this immortal
life will be in some sense a "deification". The word and
notion became familiar to mystical theologians, however
alien and even repellent they appear to us; and it was
Clement who brought them over first from Paganism into
Christianity. τὸ μὴ φθείρεσθαι θειότητος μετέχειν ἐστί,[1]

[1] "To be immortal (imperishable) is to share in the Divine nature."

he says in the *Stromateis*. But in this and other matters he evidently delights in his work of synthesis. The Church is heir, he thinks, of all that is best in thought and life, not only Hebraic, but Greek, which has gone before it. Perhaps to act as pioneer in this great-hearted task of comprehensiveness, of which the Church at its best has always shown itself capable, was the real achievement of St. Clement of Alexandria. In the West, at any rate, the note he struck vibrated on and never wholly died away. Even in the Dark Ages, men looked on Socrates and Vergil, on Plato and Plotinus, as half-canonized prophets or seers of the true Light of the world.

It may very well be, however, that depreciation of Clement's personal mysticism has been carried too far. Cultivated, cheerful and serene, he was certainly no mystic of the cloistered or ascetic type, nor, one would suppose, had his soul ever been scarred by some devastating experience, whose memory would afterwards make the contours of the world more shifting, and its hues paler. Nevertheless, in his thought of God he shows that his own approach to the subject was that which became common to a vast school of Mysticism in later days ; and in his use of " mystery " language, it is not only on the ideas of secrecy and of sacramentalism, but on the ideas of brotherhood and of right conduct required of the initiates that he lays vital stress. So that it was his mysticism that helped him to his comprehensiveness of thought. Meditation on God reduces the discords of earth to a great stillness and is in itself a feeling through confusion to the Unity that waits behind. Clement's meditation on God took the form of " analysis ", that is, like Augustine, he can but say what God is not, rather than venture to define what He is. God is indeed, he confesses, Being, rather than above Being, but he pursues refinement on refinement so far that at last only a nameless point of Being is left. But the idea even of the Monad must be discarded, for God is above or beyond it. In fact, here it is that the second Person of the Trinity is necessary to man, as also to God. For the Second Person is the " Idea of Ideas ", That in Which God comes to the knowledge of Himself, to self-consciousness, and also That in Which God sees the world ; and, needless to say, He it is also in Whom in turn we see God.

Such a mode of thought is daring and would be, perhaps, dangerous, or at least barren, if Clement stopped there. But he does not stop short at meditation. The true knowledge of God is no mere intellectual speculation. It mainly consists in growing like God. A man " knowing God will be made like God." The Divine Idea, or Word, is ever being born anew in the hearts of saints. It is communion with God, as revealed in Christ, which again and again he urges on his readers if any one will become a " harmonized man ". So Prayer is intercourse with God ; Faith a " divine and human reciprocal correspondence." Again, " He who would enter the shrine must be holy, and holiness is to think holy things " ; and, once more, " In proportion as man loves, so the more deeply does he enter into God."

Origen, Clement's pupil, who died in 253 after a bold confession of his faith in the Decian persecution, finished the structure and placed the coping-stone of the Alexandrian school of theology. Far more logical and systematic than his master, he modified some of his doctrines, and pursued others to an extreme which, despite the vast services which he rendered to the thought of the Church, earned for his writings partial condemnation and wholesale neglect for centuries. Like St. Clement he says that God is beyond or above Being, but He is not above such distinctions as goodness and wisdom. Again he modifies St. Clement's teaching as to the Son. The Son is still the " Idea of Ideas ", but He is the Activity of God, That whereby the One becomes manifold, rather than the Self-consciousness or Reason of God. God can be approached by the human reason as well as by the mystical ecstasy. A mysticism drawn from the thought of the age finds its place in Origen's conception of the Incarnation. We have the idea of the mysteries and their initiates in a more sharply defined form. Those who look to and value the Scripture facts, and especially the Gospel history, as the basis of their faith merely have according to him " somatic " or outward Christianity. Even the Cross is but teaching for babes. The acts of Christ are *αἰνίγματα*, —" riddles "—symbols that shadow forth the " pneumatic " or spiritual Gospel, for the real life, death, and resurrection of the Christ are part of a universal law enacted beyond time, in the counsels of eternity. The results of this undervaluation of the historical Incarnation, as of all the affairs of time, are often seen in Origen's system. As regards evil, he inclines, like all his Greek contemporaries, to the belief that evil is unreal, has no substance ; only the good exists. This leads him towards a confident Universalism, and he contributes the doctrine of a remedial purgatory, to bear fruit in a modified form among the future tenets of the Church. Much of Origen's teaching, and not least that of a " mystical sense " underlying the narratives of the Old and New Testaments, was also pregnant in this way. But we may trace to his evacuation of much of the meaning of the Incarnation and of the Cross for a world to which, after all, sin will always be a momentous tragedy, that undue subordination of the place and office of the Son which indirectly encouraged the advance of Arian heresy. On the other hand, to Origen, more than to any other theologian, may be ascribed the deliverance of the Church from the feverish dreams of Gnosticism. Something like a reasoned Christology, something defined and intellectually cogent took the place of the crude and bewildered speculations of Valentinus and Basilides.

That is how we may sum up the merits and defects of the great Christian Platonist school of Alexandria. It made the Christian Faith a Catholic faith in a sense it had never been before, by bringing it into relationship and harmony with the best and deepest thoughts of the day ; its mystical consciousness and expectation of direct communion with God was to be an inspiration, a breath of life within the Church, in darker ages than its own. On the other hand, it had the defects of a " school ". Something aloof and unhuman spoiled at times its most soaring thoughts and its truest intuitions. It looked on sin with Greek eyes, and so left the Atonement on one side and could find no great meaning in the Cross. Christ was the Reason of God, the Idea of Ideas, the Principle of the world, the Divine Consciousness, the Word within man, but never the Carpenter of Nazareth, the Friend of sinners, the Man of sorrows, the Saviour of the lost.

CHAPTER IV

Neo-Platonism

WE are now approaching, in our sketch of mystical thought, the strange and brilliant phenomenon of Neo-Platonism, " that splendid vision of incomparable cloudland ", as Harnack calls it, " in which the sun of Greek philosophy set ". [1] The system of Plotinus and Proclus, however, although outside the pale of Christianity, perhaps wilfully outside, cannot be passed over in any study of Christian thought. The sun of Greek philosophy might set, but it set in Athens to rise again over Christendom. Through Victorinus, who clothed sheer Neo-Platonism in Christian phraseology, and through Augustine, who had passed not unaffected through the stage of Neo-Platonic thought; through pseudo-Dionysius and Erigena, through Eckhart and his followers, Neo-Platonism found in the Church a congenial, and, it may be added, a lasting home. For the coming of its extraordinarily powerful influence—an influence with which in Western Christianity nothing can compare save that, later, of what we may call the " Teutonic Spirit "—the Alexandrines specifically paved the approach. They did this in several ways. (1) By their encouragement of the syncretic spirit within the Church; and Neo-Platonism was sympathetic to this since it claimed to be " the philo-

---

[1] Harnack : *History of Dogma*, i, p. 341.

sophy completing all systems ". Alexandria, where all
tides of opinion met, was the very place whence the belief could spread amongst Christians that the best of Pagan
philosophies, far from being really hostile to Christianity,
formed a sort of " *praeparatio Evangelica* ". (2) By their
use of the mystery terms ; and, again, with the mystery
cults the later Neo-Platonists were in close alliance. (3)
By the distinction, in Clement's case already drawn, between the two lives,—higher and lower—, which might be
followed by the Christian, the higher, the " contemplative " as opposed to the lower, the " practical ". In this
distinction which he drew too systematically, too sharply,
Clement and his followers were really in protest against
what made for formalism and materialism in the Church.
To be effective the protest had to be decisive in tone, and
an unmistakable emphasis laid on the possibility of a
higher life of thought and prayer. But the foundation
for the after mystical classification was laid. (4) Above
all, Clement prepared the way for Plotinus' doctrine of
the Ecstasy by his talk of the " Apathy " through and
by which the fully disciplined and filial soul holds converse with God. God, that is, is to be loved for His own
sake, and not for the sake of happiness or reward to be
obtained from Him. The Christian " attains to perfect
Apathy, because no thought stirs against the Saviour's
mind. He does God's Will because he cannot help doing
it : he knows, because love is the key to all secrets. He
has sacrificed even the consciousness of sacrifice. . . .
This is the Disinterested Love so famous in later mysticism. It expresses itself in the ' mystic paradox ' that
it is better to be with Christ in hell, than without Him in
heaven. The true mystic demands nothing but to be
allowed to love, and will not pray the Beloved even to
cast a glance or a thought upon him. Like all mystics,
Clement speaks of ' silent prayer ', but at this point he

stopped short." [1]   It is precisely where he " stopped short " that Plotinus, and the long line of Christian mystics who took up his thought, formulated their highest conception of the communion between the human soul and the Divine.

Plotinus " the one analytical mystic ", as M. Maeterlinck calls him, was born in 205, and, although his disciple and biographer Porphyry does not name his birthplace or race, he appears from other testimony to have been a Copt of Lycopolis in Egypt.   At the age of twenty-seven he is found in the University of Alexandria, studying philosophy and engaged with sincere and even painful eagerness in the search after truth.   One teacher after another failed him, until at last one day he chanced to stray into the classroom of Ammonius Saccas—" the porter ", as his name implies, and apparently a self-taught philosopher. " This is the man I am seeking ", cried Plotinus, as he listened to him.   Ammonius had been a Christian, and had turned away from the Faith.   Of his own doctrine we know hardly anything, but his repudiation of Christianity cannot but have had its effect on the mind of his pupil. At Alexandria, and at the feet of Ammonius, he remained for eleven years, making his choice of faith and of life. That his choice was a high one, no one, from that day to this, has doubted.   Amid the welter of beliefs that clashed and strove for mastery in the lecture halls and streets of Alexandria, Plotinus listened and mused and gradually wrought out his idealized Platonism, intellectually and morally the most perfect system of belief, outside Christianity, that the world has known.   On the death of Ammonius, about 242, he joined Gordian's expedition against Persia, so as to complete his round of mental experience by a knowledge of Persian and Hindoo beliefs.   Perhaps this step may be taken as an early indication of the attraction which the later Neo-Platonists, such as Porphyry and

[1] Dr. Bigg : *Neo-Platonism*, pp. 175–6.

Iamblichus, felt from Eastern modes of religious thought. In Plotinus' case, however, the influence of the East was destined to be very scanty and short lived. The Emperor Gordian was assassinated at the outset of the campaign, and Plotinus returned, not now to Alexandria, but, partly in the capacity of a missionary, to Rome, where he spent the rest of his life. Before we trace those features of his teaching which concern our subject, we may ask here a question which has often excited curiosity : Why was not Plotinus a Christian ? Nothing in his pure and holy life, through which there ran the charm of his modesty, his love for children, his power in turbulent Rome as a peace-maker, his contempt for wealth, his simplicity of manners, militated against his acceptance of the Faith. His philosophy, too, might seem to lend itself, by a ready adaptation, to Christian dogma. For, according to Plotinus, God is a Trinity in Unity. He is the One, the Good, the Absolute, Who is above all existence and definition ; again, He is *Noῦς*, Intelligence, Mind, God in thought, the " One-Many ", in Plotinian phrase ; and yet again, He is Soul, the " One-and-Many ", God in action, God as manifest in the realm of appearance and time-succession.[1] Again, evil is disintegration, that which is without the " Logos ", the vital and binding force of law, and is so unreal as to be unable to appear without conjunction with some very low form of goodness.[2] Here, again, he comes very close to much Christian mystical phraseology as to evil, its nature, or rather, its non-nature, the " null and void ". Again, with such doctrines of Plotinus as that the universe is a vast organism so vitally connected in all its parts that " if one member suffer, all the members suffer with it ",

---

[1] Cf. Bigg: *Neo-Platonism*, pp. 219-22. Inge: *Christian Mysticism*, p. 95.

[2] Cf. *Enneads* i, 8. 13. " Evil is still human, having been mixed with something opposite to itself."

Christianity is in fullest concord : as with much of his teaching about the virtues, when for instance he says that what we know as the four cardinal virtues, the duties of the citizen, belong really to the process of mystical ascent (though he assigns them to the lowest stage) ; that they are purgative and that they teach us the Divine characteristics of " measure and rule ". Now, as Dr. Bigg has said, " there can be no doubt that these speculations aided greatly in the clear formulation of Christian truth," and, with regard to the Plotinian Trinity, " they made it possible to understand how the Three Divine Persons of the Baptismal Formula should yet be One in Godhead ". But why, then, did not Plotinus accept Christianity ? He must have come across it, examined it, and deliberately put it on one side. Various answers have been suggested to the question, and two of these will indicate to us so well what his own mystical standpoint was, and what was his final, though indirect, contribution to Christian mysticism, that we shall do wisely to pass them in review. We may surely dismiss Dr. Bigg's not very happy suggestion that, since the strength of the Church lay in its possession of a revelation, " one, and probably not the least, among the motives of Plotinus was the desire to outbid it ". [1] This does violence to our knowledge of Plotinus' gentle and exalted character. Besides, he was never, like Porphyry, a professed opponent to Christianity : he simply ignored it. It has been surmised that Plotinus only knew of Christianity under some of the repellent Gnostic forms that affected it in Alexandria. That might very possibly be true of the Alexandrian stage of his life, when, too, he was under the domination of Ammonius Saccas ; but later he also knew Christianity during the Decian persecution and in times of tranquillity as a *religio licita* under Gallienus. There is something far more plausible in the idea that the

---

[1] Bigg : *Neo-Platonism*, p. 291.

synthetic aspirations dear to the later Platonists and rife in Alexandria, which bred in Plotinus the missionary zeal to found a philosophy that should sum up and reconcile all other systems, felt themselves in immediate and lasting revolt to the exclusive claims of the Christian Faith. But in truth there was in Plotinus' system of thought—a system remarkable as being not speculative merely, but, the nearer he gets in his thoughts to God, instinct with experience—something directly alien from the central idea of Christianity. That central idea is the Incarnation; and it was on the conception of God coming down to man, in love to man, that Celsus had rained his scorn. Plotinus rains no scorn; but none the less the Incarnation, with all that it implies, was out of the range of his thought. He was on fire with love for the One, the Absolute, it is true, and with desire for that knowledge of the Divine which to him, as to all the Platonists, was eternal life. But, like Spinoza, ages afterwards, he would have said, " He that loves God must not expect to be loved by Him in return ". " According to Plotinus, God is Goodness without love. Man may love God, but God cannot love man. Religion is the desire for the star. Man can reach the star and cannot be happy unless he does; but the star does not know anything about him and does not care whether the reaches it or not ". [1] This inward disinterested drawing owards the Good, the One, was a true mystical trait. But that for which Plotinus is beyond all else important in the evolution of mystical thought was his doctrine of the Ecstasy. Plotinus' psychology was his strongest point: it is because we can discover, as Dr. Bigg says, in the human mind the shadow or reflection of the Plotinian Trinity, [2] that his work in defining that Trinity has lasted. It is experiential, in fact, not_merely speculative. Hence what

[1] Bigg: *Neo-Platonism*, p. 248.   [2] *Ib.* p. 222.

he has to say about the highest stage of his own psychological experience must be received with respect, not only because he himself laid emphatic stress upon it, but because the experience he described passed over into the Church as the goal of the contemplative life.

It must be remembered again that Plotinus, as a Platonist, put the knowledge of God, the Beloved, as the condition of life. Now at each end of his category there is a stage which can but be described as Formlessness. Just as evil is disintegration, the somewhat beneath Being, so the One, the Good, is above and beyond Being. Yet it is necessary to the highest attainment of the soul that there should somehow, impossible as it seems, be correspondence or contact between this Ineffable One and the soul. For " if the One is a mere hypothesis, everything becomes uncertain. He must be in some sense knowable, and He could be known only by being seen or felt ". In one sense every good man, craving for ascent to God, attains to communion with Him. For " Intelligence (*Noûs*) is our King ", says Plotinus, " and we are kings when we are like Him. Life is never weary when it is pure ". This is to know God as Another, as something that we possess ; it is communion with the Second Person of the Triad, the *Noûs* or Intelligence. And this *Noûs* corresponds exactly to Eckhart's " God ", as distinct from the Godhead.

Is there a higher stage ? Plotinus thought there is. " We must go up further to the Good, for which every soul craves. . . . Let us fly to our dear fatherland ! " [1] " Using the pure Intelligence " we must look, as it were, from that standpoint, and see God, as the Second Person of the Trinity beholds the First. Plotinus illustrates the difference between the two sorts of vision by the act of sight. We see a form ; we also see the light that makes it visible ; and the very sight of the form makes us con-

[1] *Enn.* i. 6.

scious of the light by which we see it. Intelligence must
turn away from the form and concentrate itself upon the
light. Or the vision can be described in terms of sensation, such as the pervading yet unanalysable feeling of
good-health. The soul may make preparation for the
vision by moral purity, knowledge, the pursuit of beauty,
but must in no way try to force the experience. Indescribable when it comes, incommunicable to others, the
Ecstasy may not be induced by conscious emotional effort,
or wrought-up feeling, or thought, or prayer. Here St.
Clement's doctrine of Apathy comes in; and it is important to note that with Plotinus the experience was never
self-induced, still less attained by mechanical means such as
self-hypnosis or fasting, or such dubious methods as Professor James has instanced in his " Varieties of Religious
Experience ". So far from this being the case, it came
at its own will entirely, and all the subject could do was
to be in a normal state of preparedness.[1] It was, in fact,
a special grace, and was given by, not obtained from, Him
Who is self-manifested. " We cannot force God; we
must be quiet ". In a characteristic passage[2] Plotinus
tries to describe the ineffable. " He is within, yet not
within. We must not ask whence He comes; there is
no whence. For He never comes, and He never goes;
but appears, and does not appear. Wherefore we must
not pursue Him, but wait quietly till He show Himself,
only we must make ourselves ready to behold, as the eye
awaits the dayspring. And He swims above the horizon

---

[1] In fact, the stillness or " apathy " of soul which Plotinus predi-
cates does not mean idleness or vacuity, a sitting, as it has been
put, " with eyes shut and hands folded ". That in itself would be
a kind of pressing of God. Rather, it is a luminous awareness,
and habitual meditation, together with a complete resignation of
the self into the Hands of God.

[2] *Enn.* i, 5, 8.

. . . and gives Himself to our gaze ". Elsewhere there is a lovely passage likening the soul to one who had entered a palace rich and beautiful, who would gaze with wonder on all its varied treasures till he had caught sight of the Master of the House. But when he beholds Him Who is far more lovely than any of his statues and worthy of the true contemplation, he forgets the treasures and marks their Lord alone. He looks and cannot remove his eyes, till by persistence of gaze he no longer sees an object, but blends his sight with that which is seen, so that what was object becomes sight. Or again, the One suddenly appears " with nothing between ", " and they (the soul and the One) are no more two but one . . . and the soul knows that she would not exchange her bliss for all the heaven of heavens ". [1]

Plotinus believed himself to have experienced the vision of the One, or the Ecstasy, several times ; Porphyry enumerates three occasions, and tells us that he himself had known it once. It came, we gather, suddenly ; it was accompanied by a suspension, more or less complete, of external consciousness ; it conveyed no sense of fear, but rather of unutterable joy ; it was no dream, hallucination, or " vision " in the lower sense, inasmuch as nothing of definite form or scene was presented ; it was therefore indescribable, but it left a sense of certitude and the heightening of the spiritual faculties. In this contact (ἐταφή) with the Divine the perfect soul conceives, " when filled with God ", beautiful thoughts and graces.

What are we to think of Plotinus' ecstasy ? A great deal depends on the answer, because Plotinus regarded his ecstasy as a true revelation of the Divine, and was, in fact, the first thinker to bring the idea of a revelation into Greek philosophy. We may begin by saying, tentatively, with Dr. Bigg, that " Revelation is the revelation of a

[1] *Enn.* vi. 35, 34.

Presence, of a Personality ; and without denying the possibility of revelation altogether, we can hardly say that
the vision of Plotinus is inconceivable ". [1] But the question, which, if it merely concerned Plotinus, would have
for us but a passing interest, becomes of immense importance when we note that in all its essential characteristics
Plotinus' experience was identical with that of the great
Christian mystics of after time, and indeed came, through
his Christian interpreters, to exercise a momentous influence on Christian mystical theology. Thus, from all the
natural or abnormal conditions which may give rise to
seemingly mystical experiences—disease, hysteria, nerve
excitement, memory-associations, of which Professor James
makes mention and most of which, it may be added, Pope
Benedict XIV in his *De Canonisatione* enumerated before
him,—Plotinus' trance-experience was absolutely free. Fr.
Sharpe, in his recent and striking treatise on the nature of
Mysticism, notes candidly the resemblances between the
ecstasy of Plotinus and those experiences of the great contemplatives on which the Church has set the seal of verity.
" We find ", he says, " in Plotinus the most advanced conceptions of the great Christian mystics. There is no vision
or locution ; all is abstract or purely spiritual. But Plotinus tells us almost in identical phraseology of the Mansions of St. Theresa, of the prayer of quiet,[2] of St. John's
dark night of faith, and of the spiritual marriage ; the
" ground " (κέντρον) of the soul is with him as familiar
and as necessary an idea as it is with the German mystics.
Quotations might be multiplied and coincidences noted
to almost any extent." [3] He comes to the conclusion

---

[1] Bigg : *Neo-Platonism*, p. 288.
[2] Cf. St. Teresa. " Our Lord does not require the faculties or
senses to open the door of the heart to Him : they are all asleep.
We can do nothing on our part ".
[3] Sharpe : *Mysticism, Its True Nature and Value*, p. 151.

that " we must accept the experience of Plotinus as one of those manifestations of divine grace outside its regular channels, the occurrence of which from time to time, has been quite unmistakable," and he bids us therefore consider Plotinus, " magnus ille Platonicus ", as St. Augustine called him, " an involuntary witness to the truth of the Christian view of mysticism, and the reality of the experience of Christian mystics ". [1]

Plotinus died in 269 with the characteristic farewell on his lips, " Now the divine in me is struggling to reunite with the Divine in the All ". During the next 150 years, the school of philosophy of which he had been the chief light suffered a long process of degradation from within, and, as time went by, of discredit and even oppression without. Plotinus' message had never been a gospel for the simple and the poor in spirit ; it was at once its boast and its weakness that it appealed only to the wise, the learned, and the lofty-minded. It offered, not cleansing as its way of salvation, but knowledge. Under Porphyry, and still more under Iamblichus, who died in 330, Neo-Platonism suffered from the inrush of all kinds of Oriental superstitions, the practice of magic, the use of divination by numbers, and a good deal of dabbling in what the present day would call spiritualism. In Porphyry's writings beautiful mystical sayings are to be found, such as " True religion is to know God and to imitate Him ", " God looks not on the lips, but on the life ", " The true temple is the soul of the wise ",

---

[1] Sharpe, *op. cit.* p. 157. This writer has an interesting theory of the mystical experience. He thinks it a real sense-contact (cf. Plotinus' ἐπαφή), an immediate intuition of and communication with the divine Being. This happens in the " transmarginal " sphere, and " the way, whatever it may be, in which we become conscious of ideas derived from unnoticed sense-impressions may be identical with that in which the mystic becomes conscious of the immediate divine presence ". p. 116, *et seq.*

and (though this itself is an older quotation) " He that wills to enter the fragrant shrine must be holy, and holiness is to think holy thoughts ", but along with such teaching goes a belief in magic, in spells, in the baleful power of demons, against whose maleficence even divine philosophy offered no reliable safeguard. Well might Augustine say, " Thou didst learn these things not from Plato but from thy Chaldaean teachers ".

Over Iamblichus, with whom arose what was definitely known as the Syrian school of Neo-Platonism, and his successors, Maximus and Chrysanthius, it is unnecessary to .linger. Maximus is famous as the man who brought about the Emperor Julian's apostasy, but it was the Imperial disciple who lent to his circle what nobility it had. The world, to these men, was a troubled dream, which at any moment might become a nightmare, of apparitions and portents. Magic, white, and also black, was the sort of *gnosis* in which they chiefly dealt, prayer became a mere succession of formulas, often a jargon of syllables with no meaning at all. God Himself was mainly manifested as Miracle, acting in response to such invocations. The soul, which, in opposition to the teaching of Plotinus, was out of all touch with the Divine Intelligence, dwelt on earth amongst many foes, and was shadowed over by a bewilderment of world-powers. For Iamblichus had split up the Intelligence or Νοῦς into a triad, Thinking, Thought and the Thinker, each of these begetting another triad with a hebdomad alongside it, and so on *ad infinitum*. Then, as a last gesture of defiance against victorious Christianity, he had reconstituted the twelve old Gods of Olympus, and equipped them with a vast family or court of ever-descending orders and world-rulers. It was in the midst of this confusion that, on every hand, signs of the fall of heathenism flared out like the writing on the doomed wall of Babylon. In 368, the old creed had been so far

driven from the civilized and cultured towns into the rude
"pagi" or rural districts that the word "Paganism"
appeared for the first time to describe it in a law of Val-
entinian. Then came the reign of Theodosius, and the
traditional dying words of Julian, five and twenty years
before, "Vicisti, O Galilace!" were realized in fact. In
391, the Serapeum at Alexandria was destroyed, and the
schools of Hellenism there were occupied by communities of Christian monks; and in 394, the Senate of Rome
was formally converted to the Faith.

Yet Athens still remained consistent in fidelity to a
philosophy that seemed on the point of dissolution. Plu-
tarch was still teaching there, and one night, two years
before his death, a stranger arrived at the gates, just as
the porter was closing them. The porter's words, "I
should have shut up the place, had not you arrived", were
afterwards looked upon as prophetic. For the stranger
was Proclus, who with some judges is still ranked as among
the first of ancient thinkers, who certainly delayed the
final fall of Hellenism and of Polytheism in its ancient
haunts for a century by the force of his genius, and who,
like Plotinus, was destined to exert no little influence on
Christian thought.

Proclus was born about 410, and it was at the age of
nineteen that he journeyed to Athens, where, with the
exception of one enforced flight, perhaps on account of
his opinions, he lived a blameless life, and where he died
in 485. The relation which he bears to Plotinus in some
way resembles the relation which Medieval Scholasticism
bore to Mysticism. There was much more of the scholastic than of the mystic about Proclus. The distinction
is probably correct that the true province of Mysticism
is psychological and experimental, but that anything like
dogma must be left to the *magisterium* of the Church,
or if the phrase be preferred, to the common Christian

consciousness. So the after scholastics did not reject
the mystical experience and discipline, but sought to cor-
relate them with the whole *summa* of Church doctrine,
to find them their place, in fact. In his lesser way, this
is what Proclus sought to do with the Plotinian and Iam-
blichan systems that had preceded him. The result—
his " Rudiments of Theology "—was in many ways a
great piece of work, for its author was a great metaphysician : but it suffered from two defects. (1) Proclus
had no touch of intimate personal communion with the
Divine to lighten up and vitalize his severe deductive
processes. This absence of personal experience leads
him to put up, high out of reach, the Plotinian Trinity,
which had had the justification of possessing a true reflection in the human soul. With Proclus, the Good, the
Intelligence, and the Soul are not of course denied, but
" cease to be fountains of life, or causes, at all ". They
are indeed, incommunicable, and any knowledge of God
on the part of man is abandoned. Neither by opinion,
nor by science, nor by reason, nor by intuition is God known.
Such knowledge as the soul has of the Divine only comes
" necessarily " or automatically. How this is accomplished is through every soul belonging to one particular
chain of life, dependent on some under-cause or God. For
Proclus was burdened by the system of Iamblichus and
his successors, and, while rendering lip-service to Plotinus,
forsook his idea of one great chain of Life reaching through
all that is, and substituted for it the cumbrous and intricate system of triads. His principle of the division of
everything into threes had, and has, justification. It is
the " Law of the Ternary ", as Vacherot has named it,
and it was making itself felt in the theology of the Catholic Church. But in this respect it was Plotinus, and not
Proclus, who was the helpful outside force. Proclus made
it the excuse for an infinite series of chains of existence,

each of which sprang from a "Henad", having the character of absolute being, and derived in some inexplicable fashion from the "incommunicable" hypostases of the Neo-Platonic Trinity; and each in turn subdividing and ramifying endlessly as it ran down. Now, it was, he taught, by belonging to some one of these chains of existence that man necessarily and by affinity of nature knows God. Between him, therefore, and the Good, the One, there was interposed a multitude of mediated forms of being. Proclus differed also from Plotinus in crossing that Rubicon which simply speculative, as apart from experimental, mysticism ever longs to cross. The existence of evil is always a worry to the mind that wants an exactly formulated system; it comes in the way, and spoils the symmetry of the system. Plotinus, it will be remembered, recognized evil as disintegration, formlessness. Proclus denied any existence to such disintegration, and left in his system no place for evil, even in that modified form. Matter has no independent existence. (2) Proclus was hampered by being the champion, and one of the very last champions, of the falling cause of Paganism. This he took under his wing, finding places for the gods much as Iamblichus had done. Plotinus had merely tolerated a belief in them as necessary to the vulgar and ill-instructed: but Proclus was a Pagan religionist, as well as a philosopher, and, instead of smuggling away the ancient deities in this fashion, re-enthroned them with full purpose. The result is seen in a comparison of the lives of the two men. Proclus lived out his days morally and sincerely, but there is wholly lacking in his life that clear and gracious charm, the "inner light" which had something veritably Divine in its radiance, and enabled Plotinus to cast an enduring spell on human thought. With Proclus we are back amongst a crowd of discarded and repellent superstitions.

But why has it been necessary to sketch, however roughly,

the teaching of these two philosophers who were outside the pale of the Catholic Church? Because their teaching produced effects which are directly traceable within it, and which for good, and also for ill, left deep marks on the history of Mysticism, in the East for a time, and then decisively and ineffaceably in the West. What was certainly good, and strengthening to Christian thought at an era when the thoughts of the Church needed such reinforcement, found its way thither through the converted Neo-Platonist philosopher Victorinus, and his great pupil, St. Augustine; and this we owe to Plotinus. To Proclianism with its minimizing of evil and its immense series of hierarchies in the spiritual world, we can ascribe a good deal of the more doubtful doctrines of the mysterious Hierotheus, and of his disciple, destined to exercise so enormous an influence in the Western world, Dionysius the Areopagite.

CHAPTER V

The Influence of Neo-Platonism in Christianity

OF the "profound and many-sided" influence of
Neo-Platonism on Christianity there can be no
doubt whatever. The system of Plotinus, with its intellectual Trinity, that perfect flower and sum of Greek philosophic thought, could not but assist strongly, if indirectly,
the formation of Christian dogmas concerning the Being
of God, while as yet Christian formal theology was
inchoate, and Christianity itself was not "walking in silver
slippers". Besides, it is always uncertain how much,
in the first instance, Christianity gave, by unrecognized
processes, to the teaching of Ammonius Saccas and perhaps, for all his unconcern, to Plotinus himself. Certainly
another Neo-Platonist leader, Amelius, availed himself
of the prologue to St. John's Gospel; while yet another,
Numenius, appears to have been acquainted with the Gospels in general, and with St. Paul's Epistles. Christianity
may, after all, have been but receiving back its own with
usury. But with this doctrinal side of Neo-Platonist influence we are less concerned. It was, chiefly, through
its psychological and mystical teaching that Neo-Platonism
was destined to survive, and this because the two went
together. Despite all accretions and exaggerations, the
Neo-Platonists' knowledge of God was experimental, not

merely speculative, and as all "that is life indeed" was destined, sooner or later, to find a home in the Christian Church, the true spirit of Neo-Platonism, although its last professors were expelled from Athens and the doors closed upon them by Justinian's orders, found its refuge there also. Maybe the formal ruin of Neo-Platonism would have been at least delayed had not its later doctors quitted experience for speculation, and become arid scholastics—scholastics too, in part, of a dead creed.

The first link in the chain which directly connects Neo-Platonism and Christianity was the work of Victorinus. Victorinus was a Neo-Platonist philosopher and tutor in Rome, so much revered that he received the honour of a statue in the Roman Forum. He translated the "Enneads" of Plotinus into Latin, and this turned out to be a literary achievement of the highest moment, inasmuch as his translation fell under the eyes of Augustine, and was the means of the latter's deliverance from Manicheeism, from that pessimistic teaching which averred that evil is a power equal and in eternal opposition to God, and that matter, man's body and half man's soul, is under its unescapable domination. Neo-Platonism taught the exact opposite of this, in its studied, and at times anxious, evacuation of any principle of existence from evil, so as to render it mere privation, defect of good. The swing of the pendulum might range too far, yet to Augustine the perusal of the "Enneads" was a real deliverance from bondage, an upward step into a world from whose enthralling influence he never wholly freed, or perhaps wished to free, himself. Although Victorinus' teaching could not give him what every soul, sooner or later, must experience, "the tears of confession, the troubled spirit, the broken and contrite heart", although there was no Voice therein crying, "Come unto Me, all that labour and are heavy-laden", yet the atmosphere of Plotinus was an air in which the soul could at least breathe. God, he learned as he read, is the all-comprehensive Unity, the Soul of souls, the Life that permeates the whole world and quivers in the very leaves on the trees. He is incorruptible and changeless Spirit, the Immortal, the Good, the One. From one passage in the " Confessions " we may infer that Augustine, during his Neo-Platonic mood, actually attained in a fleeting glimpse to the vision of " That which is ", and from later incidents we know that the capacity for the Ecstasy, even as the capacity for so many other and varied experiences of the search after the Divine, in which he was ever " restless ", to use his own word, was certainly latent in him.

Victorinus was converted to Christianity in his old age, about 360, and there was naturally immense rejoicing in the Christian community at the conversion of so prominent a personage.[1] He set himself to the important and very difficult task of transmuting his Neo-Platonist doctrines of the Trinity into a body of Christian theology, and that in the Latin tongue. The delicate *nuances* of the Greek language are exactly suited to the refinements necessary in treating of such a subject, and it is not surprising that a great deal of Neo-Platonism got itself worked thoroughly into Christian acceptance sometimes in a more unqualified and daring form than Plotinus himself would have countenanced. The Father is " cessatio ", " quies ", " silentium ", nay, Victorinus goes further and says, comparing the Father to the Son, that the Father is ὁ μὴ ὤν, the Son ὁ ὤν, reminding us here of Clement with his ultra-refinement of the Monad past and beyond even " a point ", and reminding us too that Plotinus would never go so far for fear of confounding That which Is—supra-essential God—with matter, disintegration, that which is not. Yet with Victorinus, this " cessatio ", the ὁ μὴ ὤν, the Absolute,

[1] Cf. *Conf.* viii. 2–5.

is also "motus", and there is for him no contradiction in terms in this. "Motus" is not "mutatio ";¦ motion is not change. But in what does this "motus", necessarily eternal, consist ? In the eternal generation of the Son. The Son is That in which the Father sees Himself, or, we might say, with Clement, comes to Self-consciousness. He is the Word of the Absolute, the "forma" of God—it is the synonym of the Greek phrase πατρὸς μορφή. The Son is also,—a familiar thought—the cosmic principle, the "elementum", "habitaculum", "locus" of the universe. All that is potential is actualized in Him. Very important, as occurring for the first time in theology, and recurring as an accepted proposition ever since, is Victorinus' definition of the Holy Ghost as the "copula" of the Trinity. So Newman wrote in Victorinus' own phrase, "As Thou in perfect love dost join the Father and the Son". The theology of Victorinus was destined to be exceedingly pregnant in the thought of Christian Mysticism. Many of the later philosophical mystics caught up, and pushed to their fullest extent, not in the speculative, but in the psychological sphere, his ideas of the "ground" of the Godhead being "quies", "cessatio", "silentium"; a further, and more curious, doctrine of his, that the Holy Spirit symbolizes the female principle in the God-nature, that He is in fact the "Mother of Christ", has had echoes, here and there, amongst mystics since, although the Church refused it sanction.

We have already spoken of Augustine as a student, during his second great spiritual stage, of Victorinus' translation of the "Enneads". In truth, just as well-nigh every school of Christian thought can make an appeal for a favourable verdict to the teachings of his many-sided genius, so in a specially marked fashion can Christian Mysticism. Harnack goes so far as to say, "St. Augustine became the father of that mysticism which was naturalized in the

Catholic Church, down to the Council of Trent ". [1] Dr.
Rufus Jones calls him " the real father of Catholic mysticism ". [2] But Harnack goes to the root of the matter—
for there is much, of course, that has always militated
against the free play of Mysticism in Augustine's hard
orthodoxy—by pointing out that Augustine was the first
real Christian psychologist, and that it is the quality of
his psychological analysis that makes also the intensely
real and intimate quality of his mysticism. The " Confessions " precede the " City of God ". It was Augustine's unfaltering fidelity to a true psychology that led him
in the first instance to his Manichœism—" his massive
experience and even excessive realization of the destructive force of Evil and of the corrupt inclinations of man's
heart . . . hot and concrete ", as Baron von Hügel expresses it. [3] His Neo-Platonic studies saved him from
the ultimate pessimism of Manichœism, and brought him
into a new realm of light and life, a true " *praeparatio
Evangelica* ", yet enough of that " hot and concrete " sense
of sin remained with him to keep him from a permanent
residence even in that fair realm, where Evil was reduced
to a mere subtraction of good, almost to a nothingness.
Augustine's cravings were still unsatisfied, and at last
Christianity " spoke to his condition ". Yet it is strange
to note how, even after his conversion (that is, as late as
397), in his acute and balanced record of his own convictions, the judgement of the born psychologist, he can
still note the existence of his Neo-Platonist conception
of sin. " All things that are corrupted are deprived of
good. But, if they be deprived of all good, they will cease
to exist. . . . Evil is no substance ". But that is just
an instance, and a very good one, of the secret of Augus-

[1] *History of Dogma*, v. p. 86.
[2] *Studies in Mystical Religion*, p. 87.
[3] *The Mystical Element of Religion*, vol. ii. p. 293.

tine's greatness. He recognized opposing, seemingly contradictory, tendencies, in human thought on the highest matters, even in the best human thought, and he gave them a place and a consideration in the synthesis of his own mind, but he did not attempt to harmonize them, an attempt which, as Harnack notes, leads to mere " theological chatter", and is usually doomed to be summed up in some passing " —ism ". In more senses than one, Augustine was the great Catholic doctor. Of two things he was sure, God and his own soul. " Si enim fallor, sum " —" Even though I err, still I am ", he cried, and his desire was to " know God and the soul : nothing more ". One factor there was in Augustine's life and age, which helps much to account for his early and enduring sense of the reality and terror of sin, and also for his consciousness of the inner push of the soul to escape upwards and find a home, a " City of God ". He was at one moment in his earlier career at one with the Manichees in their conception of the concrete evil of matter, their pessimism and fatalism ; at another moment we can almost hear him echoing the desirous cry of Plotinus, " Let us fly hence to our dear fatherland ". Why ?

Because the world in which Aurelius Augustine lived was visibly changing and crumbling around him. The older civilization, that seemed rooted to endure for all time, the vast world-empire of Rome, the City that all men looked to as the centre and mainspring of the machinery of life, all were alike threatened. When Rome itself was menaced again and again and at length taken and sacked by the hordes of Alaric, when new barbarian forces of incalculable potential strength were pressing in on every side on an Empire whose very helplessness was largely due to luxury, idleness and lust, no wonder that it seemed more than ever necessary to reassure oneself of a " City that hath foundations ", and to reveal to souls shrinking before the outward portents of change and disaster the changeless refuge of the Eternal Love. Augustine was great in himself, but that his voice, with its variant cadences of severity and tenderness, and its unfaltering certainty of God, should sound at the crisis of two eras, two civilizations, two worlds,—this gave him his position of unexampled authority in the councils of the Church, and over the hearts of men.

To come directly to the mysticism of St. Augustine,— and it is this quality in his religion which appeals to the heart and has made the " Confessions " a spiritual classic— we may note as an interesting point that what would now-a-days be termed the psychic faculty was without doubt present in him. This is evidenced by the famous story of his conversion, which ranks with those of St. Paul, of St. Francis, of Bunyan, and of Fox in dramatic intensity, as in lasting effect. Augustine, sitting in his garden, the roll of the New Testament in his hand, hears a voice that bids him, " Tolle ; lege ". He opens at the passage of the Epistle to the Romans, " Put ye on the Lord Jesus Christ ", with the words that follow, and it makes of him a new man, or rather, probably, finishes with one decisive touch a process of gradual illumination and change of whose length and significance he had himself been but partially aware. But this is not the only place in which his talk of things unseen has something psychic about it. He tells us, for instance, that before his conversion, when on the Neo-Platonic track, he once " in one trembling glance . . . arrived at That Which Is "—the experience, in exact phrase, of Tennyson centuries afterwards—though he " lacked strength to fix his gaze thereon ", [1] and he tells us too that his mother Monnica could discern God's communion with her soul " by a certain indescribable savour ". Augustine's own conceptions about God and the soul retained

[1] *Conf.* bk. viii. ch. 17.

in many particulars distinctly Plotinian characteristics.
He was always " half a Platonist ", though, needless to
say, he wholly and absolutely discards such later Neo-
Platonist aberrations as theurgy and necromancy, pouring
rough and wholesome scorn upon them. God, to repeat
Dr. Inge's summary of Augustine's teaching on this point,
" is above all that can be said of Him. We must not even
call Him ineffable ; He is best adored in silence, best known
by nescience ; best described by negatives ". [1] He is absolutely changeless, and this colours all Augustine's well-
known theories on predestination. The soul is drawn
God-wards by an irresistible impulse, and must scale seven
stages of ascent, the highest three of which are, as with
all mystics, purgation, illumination, and union. It is
perhaps in his insistence on the last named, on Union rather
than on Knowledge, that we feel the parting of the ways
between Augustine's and Plotinus' souls. The difference
was made by Augustine's acceptance of belief in the Incarnation, and the key to that indescribable change of
method in the soul's intercommunion with the Divine
which parts the personal part of the " Enneads " from
the " Confessions " is the word Love. From beginning
to end Love—a Love responded to, or rather, a Love which
has itself evoked the soul's love—thrills through the Confessions. " Oh Love, too late have I known Thee ", he
cries at the outset, and all the mystic's yearning and regret are to be found in that sentence. Even illumination
knowledge, are bound up with love. " I beheld with the
mysterious eye of my soul the light that never changes
above the eye of my soul, above my intelligence. It was
something altogether different from any earthly illumina
tion. . . . He who knows the truth knows that light
and he who knows that light knows eternity. Love

[1] Inge : *Christian Mysticism*, p. 128.

knows that light ". [1] And again, " What do I love when I love Thee ? . . . I love a kind of light and melody and fragrance and food and embrace, when I love my God . . . where there shineth upon my soul what space containeth not, and where there soundeth what time doth not steal away, where there is fragrance which a breath scattereth not, where there is savour that eating doth not minish, and an embrace that satiety doth not dissolve. This I love when I love my God ". " Thy God ", he tells his soul, " is the Life of thy life ". [2] And yet, with all this wonderful familiarity of intercourse there goes the " holy fear " which makes Augustine the mystic also Augustine the saint. " What is this which flashes in upon me, and thrills my heart without wounding it ? I tremble and I burn ; I tremble, feeling I am unlike Him ; I burn, feeling I am like Him ". [3] But best of all, as well as best-known by picture and by description, was that hour when Augustine sat in contemplation with his mother Monnica, all her long prayers for her son at length and fully answered, and when together they sought and found communion with the Ineffable Love, mounting beyond time and space till their souls " for an instant touched " " that Eternal Wisdom which abideth over all things ". There is something so exquisitely Christian in this mutual contemplation and rapture of mother and son, touching the heart as it does more nearly than the most exalted ecstasy of some saintly solitary, that a few sentences of its description in the " Confessions " [4] may be quoted. " As now the day drew nigh, when she should depart out of this life . . . together we held converse very sweet and ' for-

---

[1] *Conf.* vii. 10, transl. by Dr. Bigg.

[2] *Conf.* x. ch. 6.

[3] *Conf.* xi. ch. 9.

[4] *Conf.* ix. ch. 10, quoted in part from Jones' *Mystical Religion,* pp. 93—95.

getting those things which were behind and reaching forth unto those things which were before ' (Phil. iii. 13) we were discussing between us in the presence of the truth, which Thou art, of what kind would be that eternal life of the Saints, which ' eye hath not seen nor ear heard, neither hath it entered into the heart of man ' (I Cor. ii. 9). . . . And when our converse drew to such an end that the utmost delight of the bodily senses, in the clearest material light, by the side of the enjoyment of that life seemed unworthy not only of comparison with it, but even to be named with it ; raising ourselves with a more glowing emotion towards the ' Self-same ' (Ps. iv. 8, Vulg.), we wandered, step by step through all material things, and even the very heaven whence sun and moon and stars shed their light upon the earth. And further still we climbed, in inner speech and thought, and in the wonder of Thy works, and we reached to our own minds and passed beyond them, so as to touch the realm of plenty, where Thou feedest Israel for ever in the pasture of the truth, and where life is that Wisdom, by which all things are made, both those which have been, and those which shall be ; and Itself is not made, but is now as it was, and ever shall be ; or rather in It is neither ' hath been ' nor ' shall be ', but only ' is ', since It is eternal. . . . And while we thus speak and pant after it, with the whole stress of our hearts we just for an instant touched it, and we sighed, and left there bound the ' first-fruits of the Spirit ' (Rom. viii. 23), and then returned to the broken murmurs of our own mouth, where the word hath its beginning and its end ". And he adds : " We were saying then : If to any one should grow hushed the tumult of the flesh, hushed the images of earth, and of the waters, and the air, hushed, too, the poles, and if the very soul should grow hushed to itself, and were by cessation of thought to pass beyond itself ; if all dreams, and imaginary revelations, every tongue and every token, were hushed, and whatsoever falls out through change . . . if now He by Himself should speak, not through them, but of Himself, that so we should hear His Word, not uttered by the voice of angel, nor by thunders of a cloud, nor by a parable of comparison, but Himself, Whom in these we love ; if, I say, we should hear Him, without these, as now we strained ourselves, and in the flight of thought touched upon the Eternal Wisdom that abideth over all things ; if this were continued and other visions of nature far inferior taken away, and this one alone should ravish and absorb and enwrap the beholder of it amid inward joys, so that life everlasting might be of such a kind, as was that one moment of comprehension for which we sighed ; were not this an ' Enter thou into the joy of thy. Lord ' ? "

There was another chain of teaching besides that of Victorinus and Augustine whereby Neo-Platonist Mysticism found its way into the Western Church. The Oriental influences which may be detected in parts of Plotinus' teaching, and are undisguised in the writings of such men as Proclus, who used to say that a philosopher should be the hierophant of the whole world, were not confined to the moribund schools of Athens. Among the Syrian monks of the third to the fifth centuries Oriental speculation was both rampant and daring. The writings of one of these mystics, the Book of Hierotheus so-called, which the canonized Dionysius the Areopagite named " a second Bible ", and which he regarded as nearly inspired, have come down to us. According to a steady Syriac tradition, and according to the actual evidence of Gregory bar 'Ebraia, a Monophysite patriarch of the twelfth century,[1] Hierotheus was in reality a Syrian mystic of Edessa, Stephen

---

[1] Gregory in turn based his assertion on the witness of Cyriac, Patriarch of Alexandria, 793–817.

bar Sudaili, who lived late in the fifth century. Cyriac called him a heretic, and Dr. Inge regards his system as a sort of Pan-nihilism, whose true parentage was Indian Brahminism. All Nature is consubstantial with the Divine Essence, which is an Absolute of " bare indetermination ", beyond distinction of Self or Other. The process of Nature is an emanation from this Absolute, which is Motion, the present world ; union with Christ, which is rest ; and a final fusion again with the Absolute. Union with Christ is progressive and consists of four stages, of which the fourth and final stage may be temporarily sighted or attained even here. Stephen claims this experience more than once. (1) The soul must by self-purification unite a certain spark of the Good which belongs to it by nature with the Universal Essence from which it has sprung. (2) It undergoes a sort of spiritual crucifixion, with the soul on the right and the body on the left ; it descends into Hades, and reascends to Paradise. (3) It receives a baptism of the Spirit and of fire, and enters a perfect sonship. (4) It is wholly and utterly absorbed into its own original " luminous Essence ". Here once more is the quiet and silence, the stage beyond all distinctions, of the Absolute. The second and third stages are interesting, as presaging mystical doctrines which had much vogue later. The third especially is familiar in our own day.

Apart from the curiosity of finding doctrines of an almost Indian cast promulgated within the Church of the fifth century,[1] Stephen bar Sudaili, if we identify him with

---

[1] Philosophy, however, both within and without the Church, had often turned its eyes longingly to the East. Origen and Philostratus both commended the example of " the Indians " and it will be remembered that, on their expulsion from Athens, the remnant of the Neo-Platonic school made its wistful and futile pilgrimage to the Persian court.

"Hierotheus", is chiefly important as being one of the sources from which a writer, almost as mysterious, and infinitely more influential, drew his inspiration. In scarcely less degree than the great Augustine, Dionysius the Areopagite from the end of the sixth century onwards was quoted and deferred to by the Medieval Church as an indisputable authority, especially in the domain of mystical theology. How immense the weight of that authority was we may best judge when we find the Scholastics, (usually though erroneously supposed to be in opposition to the Mystics), headed by St. Thomas Aquinas himself, making copious references to him. Indeed, Balthazar Corderius, the great Jesuit editor of Dionysius, goes so far as to say, "Observatu dignissimum quomodo S. Dionysius primus Scholasticae Theologiae jecerit fundamenta, quibus ceteri deinceps theologi eam quae de Deo rebus-que divinis in Scholis traditur doctrinam omnem inaedificarunt ". [1] The story of the winning of this vast influence is one of the strangest in Church history. The facts, as known, are these. At a council held at Constantinople in 533, Severus, patriarch of Antioch, and his followers upheld Monophysite doctrines and appealed for confirmation to the writings of Dionysius the Areopagite. This, one would suppose, would be an unfavourable introduction to the Church's notice, but the quotations were taken as garbled, and henceforth increasing respect was paid to the Areopagite's works, and heretics and orthodox alike vied in culling extracts from them. Pope Gregory the Great in the West, and Maximus in the East, wrote notes on them, the Lateran Council of 649 used them as a bulwark against Mono-

---

[1] *Observ. generales in Dion.* 12. " It is very worthy of observation how S. Dionysius first laid those foundations of Scholastic Theology, on which afterwards other theologians built up that doctrine which is handed down in the Schools concerning God and Divine things."

thelitism, and in the eighth century they reached France. Then a fresh and patriotic *furore* arose, owing to Hilduin, Abbot of St. Denys in Paris, setting out to identify the Areopagite with the French patron saint ; this identification, though of no historical value whatsoever, did much to promote the popularity and authority of Dionysius in France, and it was at the Court of Charles the Bald that the Irishman, John Scotus Erigena, himself a great mystic, made his celebrated translation of Dionysius into Latin, and thus fairly started his enormous vogue in the Western Church, by bringing his teaching within the reach of all.

Dionysius claimed to be the disciple of St. Paul mentioned in the Acts ; one of his books, on the " Divine Names ", was dedicated to the παῖς (or " child ") Timothy, another to Titus, a third to " John the Divine, Apostle and Evangelist exiled in Patmos ", which, were it a contemporary work, would indeed settle much that is perplexing to modern thought about the authorship of the Johannine books. Again, he claims to have remembered the eclipse at the time of the Crucifixion, and to have stood with St. Peter and " his master Hierotheus " by the tomb of the Blessed Virgin. All this is, unfortunately, incompatible with several glaring anachronisms in his works, which, although not entirely unnoticed by antiquity, did not affect its reverent belief in the authenticity of the writer's assumed name as they affect our judgement nowadays.[1] For instance, ὑπόστασις is used in its post-Nicene sense ; mention is made of monks ; ecclesiastical tradition is called ἀρχαία παραδόσις : Ignatius's phrase, " My love is crucified ", appears in the " Divine Names ". Further, no mention of Dionysius is made by either St. Jerome or Eusebius in their lists of Church writers,

---

[1] And this, as Fr. Sharpe acknowledges, in spite of Archbishop Darboy's vindication, which urged all that could be urged, of the traditional authorship. See *Mysticism: Its True Nature and Value,* pp. 197–9.

nor any notice at all taken of him before the sixth century. But what weighs most of all is that Dionysius is saturated with later Neo-Platonist doctrine, his style is that of the later Neo-Platonists, his ideas are theirs, and he quotes directly from Proclus' book, "De Subsistentiâ Malorum". He was, in fact, almost certainly an Athenian student, a pupil perhaps of Proclus, more likely of Damascius, the last master in the school. He assumed his *nom de plume* according to a custom not considered censurable in that age, and the name he chose was naturally that of a distinguished Athenian convert.

Dionysius' thought in several particulars, as we shall note, became inextricably interwoven with the Christianity that accepted it with such eager readiness, and the normal religious mind even of the present day bears unconsciously traces of his teaching, yet his system is " far removed from the simplicity of the primitive message. It is a religion of ripe speculation, and, spite of the abundance of Bible texts throughout the writings, it is . . . Neo-Platonic philosophy slightly sprinkled with baptismal water from a Christian font ". [1] Thus Professor Rufus Jones ; and Dr. Inge agrees with him. " His philosophy is that of his day—the later Neo-Platonism, with its strong Oriental affinities ". [2] Like the Alexandrines, " his object is to present Christianity in the guise of a Platonic Mysteriosophy ". He employs many mystery-terms, and in his philosophy goes to the furthest extreme of refinement in definition, using in his doctrine of God every subtlety of which the Greek in which he wrote was capable. God the Father is identified with the Neo-Platonic Monad, as might be expected, but unhappily, Dionysius parts company with Plotinus and associates himself with Iamblichus and Proclus in exalting the " One " even above Goodness. But

[1] *Studies in Mystical Religion*, p. 110.
[2] Cf. *Christian Mysticism*, p. 105, *et seq.*

He is exalted above all possible thought, all conceivable differentiation and relation. He is " superessential Indetermination ", " superessential Essence ", " irrational Mind ", " the absolute μὴ ὤν above all existence ". He is the Being of all that is, and all Being is in Him ; therefore Dionysius, like most speculative mystics, taking the rejection of duality as an axiom, can find hardly any definition, let alone location, for evil. Evil, he finally decides, is good which has got into the wrong place by a sort of accident, it is in itself " nothing, nohow, nowhere " ; God sees it as good. This is not by any means an untenable theory, and, above all, it is not Pantheism, which Dionysius was anxious to avoid, for Pantheism holds everything " equally Divine as it stands ", whereas, by the Dionysian theory, evil is " inharmonious, disorderly ", it needs transmuting or rearrangement before it can be recognized as Good. If God " sees it as good ", we cannot do so at present.

Dionysius accepted the doctrine, dear to the East, of the out-flux of things from God and their final reflux to Him. Yet all will not be absorbed in the Divine at the end, to the extinction of individuality. A persistence of individuality is one of the powers granted by the highest Unity. The first of emanations from the One—an eternal emanation —is the Son, who is identified with the Logos, and the Plotinian Νοῦς. He is also the " Thing in itself ", " Life in itself ", " Wisdom ". The Father is One ; the Son has plurality, namely, fore-ordaining reasons, or words, and these create existences. The world is to God as necessary as the sunshine to the sun.

It will be noticed how in several places this canonized mystic avoids the special heresies or pitfalls of mysticism— Pantheism on the one hand, Nihilism on the other. Even in his over-refinements of definition of the One,[1] it must

---

[1] Cf. Dion. Areop. *De Mysticâ Theologiâ*, chs. iv. and v. for a torrent of negations as to the Divine Being.

be remembered that the subtleties of the Greek language made possible to the theologian expression of thought for which Latin is cumbrously inadequate, and of which English is incapable. In any case, his attempts to convey how infinitely the Being of God surpasses the utmost efforts of human comprehension are to be preferred to the anthropomorphic and often puerile conceptions of God current in religious literature of the present day. It may be objected that Dionysius' writings in no way correspond to " current religious literature". There was, of course, no current literature in his day, but his influence was so wide-spread and profound that his ideas come as near as is possible to that description. In four particulars, especially, he influenced the thought of generations after him, and in one, the last, the popular religion even of the present time. (1) It was Dionysius who more than any other taught the *Via Negativa* as the true way of approaching God. This was nothing new. The process of arriving at the Divine by abstraction, by stripping away from the mind all human ideas as to aspects, virtues, or qualities, had been familiar to Clement of Alexandria, with his soul's " apathy " in communion with God, and to Basilides who taught it in an extreme form stamped with Augustine's approval, " We must not even call God ineffable, since that is to make an assertion about Him ". Amongst the Neo-Platonists Plotinus had taught it, but his positive experience of contact with the Divine, however explained, prevented in his case such a whole-hearted assertion of the negative method as that of Proclus, the pure scholastic, who first presents us with phrases about " forsaking the manifold for the One ", and (a term afterwards famous in Christian Mysticism) " sinking into the Divine Ground ". Dionysius teaches his *Via Negativa* by a beautiful analogy. " Truly to see and know (Him is) by the abstraction of all that is natural ; as those who would make a statue out of the natural stone abstract all the surrounding material which hinders the sight of the shape lying concealed within, and by that abstraction alone reveal its hidden beauty ". [1] (2) The expressions " the Divine Dark ", the " super-luminous gloom of silence ", [2] " this most luminous darkness " in which " we desire to abide ", appear in Dionysius, and became common with his successors. This " super-essential ray of the Divine Dark " must be found with " the eyeless mind ". (3) In other words, communion with the One Who is above nature and knowledge must be by supernatural contact, beyond ordinary modes of consciousness, that is, by the Ecstasy. This is described in Chapter i. of the " Mystical Theology ". [3] (4) The fourth legacy of Dionysius to the future was of a curiously different kind. His study of Proclus and his triads had filled him with the idea of an endless procession of descending Existences and Powers from God. God, by a positive process, " unveils Himself from His hiddenness ", and manifests Himself through nine-fold ranks of Cherubim, Seraphim, and Angelic beings, and then on earth through nine-fold orders of sacred ministers and symbols. These orders are explained in his books on the " Heavenly Hierarchy " and the " Ecclesiastical Hierarchy ". The celestial orders are as follows—(1) Seraphim, Cherubim, Thrones ; (2) Dominations, Virtues, Powers ; (3) Principalities, Archangels, Angels ; and they have lived on with a curious authority in human thought. Nobody questioned either their reality or their order ; in later days poets such as Dante and Spenser wove music on the theme of their " trinal

[1] *Mystical Theology.* Ch. ii. transl. Fr. Sharpe.

[2] This is the darkness of excess of light. " The divine darkness is the inaccessible light ". Cf. *Letter V. to Dorotheus the Deacon.*

[3] " Leave thou the senses, and the operations of the intellect and all things sensible and intelligible, and things that are, and things that are not, that thou mayest rise . . . by ways above knowledge to union with Him Who is above all knowledge and all being ".

triplicities "; they were part of the inspiration of medieval Art ; now-a-days we sing hymns about the " Orders nine ", and " thrones, principalities, virtues, and powers ", which derive directly from the Dionysian theology. It is strange that one so " in love with the Absolute " and with abstract methods of thought should have bequeathed to the devout imagination so concrete and definite a picture of the scheme and the work of the world to come.

We cannot end this chapter without a reference to the strange great name of John Scotus Erigena. John the Scot, or the " Irish-born "—the two designations were synonymous at that day—was first known as an Irish scholar of eminence at the Court of Charles the Bald in 847. This grandson of Charlemagne gathered round him most of the light and learning of his times, and to these Ireland with her " troop of philosophers " made a notable contribution. Erigena was called upon in 851 to answer a tract by Gottschalk, a monk of Orbais near Rheims, which pushed Augustine's doctrine of Predestination to its furthest limits, and had been condemned. In refuting this Erigena in turn got himself into serious trouble. He had deeply imbibed Neo-Platonist teaching, and the gist of his response to Gottschalk was that God could not predestine to evil, since evil itself was a negation, had no meaning except in the sphere of time, and, for God, " was not ". The Scot was condemned for heretical teaching,[1] one critic discovered not less than 106 heresies in his tract on Predestination, while another labelled it as " barbarous barking ". Un-

---

[1] It is curious how both extremes of thought—Gottschalk's and Erigena's—struck a blow at the reality of the power of the Church on earth. For, if souls were predestined irrevocably to salvation or damnation, it was difficult to find place for the Church's office of seeking and saving ; as difficult as to find justification for the solemn significance of the " power of the keys " if evil were null and void.

abashed, however, Erigena went on his way, and, soon after, by his translation of Dionysius the Areopagite into Latin, introduced and endeared that mystical master to the mind of the Middle Ages. Of Erigena's own system, which he elaborated in a book, " On the Division of Nature ", we may note that he not only interprets Dionysius and the Alexandrines, but puts an emphasis on the most exaggerated parts of their systems. God is above all categories of thought, even that of relation. The dogma of the Holy Trinity disappears, for the Three Persons are but " relative names ", and are absorbed in the Absolute. All our statements about God are merely metaphors ; but what we deny about Him, we always truthfully deny. This, as Dr. Inge observes, is the " negative road " of Dionysius carried to its last term. The consequence is that, although Erigena tells us that Creation is so necessary to God, as His Self-realization, that " He was not, before He made the Universe ", he will not acknowledge that the visible world can teach us anything about God save that He exists. We may not infer, for instance, from the world attributes of His such as beauty and order. Evil, as he conceived it, has no substance and will disappear. All this was arid enough, and was worked out drily and logically ; for the importance of Erigena lay partly in the fact that his book, although heretical, was the pivot on which Greek Mysticism began to turn into medieval Scholasticism. But he had other importance besides. In some of his doctrines he was far before his time, " a great light in a dark age ". Thus, his belief that man's soul is a microcosm, that all Nature,—corporeal, vital, sensitive, rational, intellectual—is represented in him ; that man understands the world, and so gets his glimpse of God, because the forms or patterns of that world, which is God's self-realization, are in him ; and that one day man will " become what he beholds "—this belief has a profound truth in it and takes us far. In single pregnant sayings Erigena will always live. Thus: " Thought and Action are identical in God ": " The Word is the Nature of all things ": " The loss and absence of Christ is the torment of the whole creation, nor do I think there is any other ": " There are as many revelations of God as there are human souls ".

CHAPTER VI

Three Types of Medieval Mysticism

THE Mysticism of the East, through Augustine and Erigena, had been transplanted to its new and more fruitful soil in the vigorous West. In its exaggerated, though suggestive, form, as developed by the latter, it was destined to lie dormant, a seed of future growth, for one or two centuries. Erigena was simply not understood by his contemporaries, who, beyond feeling vaguely that there was "something wrong" in his speculations, left him and his works, after a few groping "refutations," severely alone.[1] But this neglect of Erigena and his kind wears also another complexion. The curious and hearty acceptance of Dionysius hardly contradicts what is about to be said, when it is remembered how congenial his doctrine of the celestial and earthly Hierarchies was to the Medieval mind, and when his unquestioned identification with the Areopagite, and his confusion, in France, with the national patron saint, are taken into consideration. The truth was that in the world of mystical thought a reaction, and a very natural reaction, was taking place. It was helped on by the practical and unspeculative bent of the West.

[1] It was not till 350 years after his death that a general condemnation of his doctrines was promulgated by Honorius III, on the appearance of Amalric of Bena and his strongly Pantheistic school of thought at Paris. In the meantime, however, his Eucharistic doctrine, as developed by Berengar, had been proscribed in the middle of the eleventh century.

Augustine was studied, but his teaching on Predestination stirred men's minds far more than the gleaming traces of his Neo-Platonism. Dionysius' Hierarchies took immediate hold of ecclesiastical thought ; his Proclianism had to bide its time. The reaction was towards a far more definite Christology, an emphasis, too long neglected by speculative Mysticism, on the Person and work of the Redeemer. That was bound to come. The contact between the Christian Faith and the ripest development of Greek philosophy had taken place, and in that contact the Faith passed through a crisis subtler and more momentous than that of the agonies of persecution, or the after-smiles of a complacent and persuasive world. The best intellects on both sides were so keen for a synthesis of all that was good that it seemed at times as though the dogmas of the Blessed Trinity, of the Incarnation and Atonement must suffer some process of transmutation and attenuation before being assigned places in the mystical temple. Again and again in these pages we have noticed a kind of conscious effort to find room for the Second Person of the Trinity ; how anxiously he has been de-humanized into the cosmic Principle, or the Thought of the Thinker, or the Consciousness or the Self-realization of the One. Partly owing to the Eastern pre-occupation with the idea of the Absolute, partly owing to the habitual Greek notions of sin, the revelation of the Incarnate Life and the message of the Cross dropped nearly out of sight. Now in the twelfth century a great change passed over the spirit of Mysticism. It seemed to undergo a kind of intensely Christian reaction, and at the same time to take to itself a practical aspect which hitherto it had lacked. We may say, with every probability, that the latter was due to the former. But whence did this new activity arise, an activity which manifested itself in the spheres of ecclesiastical and even political influence ; which gave to the imagination a new Symbolism, to the intellect

the reconciliations of Scholasticism ; and to the Church at
large an ardent and missionary sympathy with the sick-
nesses and sorrows of mankind ?

Such an activity, distinctively and enthusiastically Christian, and seeing before it everywhere the figure of the
Redeemer, may be traced to three sources. First, the long
life-or-death struggle with Mohammedanism, challenging
the essentials of Christianity, the shock of whose onset had
only at length been stayed upon the plains of France itself.
Secondly, and arising directly from this, the extraordinary
movement, later, of the Crusades, a movement which ran
like wild-fire through Europe, leavened all thought, and
permeated every class of society. Nor was it a transitory
fervour. Lasting for centuries, it left permanent effects
on the history of the Church. Of this movement, so far as
it touches our subject, we can but note here that from first
to last its power was a personal devotion to the honour of
the Saviour. The Cross and the Crucified were in all minds.
" Salve, caput cruentatum ! " was the cry of every heart.
To rescue the Saviour's home, His shrines, His relics, from
the defiling touch of the infidel was the chief aim, however
at times diverted and spoiled, which literally led men to give
up all they held dear, and to set out on their hazardous
adventure. With the Crusades, Chivalry, that marvellous
side-product of Western Christianity, took its rise—that
Teutonic form of the Faith, which, for the first time con-
secrating war and turning devotion into a passionate adventure of romance, exactly suited the Western temperament,
and has left traces, some healthful, others more dubious,
in Western Christianity ever since. Incidentally, the diffusion and veneration of relics was vastly increased ; and
the power of the Church, and so of orthodoxy in general,
set on a basis not to be disturbed for centuries, owing to
the great amount of property and wealth of which the
Church became trustee in the absence of the Crusading lords,

or sometimes absolute owner in the event of their non-return. Thirdly, the reformation and renewal of influence on the part of the monasteries had a vast share in the deepening of the Christian influences of the period.   Foundations such as Clairvaux and St. Victor played a critical part in the story of Christian Mysticism.   Even here, the Crusading and chivalric spirit must be reckoned with.   It was in the care of the great monasteries that men left their lands on setting out for the Holy Sepulchre, or to the great monasteries that they often mortgaged them to raise arms and funds.   Again, as Mr. Cotter Morrison has pointed out in his " Life of St. Bernard ", the attraction of the monastic calm, its round of duty and prayer, made itself felt increasingly on men become world-weary with adventure or travel or war.   The sound of the convent-bells was in their ears, and, as in Russia and the East now-a-days, so then, many a worn-out warrior or statesman consecrated his remaining years of life to retirement and prayer.   But these things could not have happened had not the monasteries in general been worthy of their trust.   The fiery energy of Gregory VII. and a succession of reforming Popes, the saintly practicality of St. Bernard and his followers, raised the monastic life into a real storehouse of regular devotion, homely labour, and disciplined scholarship.

It may be asked, What had this to do with Mysticism ? It had a vast deal to do with it.   The solitary life, and with it, excesses of the solitary intellect or imagination, grew steadily rarer, and, as we shall see, the great practical mystics of the twelfth century revival all chose, as their most helpful means of realizing the mystical ideal, whether in the domain of action, or of thought, the community life, with its opportunities of self-control and self-subordination and its constant interaction of soul on soul.   Even such a community life had the Saviour approved and hallowed by His own choice of the Twelve.

As representative, in nearly all particulars, of the tendencies in medieval life just noticed, St. Bernard (1091–1153) claims our notice. In many respects, we have in him medieval saintliness at its best. Profoundly devotional, shrewdly practical, mixing in the great political movements of his day, swayed by the national and religious emotions that stirred his fellowmen, the confidant and adviser of Pope and Emperor and King, he is yet " unspotted by the world ", he returns to his monks to talk out with them his deep mystical yearnings after the Eternal Love, and, as he goes along his way, sings his " Jesu, dulcis memoria ". It was he who, turning his back on the stately Burgundian foundation of Clugny, with its 3,000 monks, once so venerable for holiness but now stained with disorder and luxury,[1] entered the humbler and stricter house of Citeaux which had reverted to the full severity of St. Benedict's original rule ; and thence founded the world-famous monastery of Clairvaux. By his letters, by his journeys, and by his influence, he became the reformer *par excellence* of monastic life and morals. But it was also St. Bernard who preached, in 1146, the Second Crusade at Vezelai in the presence of Louis VII. and a multitude of his subjects, and who afterwards travelled up and down the Rhineland, stirring up people by his fiery sermons wherever he went and finally persuading the Emperor Conrad III. himself to join the march.[2] What, meanwhile, is to be said of his mysticism ? This, of course, chiefly appears in his " Sermons on the Canticles ", and they, for better or for worse, mark an epoch in mystical thought. They introduce the romantic side of mysticism ; they also bring to bear a thorough-going and sometimes far-fetched Symbolism to the interpretation

---

[1] See Morrison's *Life of St. Bernard*, pp. 119 *et seq.*

[2] Morrison, *op. cit.* Bk. iv. Ch. ii. gives a spirited account of the preaching of the Second Crusade.

of Holy Writ. Their aim was to teach devout and loving contemplation of the Crucified Christ, and the worship of our Saviour as the " Bridegroom of the soul ". This was nothing new ; nearly all the Greek Fathers, and one or two of the Western, had touched on the imagery. But there is no doubt that St. Bernard, with his immense influence over his times, did more than any one else to perpetuate this marriage symbolism. Yet here, as elsewhere, Bernard preserved a great deal of caution. With him, it was the Church, not the individual soul, as so often afterwards, which is the " bride " of Christ. This same caution is seen in another part of his mysticism. Like most mystics, he has his scale of stages (four, with him) in the soul's love to God, of which love he says beautifully, " Verus amor se ipso contentus est ". Yet of the fourth and highest stage, " that transformation and utter self-loss in which we love ourselves only for the sake of God ", he says that he believes it unattainable in this life, and quite beyond his own reach.[1] In another matter Bernard's caution is noticeable and becomes even timidity. His position in time was just between the early speculative mystics and the body of constructive scholastics who were to find mysticism—in even some of its most daring manifestations, when founded on a true experience—a place within the Catholic system. Bernard, prompted and harassed by his long controversy with Abelard, the dry and acute logician, was inclined to give Reason a very subsidiary place in his theology. " Credo ut intelligam " was his motto, and his was the famous definition of Faith, " Fides est voluntaria quaedam et certa praelibatio necdum propalatae veritatis ".[2] But,

[1] " Let them talk of it who have experienced it, to myself I confess it seems impossible ". *De diligendo Deo*, XV. ; and cf. Vaughan : *Hours with the Mystics*, Bk. v. Ch. i.

[2] " Faith is a kind of voluntary certitude and foretaste of verities not yet open to demonstration."

as has been well observed, Bernard's "fides" was "no indolent or constrained reception of a formula", but "the divine persuasion of the pure in heart and life".

St. Bernard had shown by his life of incessant activity and his wide-spread influence that the mystic's temperament is not incompatible with a very shrewd and capable grasp on worldly affairs : not less practical in the intellectual province was the work of the great chain of scholastic mystics beginning with the Victorines of the twelfth century and ending with Gerson in the fifteenth. Though at times one feels that it is the careful tabulations of the soul's deepest experiences rather than those experiences themselves which were the schoolmen's main preoccupation, their importance in the history of Mysticism—for the matter of that, of psychology—cannot be over-rated. For one thing, the notion that Mysticism and Scholasticism were by their nature in inveterate opposition may be at once dismissed. To take two great representative leaders of the twin schools of thought, Dionysius and St. Thomas Aquinas ; Corderius, the seventeenth century translator of the former, gives several folio pages of Aquinas' quotations from his author and even calls Dionysius the founder of the scholastic method ; Hugo of St. Victor and Albertus Magnus wrote commentaries on him, and all the famous scholastics refer constantly to him. The mystics, in fact, were the adventurous mariners on unknown seas of spiritual experience ; the scholastics, following at times in their actual wake, were the chartists of their explorations. During the three centuries in which they worked, they were useful also, as cartographers, in another way. Up and down these unknown seas there were rocks where souls might find, and did find, shipwreck, and in them there were dangerous shoals and from them blind alleys. At the beginning of the thirteenth century, men like Amalric of Bena and David of Dinant were picking up and teaching the most pantheistic of Erigena's speculations, coupled with smatterings from Aristotle as interpreted by Arabian commentators.[1] Later on, Ortlieb of Strassbourg started a " Sect of the New Spirit," one of the first of many " brotherhood groups " of the thirteenth century, who mostly had their *habitat*, or wandered to and fro, in the Rhine valley. Of these " Brethren of the Free Spirit ", and their like, we shall hear again when we come to consider the German School of mystics of the thirteenth century. One of their chief ramifications, the societies of Béghards (men) and Béguines (women), the latter of whom, in ordered and modified form, still carry on their good work in Flanders, arose indirectly from the Crusades. The losses of life in these expeditions left large numbers of women, widows and daughters of the slain, without protection. About 1180, a priest of Liège, Lambert le Bègue (" the Stammerer ") began to busy himself in the good work of forming communities of these needy women, who, subsisting largely on charity, might tend the sick, the aged, and the poor, around them. Some of these Béguines were well-to-do ladies, who entered the community to live " the simple life ". Others were poor folk whose settlements were supported by rich patrons, and indeed, an extraordinary amount of gifts was lavished on this form of the religious life, the Counts of Flanders being specially devoted to the Béguinages. A third class of Béguines was composed of the actually poor, who had to beg to support themselves. In fact, the begging became a great nuisance later on, and was condemned more than once by the religious authorities. The cult of Poverty was widely and enthusiastically followed in the twelfth and thirteenth centuries, but then it was supposed to go with

[1] The first collection of Aristotle's works that came into Europe was a Latin translation from the Arabic : and some of the Arabian commentaries on Aristotle, strongly tinged with Neo-Platonism, were at first believed to be Aristotle's own work.

some recognized discipline and rule, and part of the attraction of the Béguines' really devoted life lay in its lack of exact rule, and binding vows. Much more was this the case with the Béghards,[1] who, imitating the women's example, began their career in Louvain in 1220. They however, wandered far more about the country than their sisters, being known widely as " poor men " and " apostolic men ", and in addition to the tending of the sick and sometimes, as in Frankfort, the insane, and burying the dead, they taught and preached. Unfortunately, this teaching, by the fourteenth century, began everywhere to show signs of an undiluted Pantheism, with two concomitants, harmful alike to religion and to morals. One was that the man guided by the Spirit, in whose special age or dispensation many of these " brethren " believed themselves to live,[2] was above any further attention to outward forms, sacraments or ceremonies ; the other that, being filled with the Spirit, any and every urgent impulse in him was Divine. Pure Pantheism always leads in the direction of Libertinism by blurring necessarily the distinction between right and wrong ; when a man believes himself to be in some realm of the Spirit, beyond law, a " perfect soul " that has risen above the practice of virtues and is on the way to becoming identified with the Divine Allness that fills him, there is no possible check to his actions. This " heresy of the Free Spirit " was condemned by the Council of Vienne in 1311,

---

[1] Some have thought that the words " Béghards ", " Béguines ", were derived from the Flemish verb " beggen ", " to beg ", or possibly to " pray hard ". But there is now little doubt that the Béguines derived their name from their founder, Lambert le Bègue, and that, if anything, the verb " to beg " came from the name " Béguine " instead of the other way about.

[2] This belief dated itself from the teaching of Joachim, Abbot of Floris in Calabria, who taught, during the close of the twelfth century, that the Dispensation of the " Eternal Gospel ", the reign of the Holy Spirit, had arrived.

but it was enormously spread in Western Europe by that
time. The curious thing is that the abstract nature of some
of its doctrines concerning the "indeterminate Absolute"
should have been so popular. For that such teaching was
popular there can be no doubt. Eckhart and Tauler both
had to preach again and again against its exaggerations,
and the great scholastics made it part of their task to com-
bat this spurious mysticism wherever they found it. At
one time it is Albert the Great who condemns David of
Dinant for holding that God, intelligence, and matter are
all one in essence, and unite in a single substance; at
another, Aquinas, his pupil, echoes the condemnation of
David's doctrine that everything in the universe is a single
thing, essentially one. Again, Gerson accuses Amalric of
Bena of teaching that the creature is changed into God,
and, sloughing off his own nature, no more sees and loves
God as somewhat beyond himself but actually becomes
God; and that this unity even on earth is so perfect that
there is no further place for Baptism, confession, the Eucharist; no further need of a mediator between God and man.
It was well that such doctrines were detected, exposed,
and confuted, though the medieval mind, to which the
Church was an *imperium* and heresy a dangerous treachery
to the spiritual nation, could not stop there, but proceeded
to its terrible logical conclusion of persecution by fire and
sword.

Such was one part of the schoolmen's service to Mysticism
—the rooting out of what was false and harmful in mystical
speculation. But the greater and nobler part of their
work was constructive, the reconciliation and incorporation
of a true mysticism, in all its wealth of religious psychology,
with the systematic theology of the Church.

The famous abbey of St. Victor, near Paris, was founded
by William of Champeaux about 1100, and speedily became
known as an abode of learning and of holiness. Hugo of

St. Victor joined the community in early manhood and passed his life there, dying early in his forty-fifth year, but not without laying foundations for the thought of his successors. The Church had to solve the problem of checking the errors while encouraging the love and faith of the mystics. Hugo's contribution to the solution was a three-fold division of the faculties of the self. "The way to ascend to God", he said, "is to descend into oneself"; and indeed, the Victorine school was always much less metaphysical than psychological in its processes. Hugo's three-fold division was, first and lowest, Cogitation; then, Meditation; highest of all, Contemplation. This last, however, has two stages, Speculation, which is the beginning of that final illumination whereby all things are seen in God, and Intuition, wherein the soul gains immediate apprehension of the Infinite. Hugo is responsible also for the doctrine of the three "eyes" of man; by understanding this we understand also the difficulty of the religious life. For only the "eye of flesh" remains intact; that of "reason", whereby we see ourselves, has been injured by sin; that of "contemplation", whereby we ought to be able to see God in ourselves, has been blinded by sin.[1]

Richard of St. Victor, Hugo's pupil and successor, was a practical mystic in more ways than one. He was an ardent reformer of the ecclesiastical abuses of his time. In his writings, his weakness lay in his proneness, like St. Bernard, to weave endless allegories out of the Old Testament writings. His psychology is more complex than that of Hugo. He divides contemplation into six instead of two stages. We need not trace their cumbrous Latin phraseology;[2] it may suffice that the first two have to do with

---

[1] For the Victorines see Vaughan: *Hours with the Mystics*, Bk. V. Ch. 2; and cf. Inge: *op. cit.* p. 140–2.

[2] The six stages are given in full in Vaughan, *op cit*. Bk. V, Ch. 2, note 13.

Imagination; the second two with Reason; the last two with " Intelligence ". Predisposing conditions for the third stage, above Reason, are devotion, admiration, and joy: the Victorines always insist on the preparation of the soul by a pure and holy life. " Let him that thirsts to see God cleanse his mirror ", says Richard. What makes Richard important is the re-emergence in his teaching of the Ecstasy, on which he lays the fullest emphasis, and which he reckons as a supernatural gift, or infusion, beyond Reason. " Reason dies in giving birth to Ecstasy ".[1] He is careful to say that in vision " the transfigured Christ must be accompanied by Moses and Elias ", that is, there must be nothing conflicting with law and authority in the communication which the soul receives and its after effect. But Dr. Inge reckons that it is to St. Richard in chief that the opposition between the natural and the supernatural, which grew up in Catholic Mysticism, is due.

There were other scholastic mystics to whom Mysticism owed ideas or doctrines of importance. Albertus (1193–1280), to whom his age gave the title " Magnus ", taught in the " High School " of Cologne, where one of his pupils was the famous Thomas Aquinas. In his treatise, *De Adhaerendo Deo*, Albertus developed the meaning of the words of the Fourth Gospel, " God is a Spirit ", and laid down, as necessary for the highest attainment of the soul's contemplation, the *Via Negativa*. " When thou prayest, shut thy door—that is, the door of thy senses. Keep them barred, and bolted against all images. . . . Let naught come between thee and God. . . . When we proceed to God by the way of abstraction, we deny to Him, first of all, bodily and sensible attributes, then intelligible qualities, and lastly that *esse* which would keep Him amid created things ".

With Bonaventura (1221–1274) union with God is repre-

[1] Cf. Sharpe: *Mysticism : Its True Nature and Value*, Ch. III.

sented as an immense series of stages in ascent. The final stage is only to be entered upon by the soul's passivity and nakedness—it is that of the Divine darkness, the darkness of excess of light. Yet, though one of the most formal of mystics, St. Bonaventura lives on in certain wonderful sentences, as is the way with many of his kind. The seemingly dull page is suddenly streaked with light. Thus, " God's Centre is everywhere, His circumference nowhere ". He is " totum intra omnia, et totum extra ", a fine expression of Divine Immanence and Transcendence ; He is the Trinity in Unity, since the " summum bonum " must by nature be " summe diffusivum sui ".[1] And if we would know the highest vision, we must " ask it of grace, not of doctrine ; of desire, not of the intellect ; of the ardours of prayer, not of the teaching of its schools ; of the Bridegroom, not of the Master ".[2] This is, indeed, worthy of a disciple of St. Francis.

Finally, there is Jean Gerson, the Chancellor of the University of Paris (1363–1429), scarcely a mystic at all, " who has no exaltations or visions of his own to tell of ", but is more persistent than any one else in drawing up a scheme of the mystical life, a ground-plan in black and white, accurately measured, of the spiritual temple. Mystical theology, with him, must rest on the negative process, and he characterizes the mystical revelation as having the quality or sensation of certainty, therein anticipating modern analysis. He is, perhaps, mainly interesting because he gives to each department of illumination—to the spirit, the reason, and the senses—an " affective faculty ", a point of contact or receptivity in the self. This point of contact in the case of mystical vision is " synteresis ", a curious word which corresponds to what other mystics called the " Divine

[1] Quoted from Inge : *Christian Mysticism*, p. 146.
[2] See E. Underhill, *Mysticism*, p. 148.

spark " in the soul, or the " apex " of the soul. Bonaventura, Albertus Magnus, and Thomas Aquinas also made
use of the word, and we shall see that Eckhart, at the head
of the German school, built a good deal of his doctrine upon
it. It is " an intuitive faculty, above the reasoning faculty
—a power of the mind for receiving truth immediately
from God ".

We have gone too far forward in the endeavour to group
the great analytical theologians of the Middle Ages, and
shall have to retrace our steps. Nevertheless, there is
that in Gerson's own life which gives us the connecting link
of thought with what will follow. Dry writer, uncom-
promising and even fierce Churchman as at times he was
(he urged the death of Hus at the Council of Constance),
there was in him a deep core of tenderness. The contrasts
of Medievalism seem to come out in him. This inveterate
systematiser and stern scholastic has been, as is well known,
suspected of writing the " Imitation of Christ " ; in any
case he was eager to feel the life of the people as well as the
atmosphere of an University. So he took a cure of souls
in Bruges in addition to his professorial work, that he
might know the practical experience of a parish priest :
he wrote in the vernacular and in the simplest words little
tracts on the truths of religion, such as the treatise, " De
scavoir bien mourir ", much used in parish churches, and
" L'A.B.C. des simples gens ". Hence he was lovingly
called " le Docteur du peuple et le Docteur des petits en-
fants." [1] As he lay dying, in exile at Lyons for righteousness' sake, a band of children crowded around to hear his
last words of counsel and to pray " for our dear father,
Jean Gerson ".

All through the later Middle Ages, despite very much
that was of evil omen in Church life, formality in religious

[1] See J. E. G. de Montmorency. *Thomas à Kempis*, p. 22.

observance, worldliness, luxury, or cruelty in high places, this spirit of a primitive childlikeness, exquisitely tender and winning, makes itself seen and heard. Often it takes the form of some legend, of infinite grace and meaning, repeated mysteriously from mouth to mouth, as when the story of the Holy Graal was told, and, under varying forms, but always with its significance of a high Quest and Adventure after Christ, became to countless hearts a Gospel within the Gospel. Often again it issues in splendid deeds or lifetimes of self-surrender, such as the strange Cult of Poverty, which, coupled with the care of the sick and dying, became a generous passion in the Low Countries and the Rhineland of the thirteenth and fourteenth centuries.

Whence did all this arise ? the Vision that so many men saw, the practical mysticism of daily service to which so many gave themselves ? The Crusades were in part the cause of the deepening and strengthening of this fervour, but the Crusades would have been impossible had not the essentials of this spiritual chivalry already existed, and the Crusades were not spotless enterprises, and left many wounds to heal.

The causes were surely a doctrine, and a man.

(1) The doctrine was the belief, almost universal in the Middle Ages, if we except a few obscure sects, in the Mystery of the Mass. " It is the Mass that matters ", says Mr. Birrell somewhere, and certainly it was the Mass that mattered to medieval Europe. The doctrine concerning the Eucharist began to harden during the age of Charlemagne, but when the dogma of Transubstantiation was defined by the fourth Lateran Council in 1215, it was only the summing up, with the remorseless logic of the West and according to the philosophy of the period, of the long and eager controversies, and still more the unwavering popular prepossession, of centuries. But more than this ; the Lateran Council, in its emphasis on the tremendous reality

underlying the Holy Sacrament, expressed a debt of gratitude on the part of the Church. To " the belief in the real presence of the King of kings in the consecrated wafer and in the power mysteriously given by the imposition of hands to the humblest priest to work this stupendous miracle " had been due more than to any other force the conquest and taming of the barbarian nations by the Church. " Whatever be its theological truth ", says Dr. Workman, " it must be confessed that the medieval doctrine of the Sacrament had accomplished wonders for civilization where a more spiritual conception might have failed ".[1] While Radbert and Ratramn and Rabanus had argued and discussed in the ninth century, and Berengar and Lanfranc in the tenth, there beat beneath all arid dispute and definition the pulse of a vast awe and faith in the Mystery enthroned on every Altar. Perhaps nothing else would have kept in any sort of check the welter of violence, fraud and cruelty that too often surged up within the outward show of Christianity. Rossetti's picturesque phrase, " High do the bells of Rouen beat, when the Body of Christ goes down the street " gives us, in one stroke of colour and sound, the medieval conception of the great Sign which, wherever it was upheld or carried, brought hope to the helpless sick, truce to the fray, asylum to the refugee, and its Viaticum to the parting soul. When around the Mystery there began to cluster the hues of spiritual romance which the Crusades in their longing touch on the far-away land of the Last Supper brought to it, and of which the mysterious relics of the Blood in Bruges and Hailes were witnesses, what wonder that some great legend like that of the Graal should arise, in which belief in the Mass, and yet of a Mystery within and beyond the Mass, the rumour of a Quest, the unsatisfied desire of the human soul for That Which the most august Sacrament could only symbolize, should all find expression ?

[1] *Christian Thought to the Reformation*, p. 146.

(.) What was needed still was something like a Life that should correspond to this enthusiastic veneration for its sacramental expression. That such a life—in truth a reversion to the Christ type—did actually begin to lift itself and spread its beautiful influence, an influence still felt, in the cities and lanes of thirteenth century Europe, was due to one great saint above all others, Francis of Assisi.

It is unnecessary to sketch again a life which has been written and re-written so often and so well. It may be said, however, that, despite all after efforts, capable and sympathetic as many of them are, the " Fioretti " still holds its indisputable pre-eminence as the source whence we may win the actual fragrance, the first childlike freshness and joy of the Franciscan ideal. Many times has the cry, " Back to Christ ! " been raised, but no one ever came more closely to the Galilean ministry of love, its hand of helpfulness for all in distress, its simple hold on the Fatherhood of God, than Francis of Assisi. Born in 1182, the true spiritual life of the thirteenth century, especially among the poor, the sick and the outcast, largely owed itself to him ; and from his simple following of the Saviour a vast missionary movement, that of the Friars, radiated far and wide. Let us recall the chief notes in St. Francis' mysticism, one or two of them wonderfully new and clear to the age in which he lived. There was first the personal attachment to his Lord, Whom he saw not " coming in the clouds " of dogma, nor even only as a sacramental Presence, but as a vivid Reality in the paths of the world. He was praying, a young man of twenty-two, before the little altar of St. Damian, near Assisi, when, so Bonaventura his biographer tells us, he found that he could not take his eyes from those of the Image on the Crucifix. They seemed to burn into his soul, and to ask for his life. The Jesus of the Gospels had become for him alive again. Therefore he wedded " his lady Poverty " and, much to the wrath of his father, a rich merchant, went out into the world a poor man. One of his first acts was to range himself with a line of outcast beggars in Rome, and next (we cannot doubt with the passage of St. Matthew viii. in his mind) he kissed a leper by the wayside. One day, soon afterwards, he heard a priest at Mass read the Gospel which contained our Lord's commission, " Preach, saying, ' The Kingdom of God is at hand. Heal the sick, cleanse the lepers. . . . Provide neither silver nor gold in your purses '." The words sounded to him, as those of the Epistle to the Romans to St. Augustine, like an imperious command. Henceforth this was his life and the life of his followers, the Friars Minor. Pope Innocent III. allowed their rule—the apostolic life—in 1210, and in 1212 the Second Order for women came into being, named, after its foundress, the Poor Clares. More significant still was the formation, forced on St. Francis to meet the needs of the eager crowds who hung upon his teaching, of a Third Order, the Tertiaries, who were vowed to live the gospel life of unselfishness, love, and devotion in their own homes and in the world. Now we can understand the spread of the enthusiastic cult of Poverty already noticed, and the restless yearning of the manifold groups of men and women whose movements in the thirteenth and fourteenth centuries we can dimly discern, after a more primitive faith and practice. For the spirit of Francis spread far and wide. In Francis himself we see two developments of the mystic sense very rare in his age. One was his recognition of God in the beauties and wonders of Nature. He preaches to the birds and the fishes ; the sun is his brother, the trees and flowers are his sisters. To this love of Nature the close, attentive following of the Master of Galilee had led him, and it led him, unconsciously, for Francis was no theologian, into the path of safety. Man and Nature are to him brother and sister, indeed, he is often playful with Nature as with a little sister, for Man is higher and holier in destiny than

Nature. There is no temptation to Pantheism, to shut up God in Nature, of which man is a segment, to translate the whole Being of God from the hints, sometimes to us confused and contradictory, given us by Nature. The soul of man, as redeemed, is, after all, the greater hieroglyphic of God. Then, again, as directly caught from the early days of Galilee, there is Francis' joy. Whatever his circumstances, of outward hardship or of bodily pain, that fountain of radiant joy never failed him, and, in the dark times of the Italy in which he worked, was an infectious means of his influence.

Several of his followers showed very beautifully these special characteristics of St. Francis. There was St. Douceline, a lady of Genoa, who joined the Béguines of her neighbourhood (and whom the song of a bird, or the beauty of a flower " drew straightway to God ", just as Francis once ordered a bed of flowers to be laid out " that all who beheld them might remember the Eternal Sweetness ".[1] There was Jacopone da Todi, the converted lawyer, who turned poet of the infinite light and joy, and became, like his master, " a troubadour of God " ; and St. Bonaventura himself, the great scholastic mystic, was a disciple of Francis.

It may be wondered at that in one chapter, there should be grouped together three such different types of the mystical life. The answer is that each type was, for the age, a practical type, and that only in considering the three types together can the religious life of the Middle Ages be really understood and summed up. The mystic who was a statesman, a reformer, and a man of affairs ; the mystics who were masters in the schools of thought ; the mystics who revived the Gospel ideal of succour to the sick and sorrowful, and mission to the outcast, all of these rendered practical service to their times ; and, at least, it speaks volumes for

[1] Thomas of Celano : *Legenda Secunda*, cap. cxxiv.

the Medieval Church that, whether amongst the statesmen, or the thinkers, or the free lances in its ranks, it knew a saint when it saw one. The slow judgement of centuries has confirmed, or is in process of confirming, the verdict passed on the life and work, whether of Bernard, or of Aquinas, or of Francis; and Mysticism, felt as a living force once again after years of neglect, is glad to find, by the example of St. Bernard, that the busy round of affairs may be followed under the unwavering light of the Divine Presence; that the labours of the great scholastics secured for its highest and dearest aspirations a home within the Church; and that, as St. Francis showed, the abiding Christ still walks with those who joy in Nature and in simple things and serve His sick and poor.

CHAPTER VII

The German Mystics of the Middle Ages

THE great German school of Mysticism of the four-teenth century—one of the landmarks in mystical history—which later ramified northwards into the Low Countries, and had no inconsiderable share in preparing the way for the Reformation, was heralded by a remarkable group of women saints and mystics. From the seclusion of convent walls they influenced the life of their times pro-foundly as prophetesses and reformers. Thus the letters of St. Hildegarde (1098–1179) condemning the abuses of the Christian world around her, intensely Teutonic in their mingling of poetic visionariness and practical plain-speaking, were passed from hand to hand throughout Germany ; and in the next century four Benedictine nuns, of the con-vent of Helfde, have left writings that are still studied. First came the Abbess Gertrude and her sister St. Mechthild (Matilda) of Hackborn ; then another and greater pair, puzzlingly enough of the same names, St. Gertrude the Great and Mechthild of Magdebourg, so called because before coming to Helfde she was first of all a Magdebourg Béguine. With regard to St. Gertrude and Mechthild of Hackborn, Miss Underhill thinks that the former was a " characteristic Catholic visionary of the feminine type ; absorbed in her subjective experience . . . her loving con-versations with Christ and the Blessed Virgin ", the latter's

" attitude as a whole is more impersonal . . . the great symbolic visions in which her most spiritual perceptions are expressed are artistic creations . . . and dwell little upon the humanity of Christ ".[1] Mechthild of Magdebourg wrote a book called " The Flowing Light of the Godhead." She was the poetess of the group, and her works were read by Dante in a Latin translation, and are thought to have influenced the " Paradiso ".

It is one of the old scribes who penned a couplet about " Meister Eckhart, from whom God kept nothing hid ", and it has been truly said by a modern writer that " one soon finds he cannot touch the surface of fourteenth century Mysticism in Germany without making up accounts with Eckhart ". He was, indeed, one of those extraordinary persons in whom two ages seem to meet, and who sum up in themselves and their teaching qualities seemingly the most contradictory. Thus, he had absorbed the theology of Augustine, Dionysius, and Erigena, and was the pupil of Thomas Aquinas, and through him of Albertus Magnus. Yet, inheritor of the past as he was, he pointed the way to the German philosophy of the future. A mystic of mystics, revelling in abstractions, he yet thought so much of practical Christianity that he ranked Martha above Mary in the scale of perfection, and taught that " even were one in a rapture like Paul's, and there were a sick man needing help, it would be far better to come out of the rapture and show love by serving the needy one ". It is hard to imagine more difficult subjects or more abstruse philosophy than those of Eckhart's sermons, yet both at Cologne and Strassbourg those sermons were eagerly listened to by enormous crowds. A great deal of credit must be given to the general level of intelligence in fourteenth century audiences, and, perhaps, some regret may be felt at the obvious modern lapse from this standard ; yet it must not be forgotten that

[1] Underhill, *Mysticism*, p. 548.

Eckhart had a singular gift of clothing his philosophy in striking epigrams. Also, he was apt to deal in rather dangerous speculations, twenty-eight of which were afterwards condemned by the Church, and the Rhine valley was at the time the nursery of Pantheistic speculation and its like. Even so, however, Eckhart's sermons and their undoubted popularity make a curious study. It is one of several instances—the Graal legend is one, the story of Joan of Arc another, the working of the great craft-guilds a third—which, just when we have settled our convictions as to the darkness of the "Dark Ages", surprise us and make us think afresh. Not the least remarkable circumstance as regards Eckhart was that the Church allowed him to preach and teach unhindered for a generation. But the Church was always very careful and very tender about a genuine mystic. It really allowed the "goodly fellowship of the Prophets" to sing in its *Te Deum*.

Eckhart's story is soon told. He was born, in Thuringia probably, about 1260. He entered, about the age of fifteen, the Dominican convent at Erfurt, and afterwards studied at Cologne, where Albert the Great had just died, and the writings of Thomas Aquinas, his pupil, were attaining their undisputed pre-eminence. Then in 1302, we find him at Paris, enrolled in the school of theology as " Brother Aychardus, a German " ; already he was Prior of Erfurt and Vicar-general of Thuringia. On leaving Paris with the title of " Meister ", he became Provincial Prior for the Dominican Order in Saxony, and had fifty-one monasteries and nine nunneries under his charge. It will be remembered that, just as the Franciscans were the Mission-preachers of the Church, so the Order of St. Dominic (the " Domini canes," or watch-dogs of the Lord, as their punning synonym went) was founded to teach and illustrate the orthodox faith. Hence Eckhart had two great periods of preaching, one at Strassbourg, the centre of "every type of Christian Society and every form of piety ", as well as of much of the best scholarship of the day, the other at Cologne whither he moved in 1320. He died seven years later, under suspicions of heresy ; " he wished to know more than he should ", was the Pope's verdict. Now for some notes on his teaching.

The Godhead is above all distinctions. " He is neither this nor that ". "All things in Him are one thing ". Yet He is the eternal Ground or Potentiality of being, and of all distinctions, as yet undeveloped. He is the great Unknowable, the " Nameless Nothing ", " the Naked, or Wordless Godhead ", " the silent wilderness where none is at home ". He is also the " Unnatured Nature ". These, startling as they sound, are only expansions of the phrases familiar to ourselves, the " Infinite ", the " Absolute ". Now with Eckhart the Godhead is distinguished from God. God is the Self-realization, or manifestation of the Godhead ; He is Triune, the Son being the Father's Word, the uttered Thought of the Thinker ; the Holy Spirit, following out the idea of Victorinus, being the bond of love between the Father and the Son. It would seem that on the whole he insisted that the generation of the Son is continuous and eternal, and therefore that the Trinity is not an emanation or appearance of the Absolute, but of Its necessary being. The universe is divided into two spheres, the sphere of Ideas, and the sphere of Phenomena. The sphere of Ideas is in reality the activity of the Son, for the Son is the Reason or Word of the Father, and Reason is the ordered sum of Ideas. In this sense Eckhart utters some of his most startling phrases such as, " Nature is the lower part of the Godhead ", and, " Before creation, God was not God ". All depends on his distinction between the Godhead and God. What is the connexion between this world of Ideas—the Son in the bosom of the Father, as it were—and the world of Phenomena, between " non-natured nature ", and what Spinoza afterwards termed

"Natura naturata"? Eckhart offers the Incarnation as an explanation. Here "the Prototype passes into externality." When the Christian soul frees itself from the phenomenal world and its imprisoning influence and gets back to the "intelligible world", there is a fresh begetting of the Son; so that the Son is twice-begotten, once into time, then spiritually, back again towards God; the spiritual process is therefore a circular one. Eckhart found it difficult to solve the problem of evil, for he steadily refused the Neo-Platonic solution of the Cosmos or Word of the Godhead being like the emanation of rays from the sun, growing less bright the further they extended from the Centre of Light. Nor had the theory of evolution, as Dr. Inge points out, yet come to help him. Eckhart is strictly Catholic in refusing any idea of subordination in Divine essence as regards the Son. He is "the Brightness of the Father's glory, the express Image of His Person". But in consequence, since he practically identified the intelligible world with God, he comes very near to Pantheism. Indeed, he does affirm (we must always remember his love for epigrammatic expression) that "in God all things are one, from angel to spider", and one of the *gravamina* of the Inquisition against him was that he taught "in omni opere, etiam malo, manifestatur et relucet aequaliter gloria Dei".[1] This, of course, if he really affirmed it, is much more serious than the "angel and spider" saying, in which we are confronted rather with Eckhart's optimism over something generally disliked, than his re-valuation of anything definitely evil. He frequently, in any case, asserted the transcendence of God, e.g. "He is above all Nature, and is not Himself Nature". Probably he tried at different times to express the two facets of truth, apparently discordant, yet each felt as truth,

[1] "The glory of God manifests itself and shines equally in every activity; yea, even in that which is evil."

which impress themselves by turns—in enduring contradiction—on the mystical mind. Evil is chiefly, with him, as with Dionysius, not-being, *privatio*, and moral evil, it follows, is the attempt of the soul to get out of God, Who is Being—the standing by one-self, self-will.

But the most important part of Eckhart's system, the part which became distinctive of his school, was his doctrine of the Divine Immanence in the soul. This is closely connected with his tenet as to the Divine " spark ", " das Fünkelein ", which is " the ground of the soul ", its means of union with the Divine Nature, the part or "apex", of the spirit whereby the spirit is gradually informed with God and becomes God-like. At first Eckhart thought that this something of God in us, whereby we respond to God, is a created function, a residue of the Divine left in man, and in this sense it had been inculcated by Albertus Magnus, Aquinas and Bonaventura ; but, later, Eckhart went further and said that the " Fünkelein " was the very true life of the soul, in fact was God Himself in man.[1] " Diess Fünkelein, das ist Gott ". He beats down all series of emanations betwixt the soul and God, all grades of ascent to God, all mediation between God and the soul. The systems of Dionysius and the scholastics alike disappear. God is simply and already there in this " spark " of the soul, the Divine essence itself. All depends upon the Will : on the Will Eckhart lays immense stress. In a sense and by the nature of things, the Son of God, the power of response to God, is born in every man coming into the world ; but by active co-operation—the imitation of Christ—and by passive contemplation the second Birth takes place in the soul. The first method he calls " the way of the manhood ", the second, " the way of the Godhead ", and it must be confessed that

---

[1] Cf. " The eye with which I see God is the same as that with which God sees me."

in treating of the latter he does fall into the snare of the mystics, the temptation to get beyond Christ, " to rise from the Three to the One ", and that there is much about the " Waste Place of the Godhead ", and the love of God as He is, " a non-God, a non-Spirit, a non-Person, a non-Form, absolute bare Unity ". It is possible to comprehend the nameless longing of such minds as Eckhart's and the attempts in words to express that which is intuition, sensation, half psychic, half spiritual, in any event inexpressible, but these were dangerous phrases to sow broadcast in the speculative soil of the day. Yet Eckhart's ordinary teaching was sound and sane enough. In any case, " the way of the manhood " must be trodden first of all ; that is essential ; and it takes the whole time of most ; he lays perpetual stress on the primary duties of a pure intention, and on love. Heaven, Hell and Purgatory are states, not places. If any one will be a saint, he must mix with his kind, avoid all peculiarity of dress or manner, rather live in a crowd than retire to a desert to fast, and accustom himself to small duties, which are harder to do than great. The spirit of the sixteenth century reformer is often felt struggling towards awakening, and sometimes to be wide awake, in Eckhart. He stands, a supremely interesting figure, at the close of one period, and the beginning of the next,—at the close of Medieval, and at the beginning of Modern Christianity.

Meister Eckhart had two great pupils, whose lives extended over much the same period of time, 1300 to 1365. The three men made up a remarkable trio with the various gifts by which they served the Church—Eckhart as a philosopher, Tauler as a preacher, and Suso, who was beatified, as a man with whom " mysticism was an intimate personal adventure ", so interesting and critical that, like Bunyan the Puritan, he left its record in an autobiography. Around all three, and knitting them the more together, moved the shadowy shapes of the members of that strange and fascinating Society of Catholic Quakers, the " Friends of God." Of this Society Tauler was a leading member.

He was born in 1300 at Strassbourg and, like Eckhart, entered the Dominican Order at the age of fifteen. He may have studied in Paris, and all that is quite clearly known of him, beyond the fact of his being the greatest preacher of his age, is that he moved about a good deal between Cologne, Basle, and Strassbourg, at which last named place he died in 1361. It is possible that at Cologne or Paris he took the degree of " Master in Holy Scripture ", but there is no evidence for this ; yet it is in virtue of this supposition that he is always called " Dr." John Tauler, and that he has been identified as the " Master of Holy Scripture " who was converted by the mysterious " Friend of God ", Master Nicholas, at Basle and visited by him on his death-bed.[1] The story of the conversion, in all its picturesqueness and its mystery, rings true of the age and is now chiefly important for that reason. It was contradicted and nearly disproved by Denifle, a learned Dominican of our own day ; re-habilitated by Preger, who wrote the history of German Mysticism from the Protestant standpoint ; contradicted again by another Dominican, von Loë, and is now regarded as extremely doubtful. So is the story as to whether Tauler and his Dominican house at Strassbourg resisted the Papal Interdict laid upon Strassbourg and other cities which supported Louis the Bavarian in 1329.[2] In any case it is really to be doubted whether Tauler needed, or was any the better for, so vast a disturbance to soul and body alike, and

[1] The whole story is told at length by Vaughan : *Hours with the Mystics*, bk. vi. ch. 5, and by Miss Winkworth : *History and Life of the Reverend Dr. John Tauler.*

[2] For a brief synopsis of these disputed points see Mr. Hutton's excellent little Introduction to *The Inner Way*—46 of Tauler's sermons.

the years of uselessness entailed on him, by Nicholas'
interference.

Tauler lays far more emphasis on sin than does his master,
Eckhart. Sin he defines as selfishness. He was a practical
instructor of souls, and therefore he bids self to be renounced
and abandoned, and mainly in its two degradations of pride
and sensuality. He holds the doctrine of the Fall of man
strongly. Separation from God, he teaches, in words
strangely enlightened, is the chief and indeed only true
misery and the veritable hell. " The human soul can never
cease to yearn and thirst after God ; and the greatest pain
of the lost is that this longing can never be satisfied."
It is natural that we should find in Tauler the doctrine of
the Divine spark in the apex of the soul, but he does not go
to such lengths as Eckhart. With Tauler it is a created
medium for a special purpose—the presence of Christ in the
heart. This work of Christ in us is one of his great doctrines ;
and there are three stages, first, of self-control, during which
the " temple courts " have to be cleared of the harsh sounds
of buying and selling, so that Jesus may be heard therein ;
secondly, a resting like John on the breast of Jesus, till contemplation changes the soul into " His beautiful image ";
thirdly, a stage attained by a few after " many a death of
nature, inward and outward ", when practically Christ
lives and repeats His experience, this " mingled web of
grief and joy " in the soul. In the third stage, Quietism,
but a noble Quietism, appears. The will and intellect are to
be passive to receive the Divine impress. Perhaps he depreciates the intellect too much, differing herein, yet on the
whole, considering his times, healthfully, from Eckhart.
" Put out into the deep ", he says, " and let down your nets
for a draught ". But the deep is the deep of the heart : it
is love, not speculation, that will learn most. But, granted
God's impress, he made much of the active will. " With the
will one may do anything ", says Tauler, and as against the

errors of the *Via Negativa*, he has striking phrases. "We must lop and prune vices, not nature, which is in itself good and noble"; "all kinds of skill are gifts of the Holy Ghost", and, "works of love are more acceptable to God than pious contemplation".

Certainly he uses the language of the advanced mystics in speaking of the goal of the soul. It is once more "deification", "rising above distinctions", "the Divine Abyss", "the Waste Place", and so on. He had forgotten Irenaeus' wise sentence. "Mensura . . . Patris Filius." Yet we may at least recall, if startled by such language, that it was used by holy and humble men of heart, who perhaps really knew of what they talked with unanimity and who used a discipline of life to which we are strangers. There was with the mystics a temptation to soar too high, but by the very strain and effort they kept before the Christian mind the fact that man is meant to soar.

There is a great deal more to tell of Suso than of either Eckhart or Tauler. He left an Autobiography, and this record, which Dr. Inge calls a "gem of medieval literature", gives us Suso's special legacy to the Church, an experience. He returns from soaring speculations as to the Unknowable and the Light of the Absolute which is, in its excess, darkness to the soul's eyes, to the Life and Sufferings of Jesus, which he endeavours to bear about in his mortal body. In this he resembles the later Spanish mystics; and there is in him an excellent example of the visionary, as apart from the ecstatic, stage. We shall probably think, and not be far wrong in thinking, that his visions were in part the product of his awful earlier austerities. There were two stages in his life, the period of outward penance and of visions, and the period of inner dereliction, which he found far harder, and which was his fruitful time, spiritually speaking, after all.

"The servitor of the Eternal Wisdom", as he calls himself, was born in 1295, and was converted to his life-long service at the age of seventeen. He had lived hitherto in careful avoidance of deadly sin, but, like the young ruler of the Gospel, had not escaped an inner reproach. Then came a voice, " Be content with gradual progress : treat thyself well". But Wisdom said to him, " If thou purpose to renounce all, do so to good purpose ". This voice, whether he misinterpreted it or not, he obeyed, and began a long series of frightful self torments.[1] No man ever exhibited this side of the mystical life to such terrible excess. What are we to say of it ? Well : let us not be too critical, at any rate. The inner pressure in this direction has in some natures been enormous ; it is never quite absent from the mystical life, any more than the voluntary Cross was absent from Christ and His teaching. With Suso, it proved to be a valuable experience, in spite of its extravagance, and in his fortieth year, when a fresh and unmistakable command came, he laid it all down as obediently as he had taken it up. This implied that he kept his sanity and self-control absolutely unimpaired. During the period of self-inflicted torture, he had visions, and one undoubted ecstasy. Curiously enough, if one may venture a criticism, Dr. Inge does not in the least distinguish them, and yet they are perfectly distinguishable. The account of the Ecstasy had best be read in Suso's own words :—" It was without form or mode ; but contained within itself the most entrancing delight. His heart was athirst and yet satisfied. It was the breaking forth of the sweetness of eternal life ". It lasted half an hour, and left certain after-gleams and touches. Now all this corresponds exactly with the four notes of the mystical experience we have earlier noted—Ineffability,

---

[1] For a long quotation of these austerities from *The Life of the Blessed Henry Suso* translated by T. F. Knox, 1865, see James : *Varieties of Religious Experience*, pp. 307–309.

Authority or Certainty, Transiency, and, we may judge, Passivity on the part of the recipient. "Eternal life" broke forth; he was not straining towards it. As regards transiency, the period, half an hour, exactly corresponds with that mentioned by other recipients of the experience, for instance, St. Teresa. Now if we compare this with the visions, the difference will at once be apparent. Once Suso saw the Eternal Wisdom in the form of a lovely woman. Another time an angel bade him look within and see how "God plays His play of love" with the soul. His body seemed then to become clear as crystal, and he saw his soul lying in God's arms, whilst beside sat Wisdom, still as a beautiful woman. Yet again, he saw his master Eckhart, soon after the latter's death, in glory. Once the Divine Child appeared to him in the Virgin's arms, and he embraced It. All this is pretty enough, but it is "of such stuff as dreams are made of". Then came the great change. He was told by an angel to discontinue his austerities. "Hitherto hast thou been God's squire. Now shalt thou be God's knight". He was to be defamed by false scandal. He was to lose the sense of God's love. "Hitherto hast thou floated in Divine sweetness, like a fish in the sea; now shalt thou starve and wither. God and the world shall forsake thee." All this came upon him. He felt he must go out and face the world; and by a not infrequent contradiction, he who feared not torments worse than death, self-inflicted, dreaded incessantly a violent death at others' hands. There were many who hated the monks. Then came a terrible accusation of loose living, which hung over him like a black cloud for several years. At last he was cleared and ended his days at the age of seventy in peace and love with all and with God. Truly he had tasted much of the Passion.

One or two sentences of his may be quoted. "This is the transit of the soul. It passes beyond time and space, and is with an amorous inward intuition dissolved in God.

M.C.   K

This entrance of the soul banishes all forms, images, and multiplicity. The Divine Nature doth, as it were, inwardly kiss through and through the soul." Again, " A man of true self-abandonment must be un-built from the creature, in-built with Christ, over-built into the Godhead ". Asked to give an illustration of the Trinity, he gave the figure of concentric circles following the throwing of a stone into a pool " : but, he added, " this is as unlike the formless truth as a black moor is unlike the beautiful Sun ".

Suso held that Christ's Humanity is the key to God's secrets. He is the Way and the source of living energy by which we walk the way. So the mystical saying comes true that " the door by which God issues from Himself is the door by which He enters the human soul ". More than any other German mystic, Suso shews us Christ, and Christ in His sorrows. This is the proof of love. " No Cross, no Crown " is the link that unites in one life of self-sacrifice Christ and his servants.

Something has already been said of the Society of the Friends of God, with which Eckhart, Tauler, and Suso were all connected. The sense of spiritual things, of which the existence of this and kindred associations was the outcome and the expression, had been greatly intensified at the beginning of the fourteenth century by two events which had, as it were, thrown people's souls back upon themselves, as well as quickened their realization of eternal things. One of these events was the awful visitation of the Black Death, which, on the Continent as in England, killed a vast number of devoted parish priests and left their flocks without regular ministry. One sign of the impression produced by the ravages of the pestilence was the appearance of the Flagellants, melancholy processions of devotees drawn from all ranks of society, who, to appease the Divine wrath, passed through the towns and villages repeating the Penitential Psalms and scourging themselves the while. A better course was that

taken by Tauler and others of his school who laboured coura-
geously and persistently among the sick and dying. The other
event that came to crown the wretchedness of the times was
a miserable quarrel which broke out between the Emperor
Louis the Bavarian and Pope John XXII. Strassbourg and
most of the Rhine cities supported the Emperor, with the
result that the whole country was laid under an interdict
that lasted twenty years. Deprived thus of ordinary ministrations, societies were formed in all directions for keeping
alive the individual spiritual life, and the fact that many
priests, such as Tauler, belonged to these societies prevented
them in great measure from drifting away from the Catholic
Church. The principles of the societies, especially of that
one known as the " Friends of God ", were set forth by a
series of remarkable writings. Perhaps the most representative writer was the mystic Rulman Merswin, to whom no
less than sixteen books, largely allegorical in character,
have been ascribed,[1] but by far the most representative
book is the *Theologia Germanica*, which has indeed survived
as one of the world's spiritual classics.

Its author is entirely unknown; he was without doubt
a Catholic, probably a Knight of the Teutonic Order, and in
all likelihood a member of the Society of the Friends of God,
as the teaching of the little book is practically a synopsis
of the body of religious thought common to the Society.
The " Theologia ", whoever wrote it, first appeared in 1350,
certainly in Tauler's life-time. The earliest extant MS.
dates from 1497. Luther got hold of it, and published an
edition in 1516. It had made an immense impression on
him; he says, " Next to the Bible and St. Augustine, no

---

[1] For a full list of these, as well as for a detailed notice of Merswin
and a singularly full and excellent account of the " Friends of
God," see Prof. Rufus Jones, *Studies in Mysticism*, p. 246, and the
entire Ch. 13 of that work.

book hath ever come into my hands, whence I have learned, or would wish to learn more of what God and Christ and men and all things are ". No fewer than seventeen editions of the book appeared in Luther's day; and since his time it has had over sixty editions in Germany, and has been translated into Latin, French, Flemish, and English.

Its author evidently thoroughly understands Eckhart, but he wants to view things not wholly " in the light of eternity ", as Eckhart tries to do, but more practically. He maintains the distinction between the Godhead,—formless, unknowable,—and God: but he is not always bidding the soul strain itself to heights that turn out often too much like empty summits if and when attained. So the soul, he says, has two eyes, the right looking into eternity and at God; the left beholding the things of time. Christ only, says this curious, suggestive passage, saw with both eyes at once. A man may leave, or try to leave temporal things and images of the true, too soon; but leave them at last he must in intent and effort. Sin is self-will, self-love; we must not love God just for what we have of Him. It is sin to stop half-way when we may go higher. " It is of sin ", the *Theologia* quotes Boethius, " that we do not love that which is the Best ". Actual experience is insisted on throughout; the new birth must be a complete and verifiable transformation of the inner nature. The little book has less in it by far of what is speculative and startling than Eckhart's teaching; but it has a deeper sense of sin, and of the contrast between light and darkness than is evinced by Eckhart, and it is less self-centred than à Kempis' great work. To rise above the " I " and the " Mine " is its outstanding message, and its ambition is " to be to the Eternal Goodness as a right hand to its owner ".

Jan Ruysbroek, " Doctor Ecstaticus ", as he is named by the Church, has an importance of his own, apart from his mysticism. He was the link that united the schools of the Rhineland and of Holland, the " Friends of God " and the " Brethren of the Common Life ". For, himself the friend and follower of Tauler, he had for disciple the famous Gerard Groote who founded the brotherhoods and sisterhoods of the Common Life, the society of which Thomas à Kempis was the greatest and most enduring ornament. Ruysbroek combined in his own character the two aspects of Christian service, the practical and the devotional, to a very remarkable degree. A hard-working parish priest till the age of sixty,—he was born in 1293—and Vicar of the great Church of St. Gudule in Brussels as well as Prior of Vauvert, he retired thence to a life of contemplation in the forest of Grönendal. But he was by no means idle or solitary even there. Many sought his advice in the forest recesses, attracted by the reports of his holiness, and the growing reputation of the mystical books [1] which he was writing. One such band of inquirers, priests from Paris, wishing to consult him on the state of their souls, got from him the celebrated answer, " You are as holy as you will to be holy ". One thing may be said at once. His intellectual powers were insignificant compared with those of Eckhart and Tauler. " Teacher had he none ", says Denys the Carthusian, " save the Holy Spirit. He was, like Peter and John, unlearned and ignorant ". This may account for the varying judgements passed upon his powers. Speaking generally, those who value intellectuality as a necessary concomitant and balance to the mystical gift, are apt to disparage him. On the other hand, the mystics themselves are enthusiastic in his praise. M. Maeterlinck, though he feels that the light of Ruysbroek's mind comes to us as through " poor double horn-panes ", yet exalts him, intellect and all, as one well-nigh

---

[1] *The Book of the Adornment of Spiritual Marriage : The Book on True Contemplation : The Book of the Sparkling Stone : a treatise, " On the Seven Grades of Love ", and others.*

beyond praise. He "receives all unconsciously dazzling sunbeams from all the lonely, mysterious peaks of human thought . . . His marvellous ignorance rediscovers the wisdom of buried centuries, and foresees the knowledge of centuries yet unborn".[1] "He is one of the rarest souls in the goodly fellowship of mystical teachers. One comes away from a study of him with a sort of reverent awe", says Dr. Rufus Jones. "Both saint and seer—one of the very greatest mystics whom the world has yet known", is Miss Underhill's verdict. Certainly, Ruysbroek's was a wonderful life : it was informed through and through with the spirit of love, love, under the figure of spiritual espousals with the Divine Bridegroom, (an idea destined to find its complete expression centuries afterwards through the great modern mystic, Coventry Patmore,) and love in the practical affairs of everyday life. This was what so influenced Gerard Groote, as we learn from Thomas à Kempis' *Vita Gerardi*, when he visited Ruysbroek at Grönendal. Ruysbroek was prior of the community, but carried out the humblest tasks in that happy family life, while all, down to " John the cook ", were treated as friends and consulted even on spiritual matters.

In his actual writings, Ruysbroek returned to what Eckhart had left, and laid out a complete chart of the mystic's progress. We have its grades and stages duly set in order. Thus his " Ladder of Love " has seven steps of progress upwards, (1) Goodwill ; (2) Voluntary poverty ; (3) Purity ; (4) Lowliness of mind ; (5) Desire for God's Glory ; (6) Divine contemplation ; and (7) unnameable, indescribable transcendence of all thought and knowledge. We may note the Eckhartian prominence of the will, the emphasis, common in his day, on poverty, and two very

---

[1] Maeterlinck : *Ruysbroek and the Mystics*, translated by Jane Stoddart, p. 12.

wise psychological counsels besides ; first, that humility is made to follow two virtues whose practice might very well lead to a certain cold pride, and secondly, how ambition for God closely succeeds to the renunciation of self. In the " *Ordo Spiritualium Nuptiarum* " there is a yet more complete chart viewed from a different aspect. Ruysbroek tells us that there are three stages of ascent, the Active life corresponding to the sensitive,—the Inner Life, corresponding to the rational—and the Contemplative Life corresponding to the spiritual, powers of the soul. The motto of the Active life is " Ecce sponsus venit ", and this Advent which is threefold, in the days of His flesh, through grace in this life, and finally to judgement, is met on the soul's part by humility, by love, and by justice. Above the Active rises the Inner life. This too has three parts. The illumination of the Intellect, in the apprehension of eternal Truth, shews us the *Coming* of the Bridegroom. The effort of the Will ensures the *going forth* to meet Him. The desire of Love to be united with Him will ensure the *actual meeting*. The last, or Contemplative, stage, is one to which only a few attain here and now. In attempting its description Ruysbroek avails himself of a great deal of Dionysian and Eckhartian phraseology, the talk of " living immersion ", of " melting away into the unknown Dark ". " In this higher state the soul sinks into the vast darkness of the Godhead, into the Abyss in which the Persons of the Trinity transcend themselves ". " There we become one and uncreated, according to our prototypes ". No one has gone farther than Ruysbroek in the use of such terms, and even more startling expressions might be quoted. Yet there are three principles to which he clings, which save this wonderful man from becoming one of those " theopaths, living in inert sloth, and putting down every impulse as Divine ", whom he strongly reprobates. One of these principles is his zeal for activity. " Laziness is not holy abstraction ", he announces, and, whatever our experience, we are not to forsake religious exercises. All his life, too, he was a vigorous reformer of abuse and an unmerciful critic of the sins of popes, bishops, monks and laity. Another saving principle was his conviction that, in all the spiritual progress made, it is the Son in us Who responds to the Father's call. " The abyss of God calleth to the abyss in us ". A third is that while like many mystics of all ages he yields sometimes to the language of absorption in God—our own Keble does so in the closing line of his Evening Hymn—he believes firmly in the retention of individual personality. The creature, as such, remains a creature, eternally distinct from God. For eternal life consists in the knowledge of God, and there can be no knowledge without self-consciousness. " If we could be blessed without knowing it, then a stone might be blessed ".

One of the most ardent disciples of Ruysbroek was Gerard Groote. Born in 1340, the son of wealthy parents, he became a professor at Cologne, an ambitious and clever man, with an eye to worldly advancement, but always with a keenness for study, and a certain vague longing for things unseen, which at first only found its vent in " dabbling with magic and astrology". His was always an attractive personality, with much brilliance and charm, and one day, an unknown stranger, after watching him wistfully for some-time while he gazed at some public fête in Cologne, came to his side and whispered, " Why standest thou here? thou shouldest become another man ". Soon after, Groote fell ill, and the strange sentence returned to his mind. He rose from his sick-bed a changed man, and went to seek Ruysbroek's advice as to the future. After a time of preparation, he set forth in 1379 to preach as a lay-evangelist, and his influence in the North was only second to that which had gone forth from Francis of Assisi in the South. Crowds flocked to hear him, whole towns neglected their business, even meals were left on one side, when Gerard Groote was preaching. Much of his teaching dealt with current ecclesiastical abuses, and in all this stir continually effervescent up and down the Rhineland and the Low Countries it is possible to see how the soil for the Reformation was being carefully prepared, and how, sooner or later, that mighty phenomenon of spiritual growth and change, far from being an accidental occurrence, was bound to come. Such preaching as Groote's was very soon stopped, and this interruption turned his thoughts into another channel. A great friend of his, Florentius Radewin, suggested the founding of a new community, in which the following of the devout life and the care for study, in the form of the copying of manuscripts, could be combined. Gerard worked out the idea, and the first house of the Brethren of the Common Life was set up at Deventer in Holland. The movement rapidly spread, and brother-houses—and in a few cases, sister-houses—were constructed in a great many towns in Germany and Holland.[1] The idea of the members' life was practical, they wore simple clothes, and their chief work lay in the education of the folk around them, and in the provision of books. The children were a special concern to them, and so was the teaching of reading and writing to the poor.

Among the children who had their schooling from the "good father and sweet master" Florentius, at Deventer, was Thomas Haemerlein of Kempen, known to succeeding ages as Thomas à Kempis.

There is scarcely any reason nowadays for refusing to identify the author of the "Imitatio" with the writer whose name is so inextricably interwoven with the great spiritual classic that with English people to talk of reading

[1] For an excellent account of these communities see G. Harvey Gem's *Hidden Saints*.

" Thomas à Kempis " is the usual way to speak of reading the " Imitation ".   Other names have been suggested, however—Walter Hylton's is one.   He was an English monk of Surrey, and a mystic, and was said to have written a book called " Musica Ecclesiastica ", but there is no very cogent proof even of this.   The Benedictines have supported the claims of John Gersen, Abbot of Vercelli. There is little proof that he even existed, and much that he is a confusion for the better known John Gerson, the Paris Chancellor.   Something, maybe, of the sadness and humiliation of Gerson's last days may be said to be reflected in the 3rd book ; and Frenchmen, keen over the controversy, have patriotically declared their interest in the matter by the phrase, " Pour Gerson, pour la France ".   Yet Renan, a judge of style and a great admirer of the " Imitation ", was against the ascription.

Thomas Haemerlein of Kempen, the usually accepted author, learned at Deventer singing and the copying of manuscripts, and copying became one of the lasting pursuits of his life, " a cup of cold water ", as he names it, in a bookless age ; and who shall say that he was wrong ?   Here is a sudden glimpse he gives us of the quiet holiness of the house at Deventer.   " One day in winter, Henry Brune was sitting by the fireside warming his hands, but with his face turned towards the wall, for he was at the time engaged in secret prayer.   When I saw this, I was edified and loved him from that day all the more ".   From Deventer, Thomas went to the brother-house of Mount St. Agnes where in his retired corner he spent, with just three years' exception, all his life, " in angello cum libello "—" in a little nook with a little book ".   In 1414, he was ordained priest, and became a Canon-regular of St. Augustine.

What did he do all this time ?   A revolt in Zwolle and Deventer against a newly appointed Bishop of Utrecht called down an Interdict on the towns, and, as the Canons of St. Agnes obeyed the Interdict, the wrathful inhabitants drove them forth for a brief exile of about three years. Then, in 1450, there was a terrible outbreak of plague in Cologne, and the St. Agnes' Canons took over a House of Regulars in the town and helped to nurse the sick.[1] Otherwise, the long years passed in an atmosphere of peace, the sort of luminous peace which pervades his book. The book was a work of years ; it was at times so much in his mind that he would lie awake in bed at night composing, and then write out his thoughts after Lauds, i.e. at about 2 a.m., and onwards. Besides, he copied the entire Bible for the use of his House, and wrote on numberless slips of vellum texts for distribution amongst the poor ; and he wrote thirty-seven textbooks besides. So he was scarcely an idler, this " little fresh-coloured man, with soft brown eyes, who steals away often to his *cubiculum*, if the talk gets too lively, with a genial humour, and not above an occasional pun, but shy, and fond of his ' angellum '."

The effect of the quiet life, and the books, and the presence of these holy households in North Germany and Holland, was deep and lasting. To take only a few of the many and very differing characters which the " Imitatio " has influenced, we hear St. Francis de Sales saying, " There is no book like it,". Ignatius Loyola read a chapter of it daily ; so did a very different thinker, Auguste Comte. Eugene of Savoy carried the book about with him in all his campaigns, and another warrior, Charles Gordon, wished it always by him and sent for a copy during the last days at Khartoum. Gladstone called it " a golden book for all time, but most for times like these ; it shows us the Man of Sorrows ". Matthew Arnold named it " the most exquisite document after the New Testament " ; Charles Kingsley, " the school of

[1] For a short and beautifully written account of Kempis' life see J. E. G. de Montmorency : *Thomas à Kempis. His Age and Book*, pp. 83–103.

many a noble soul ". Vaughan, in his " Hours with the Mystics ", called Kempis in a more discriminating passage than usual " the comforter of the fifteenth century ". Dr. Johnson liked it especially for one shrewd sentence, " Be not angry that you cannot make others as you would wish them to be, since you cannot make yourself as you wish to be ". George Eliot describes the " Imitation " as soothing Maggie Tulliver's troubles in the " Mill on the Floss ", and in one of the late Edward Cooper's books what purports to be an actual child's diary tells how the child read it to her mother, and thought it dry and hard ; but later on, in sudden terror during the mother's last illness, reads it again and finds that " it seems to suit you when you are frightened ".

So the book is a classic. Is it a mystical classic ? To some extent the answer must be, Yes. It is mystical in that it looks steadily at the unseen, and, in Browning's words, here is a man who " at least believed in soul, was very sure of God ". It adopts the mystical gradations, too ; the Three Stages of Ascent are here. Nevertheless, we miss very much some chief mystical characteristics. Here, for one thing, is no note of striving after the Ineffable, the Absolute ; here is no message of the Divine in man responding to the drawing of God ; here is scarcely the gleam " of light that never was on land or sea ". It is the human Christ Who speaks, and the soul as it were outside of Him, distinct from Him, that answers ; it is an Imitation, not a Transformation. Then there is no thought of the possibility of the Ecstasy ; all is orderly, ordinary, defined, limited—you are in a heavenly earth, it is true, but on earth still. Unlike those mystics who seem to try to pass beyond Christ, and to reach the essential Godhead, à Kempis never leaves the humanity of Christ or attempts to see what it was to which Christ pointed, and what He at one and the same time concealed and revealed, as the sunlight reveals and yet conceals the sun. Dr. Inge distinctly denies that the " Imitatio " is a mystical treatise at all, let alone " the finest flower of Christian Mysticism ", as it has sometimes been called. It is, he thinks, " the ripe fruit of medieval Christianity as concentrated in the life of the Cloister ", but there is no trace of " that independence which made Eckhart a pioneer of modern philosophy, and the fourteenth-century mystics forerunners of the Reformation ". He praises it for its teaching of humility, simplicity, and purity of heart ; but condemns it as really " a defence of the recluse and his scheme of life ". [1] This accusation of a kind of spiritual selfishness has been brought again and again ; Dean Milman first started it on its way.   Is it quite fair ?

(i) For one thing, the social side of religious life was thoroughly developed in the Medieval Church.   Never has the corporate aspect of Christianity received so vast and diversified an attention.   The Church took part in, organized, claimed as legitimate spheres of its influence pageants, merrymakings, fairs, feastings, schools and holidays, matters of commerce and trade (through the great Guilds), Art, diplomacy, chivalry and even war in a way we can scarcely realize nowadays.   ¡It was in part the development of the Teutonic spirit within its pale, in part the legacy of the dream of a spiritual *imperium* derived from Hildebrand.   An emphasis on the other side, the side of quiet devotion, inward self-knowledge, God-knowledge was the thing needful above all others.   (ii) Then, as we have seen, the lives lived by Thomas and his fellow-Brethren of the Common Life were not idle and recluse, but exceedingly useful.   Only they had their own idea of usefulness.   (iii) This idea was a reaction, in point of fact, from the Franciscan ideal.   The Franciscans had gone out into the highways and hedges after Jesus, and the life of their founder, " the child of Nature

---

[1] Inge : *Christian Mysticism*, p. 194.

and of God, half angel and half nightingale ", as Dr. Bigg has
called him, was indeed unique, on its own side as near
Christ's life as any human being has lived it. But Francis
was an exceptional man, and his rule with lesser men, as the
first love waxed cold, was open to corruption. The " cor-
ruptio optimi " was indeed " pessima ", and came frightfully
soon ; by Chaucer's time the name ' Franciscan ' was nearly
a reproach, it meant wandering idleness and sturdy beggary,
and often things far worse. So that to many, after all, à
Kempis' companions among them, the disciplined life seemed
better—the life of rules, of set hours, of thought and prayer.
His own duty lay in the reception and training of younger
brethren. There is an engraving of copper over his tomb,
which shows him coming out of the chancel to receive a
young man desirous of renouncing the world and of entering
the religious life. The youth kneels, holding a scroll on
which is written, " Oh, where is peace, for thou its path
hast trod ? " Thomas replies on another scroll, held in
his hands, " In poverty, retirement, and with God ". But
there is one sentence in the " Imitatio " which shows that
Thomas and his brethren were not unmindful of the big,
needy world around. " *Si portari vis, porta alium.*" And
again, " Learn how many times greater is the virtue that is
tested by action than the virtue which depends on thought
and imagination ". Moreover, the school of Thomas at
Mount St. Agnes became the great classical seminary of the
North ; three of his disciples visited Italy, and, bringing
from that home of the Renaissance the study of Greek, are
regarded as the founders of German classical learning. Indeed, the educational work of the Brethren as a whole was
one of the great factors in the Revival of Letters. Thomas
à Kempis died in 1471, " on the festival of St. James the
Less, after compline ", in his ninety-second year. It is
curious to think that a few years after his death the little
Erasmus was studying Greek under Hegius, not himself a

Brother, but in close touch with the Brethren, and Rector of the School at Deventer ; [1] and that some of the Brotherhood houses lingered on till suppressed by Napoleon.

[1] See S. Harvey Gem : *Hidden Saints*, pp. 115–116.

CHAPTER VIII

English and Italian Mystics

AS the Medieval mind felt more and more the disintegrating effects, first, of the Renaissance, and then of its child, the Reformation, Mysticism tended to lose its aspect of distinctive schools of thought and to become increasingly the affair of individuals. It is always possible, of course, as well as very convenient, to take nationalities, and to group the mystics under these labels. In this way, we might speak, from the fourteenth to the sixteenth centuries, of the English school, the Italian school, the Spanish school: but we could not do this in the same way as when we spoke of the Alexandrines, the Neo-Platonists, or the school of Eckhart. There is, for example, no special connecting tie between the visionary anchoress, Julian of Norwich, and Walter Hylton—Julian has more affinity, were we to seek it, with Angela of Foligno. So Teresa resembles St. Catherine of Genoa more nearly than St. John of the Cross. Premising this, however, and remembering that the chain of connexion which we adopt for clearness' sake must of necessity be a rather artificial one, we shall not do badly if we try to examine in this chapter a few types of Mysticism according to the countries to which they owed their birth.

(1) First, with regard to England. There is a certain amount of paradox in English Mysticism, a little of the odd

contradiction which runs through the English character. " Saxons, and Normans, and Danes are we ", and we show our very varied derivations by exhibiting unexpected and incongruous traits. England prides itself, for instance, and justly, on its common sense, its moderation, its love of compromise, and in religious things on its saneness and aloofness of judgement ; but it has also contrived to be a nursery of poets, and these poets have sung in greatest number and most convincingly during England's most matter-of-fact, commercial, and disillusioned periods—the periods of Elizabeth, of Anne, and of the Victorian age. Or again, the most conservative, law-abiding, and proudly constitutional nation in Europe was the first, strangely enough, to cut off its king's head in the name of freedom, and then to drive out its honoured Parliament at the edge of the sword.

So when we come to more out-of-the-way corners of English thought and history, we need not be unprepared for paradox. And we get it. One of the most distinguishing characteristics of English Mysticism is its sane common sense—a common sense that knows the world and its ways, is just a little humorous, a little caustic at times. Exaggerations of feeling, deep philosophizing we do not meet with. But then, whence did this Mysticism of common sense proceed ? Partly, at any rate, from lives lived in the most singular fashion it is possible to conceive. For three of the great English mystics, Margery Kempe, Richard Rolle of Hampole, and Julian of Norwich were anchorites. Of Margery Kempe, the anchoress of Lynn, very little is known, but Richard Rolle and Julian felt the full influence of their mystical period and exercised a great deal in return. But even in Margery Kempe we get a glimpse of the practical English spirit in her love and care for lepers.[1]

[1] See E. Underhill : *Mysticism*, p. 270, which quotes from Mr. E. Gardner's *Cell of Self-Knowledge*.

M.C. L

First, who and what were the anchorites? They were
recluses, men and women who lived under vows the hermit
life, either in the country or, more frequently perhaps in
the case of women, in cathedral cities. A favourite position
was a cell joined to the outer side of a cathedral or church
wall. The traces of one such remains outside St. Mary's
Church at Sandwich,[1] and there was in the fourteenth century a noted anchorite who lived by Westminster Abbey.
One wonders whether the great number of these hermits
in England was not a sort of medieval testimony to the independence of the English religious character taking its only
recognized and respectable outlet. For, " the life of the
recluse, now seldom chosen, and never respected . . . was
once a career, and not the abdication of all careers. . . .
It was a recognized manner of life, which, however austere,
did not at all condemn him who had chosen it to obscurity
or contempt ".[2] Hermits originally came into being after
the Decian persecution in 250, when great multitudes fled
into the deserts of North Africa, and lived the rest of their
lives there, solitary, prayerful, and safe. Thenceforth,
such recluses were never wanting to the life of the Church,
and the best of them did actually spend their days in inter-
cessory prayer, and also in counselling those who resorted
to them for advice. The hermits were stationary, and
one of the peculiarities of the life of the Middle Ages was
its restlessness. Merchants, crusaders, scholars, pilgrims,
were for ever on the move, and many a hermit's or anchoress'
cell was like a fixed star to guide the wanderer by its beam.
That they were held in a very deep awe and reverence is
evidenced by such a fact as that King Richard II went to
confession to the anchorite at Westminster immediately
before his hazardous meeting with Wat Tyler and his mob;

[1] Doubtless there are many others up and down the country.
See *infra*.

[2] Inge : *Studies of English Mystics*, p. 38.

and such a book as the "Ancren Riwle", drawn up for three ladies, anchoresses, by Bishop Poore of Salisbury [1] in the early part of the thirteenth century, also shows how widespread and ordinary such a manner of the devout life had become.

Richard Rolle, "the father of English mysticism", [2] was a highly educated Oxford scholar, and well read in Richard of St. Victor, St. Bernard, and St. Bonaventura. Perhaps the latter gave him a certain touch of Franciscan poetry, and a burning zeal for souls. For he, most mystical of mystics, was in this last particular, a very practical servitor of God. What marks him out from other mystics is that to him the apprehension of the Divine seems to take the form of Music. First there is a state of burning love, which he described as "calor", and then this is changed to "canor"—"meditation is turned into a song of joy". "Song", he says, " I call when in a plenteous soul the sweetness of eternal love with burning is taken . . . and the mind into full sweet sound is changed". The man who experiences this melody " is taken into marvellous mirth". and even " with notes his prayers he sings". In another passage he compares the soul that loves God to a "little bird that for love of her lover longs . . . and joying she sings, and singing she longs, but in sweetness and heat ". [3] One or two sayings may perhaps be culled from this writer, before we pass on, sayings of a more general wisdom and

---

[1] It is also attributed to a later Bishop of Salisbury, Simon de Ghent. For its provisions, delightful in their quaint, common-sense simplicity see the book by Dr. Inge already quoted, pp. 41–49.

[2] He is, in part, one suspects, the prototype of Fr. Benson's *Richard Raynal*.

[3] These quotations are taken from Miss Underhill's *Mysticism*, pp. 92, 234. A full and excellent account of Rolle is given in the Introduction to the *Works of Richard Rolle of Hampole and his followers*. Edited by C. Horstman, 2 vols. (Library of Early English Writers.)

application. Thus : " Love is a life, copuland together the loving and the loved ". Again, " All deadly sin is in- ordinate love for a thing that is naught ". Again, and very shrewdly, " Truth may be without love, but it may naught help without it ", and " I hope that God has no perfect servant upon earth without enemies of some men ; for only wretchedness has no enemy ".

One of the most remarkable of the anchorite mystics was Julian of Norwich, who wrote " Sixteen Revelations of Divine Love ".[1] In Norwich " the little church of St. Julian ", says Miss Warrack, who has edited the " Revela- tions ", " still keeps from Norman times its dark round tower of flint rubble, and still there are traces about its foundation of the anchorage built against its south-eastern wall ". Here from 1370 to 1450 lived a Benedictine nun of Carrow, called the Lady Julian,—the courtesy prefix was usually given to recluses who were gentlewomen. She describes her experience as revelations made to her by God ; they began at the age of thirty. Their characteristics are abso- lute candour and simplicity, happiness of temperament, humility and love of her kind, and delight in being busy— " sloth and losing of time are the beginnings of sin ", she says. It is a very attractive character that is thus revealed, and, on the psychic side, her accounts of what happened are singularly true to modern psychological knowledge. She had prayed, it seems, for three gifts from God, the first of which was a sight of the Passion of Christ. Devotion and loyalty to our Lord were strong traits in her mind, proof even against strange mystic temptations. Secondly, she had asked for a sickness or pain that would purge her of sin and self-will : [2] and thirdly, for three " wounds ".

[1] Grace Warrack : *Revelations of Divine Love recorded by Julian, anchoress at Norwich.*

[2] " For hearts that verily repent
    Are burdened with impunity
    And comforted by chastisement ".   *Coventry Patmore.*

The first two requests were made subject to God's will, but the third was made absolutely, for the three wounds were true contrition, a natural sympathy, and a steadfast longing for God.

The illness for which she prayed actually came, and her life was despaired of. It was during the crisis of her illness that her " revelations " or visions began. These, we shall do well to remember, were " visions ", and had nothing to do with the mystical Ecstasy. But they were probably as truly " visions " as St. Peter's trance on the housetop, or St. Paul's vision of Christ, and like Peter's trance, they came in what would be now called an abnormal bodily state. He was fasting ; she was ill. But she can always quite sanely distinguish the visions from mere dreams ; and they are described simply and directly without any furbishing or ornament.

The visions were of Christ crucified. There is no need to enlarge on them further than to say that they were most important as forming the beginning of her mystical experience. She was thereby stayed on Christ, and able to resist the mystic's characteristic temptation to soar beyond. The thought did come to her once that she ought to look beyond the Cross to heaven and God the Father, but she answered inwardly to her Lord, " Nay ; I may not, for Thou art my heaven ". Christ as her Friend and Master was a living reality to her, and she thus describes the soul's relations with Him in a kind of charming language of chivalry. " Our courteous Lord willeth that we should be as homely with Him as heart may think, or soul may desire. But beware lest we take recklessly this homeliness, so as to leave courtesy. For our Lord is sovereign homeliness, and as homely as He is, so courteous He is ".

For her teaching, it is grounded on love to God, and in God to all, and an intense happiness and hopefulness. She is no stranger to the high mystical apprehensions of God.

For example, here are three mystical sayings that equal anything that Eckhart taught. " I saw God in a point ". Here mathematics, philosophy, and theology all touch, though to the first and second she was in all probability a complete stranger. Again, " unmade kind (i.e. matter) is God", which reminds us of Ruysbrock's doctrine that God is *potential* force, or life, or substance. Again, "It needeth us to naughten (i.e. to make naught) all thing that is made, for to love and honour God that is unmade ".

Others will like better her more human apprehensions of God and His love. She believes in that love with a sort of saintly heartiness. " God wills that we should more rejoice in His whole love than sorrow in our often failings ". " It is the best worship of Him . . . that we live gladly and merrily, for His love, in our penance. For He beholdeth us so tenderly that He seeth all our being a penance ". She sees, and sorrows for, sin, and is cast down by the mystery of evil, but a Voice comes to her again and again, " I have done in the Atonement of Christ that which is greatest ; shall I fail in the rest, that which is less ? " and once more, " All shall be well, and all manner of thing shall be well". She sees no wrath anywhere, save in man ; and " *that* forgiveth He in us". God is revealed to her as Life, Love, and Light ; and these are one goodness.

In Walter Hylton we have a contrast, though not a discordant contrast, both in life and teaching, to Julian of Norwich. Yet in some ways he acts as her complement, just as Tauler supplemented Eckhart, or the *Theologia Germanica* some of the more visionary writings of Suso. Of Hylton himself we know little, though, as we saw, he was at one time credited with the authorship of the " Imitatio". He was Canon of Thurgarton in Yorkshire, and died in 1396, and his life was not that of a hermit, but of a working parish priest, who knew the world of his own day well. The book by which he " being dead, yet speaketh " is called the " Scale of Perfection ", and, as its name implies, is a description of the ladder of the spiritual life.[1] But Hylton's ladder has rungs quite peculiar to itself. The first step is a knowledge of the facts of religion ; this is only a shadow of true contemplation, for it may, of course, be without love. It is, we are told, like the water of Cana, which Divine grace must turn into wine. The second step is the feeling of grace—warmth without light to analyse it. This feeling at first comes and goes, but steadily increases, till the third step is reached, knowledge with love. The Second Part deals with the higher rungs of the ladder; and is persistent, by every inducement of which Hylton can avail himself, in persuading those who have reached the lower stages to press on higher. There is no standing still in the spiritual life ; not to advance is to recede, and it is dangerous for any one to aim at what is barely sufficient, for he may of course just miss it, and losing that, lose everything.

Like Julian, he puts the greatest stress on the Person of Christ, and is careful to inculcate the regular use of the Sacraments. Of the soul in Part Three he has much to say, and of the soul's relations with its " Heaven, which is Jesus God ". We must not look for our soul inside the body ; it is far truer to say that the body is within the soul. The soul is that which touches God ; it has four senses of apprehension, Wit, Memory, Understanding (who is a lady with a certain handmaiden, Imagination), and Will. Wit is the power of taking in things at all ; then you remember what you have heard or received, and set your understanding to ravel it out, and your will to act on it. The whole of this is worked out with a quaint intermingling of shrewd " obiter dicta ", and a passionate love to God, which at times soars to great heights.

God gives us Himself, and the fruits of the spirit are

[1] *The Scale or Ladder of Perfection.* Written by Walter Hylton. With **Essay** by Rev. J. B. Dalgairns.

many activities which all make up Rest. Some one has
defined rest as "unimpeded activity". Hylton would
agree with him. God's rest "is a most busy rest". There
are times of drought to the soul, but it is only special grace
that is for a time removed ; common grace remains always
entire to us. He likens the journey of the soul, in a beautiful passage, to a pilgrimage towards Jerusalem. "By some
small flashes of light which shine through the chinks of the
city walls, thou wilt be able to see it long before thou comest
to it ".

Hylton says of Prayer that it is not the *cause* of grace,
but the *means by* which grace comes into the soul. Vocal
prayer must not be too much abandoned for the " Prayer
of Quiet". Concerning sin, he tells us (surely he was one
of the first to discover this true but most difficult Christian
precept) that we must hate the sin, yet love the sinner.
"Thou shouldest love the man, be he ever so sinful, and
hate the sin in every man, *whatever he be*". "When thou
attackest any root of sin, fix thy thought more upon the
God Whom thou desirest than upon the sin thou abhorrest".

He discourages dreams and visions. Those who have
them must be cautious. Of the Ecstasy, he says that he
has never experienced it, but believes it to be possible.
And here finally, at the beginning of Part III, is the humility
of the man. " God knows that I am teaching far more than
I practise, and I would not by these discourses limit God's
working by the law of my speaking. I wish not to say that
God worketh *so* in a soul, and no otherwise. No ; I meant
not so. I hope well that He worketh otherwise, in ways
which pass my wit and feeling".

(2) " It is an insufficient criticism ", observes Mr. Algar
Thorold,[1] " that has led some to suppose that the medieval
Church weighed on the conscience of Christendom . . . as

---

[1] Thorold : *The Dialogues of Catherine of Siena*, pp. 4, 5.

an arbitrary fact. . . . Probably at no period has the Christian conscience realized more profoundly that the whole external fabric of Catholicism, its sacraments, its priesthood, its discipline, was but the phenomenal expression, necessary and sacred in its place, of the Idea of Christianity, and . . . that by that Idea all Christians, priests, as well as laymen, rulers as well as subjects, would at last be judged ". There may be a slight overstatement of the case here, as regards the common people, but it is certainly true that the painters and poets of the later Medieval period had no hesitation in exposing the faults of ecclesiastics in high places, " no difficulty in distinguishing between the office and the individual ", and no aversion " from contemplating the fate of the faithless steward ". This phase of the medieval mind comes out most clearly, perhaps, in the position reserved by the Church for the " saint," especially the saint who was a mystic. The official hierarchy was not considered the sole agent for revealing the Divine Will to humanity. Sabatier points out with much force that the medieval saint occupied much the same position as the Prophet in Ancient Israel. Take the case of the Blessed Columba of Rieti. Brought into the dubious presence of Pope Alexander VI, she fell into an ecstasy induced by devotion at the sight of the supreme Pontiff, but during this ecstasy, she denounced the Divine judgement on the sins of the man Rodrigo Borgia. To complete the amazing story, the Pope listened to her attentively, and dismissed her with every mark of reverence. This characteristic episode forms no inappropriate introduction to a consideration of the lives and work of St. Catherine of Siena, and her namesake St. Catherine of Genoa.

Both were practical geniuses, and both exhibited the mystical life in its extreme form. Catherine of Siena was the daughter of Jacopo Benincasa, a dyer, the youngest of his twenty-five children, and was born in 1347. From her earliest years, improbable as it sounds, she experienced at times the mystical ecstasy, the first taking place at the age of six, while at fourteen she became a tertiary of the Order of St. Dominic. Two desires seized her, that of the "sweetness of serving God, not for her own joy; and of serving her neighbour . . . from pure love". These twin longings were quickened by an ever deepening sense of the terrible corruptions of the Church, for it was the time of the "Babylonish captivity" at Avignon, and by a passion for our Lord, conceived in its intensest form for His humanity. In one of her ecstasies she believed herself to be united in spiritual nuptials to Christ; in another, the *stigmata* were vouchsafed to her as to St. Francis before her. Nowadays the possibility of the *stigmata* to a highly wrought nature much given to pondering over the details of the Passion is recognized, but with Catherine such meditations on the Person of the Lord were redeemed from what might have been merely morbid and fanciful, first, by the depth and clearness of her thoughts with regard to the love of God as displayed in the Passion, thoughts such as "Nails would not have held the God-man fast to the cross had not love held Him there", [1] and, secondly, by the practical work for the Church to which she conceived herself bound by her mystical nuptials. She felt herself pledged "to do manfully and without hesitation" whatever task was laid upon her, and the result was an act of momentous courage and of lasting effect upon the Church's destinies. She resolved to get the Pope away from the sumptuous court of Avignon, with its deadly influences of sloth and luxury, and its political subservience to the French King, back to Italy and Rome and a true leadership of the spiritual world. She had, it is true, no Alexander VI. to contend with; but Gregory XI, in spite of much personal charm, was vacillating

---

[1] V. D. Scudder : *St. Catherine of Siena, as seen in her Letters*, p. 8.

and cowardly, and extremely unlikely to exchange the easy-going life of pleasure at Avignon for the risks and uncertainties, however heroic, of Papal rule in turbulent Rome. First, she wrote to those who might be most influential in the Pope's circle. " You and the Holy Father ", she told one such, " ought to toil and do what you can to get rid of the wolfish shepherds who care for nothing but eating, and fine palaces, and big horses. . . . Tell the Holy Father to put an end to such iniquities. And when the time comes to make priests or cardinals, let them not be chosen through flatteries or money or simony ".[1] Finding that little good resulted, she determined to do what Columba of Rieti had done, and to visit the Pope in his own Court. In 1366, St. Bridget of Sweden had followed up a Divine intimation and had gone to Avignon to urge Urban V to return to Rome. Bridget had been unsuccessful, but Catherine resolved to try again the effect of personal pleading on the more malleable nature of Gregory XI. But first she wrote to him. Curious letters they were, for the sternness of the prophetess struggled in her with an unmistakable personal fondness for the man whom she called by turns " venerable father ", and " sweetest ' Babbo ' mine ", " sweet Christ on earth ". Yet she does not mince matters. " Quench ", she writes, " this perverse and perilous self-love in yourself . . . be so true and good a shepherd that if you had a hundred thousand lives you would be ready to give them all for the honour of God and the salvation of men. . . . Temporal things are failing you from no other cause than from your neglect of the spiritual ".[2] At another time she told him that he should strive to follow his namesake, Gregory the Great, " it will be as possible for you to quench self-love as it was for him ". Then at last, the intrepid dyer's daughter went to Avignon, overcame all obstacles,

[1] *St. Catherine of Siena, as seen in her Letters*, p. 115.
[2] *Ib.* p. 131.

and prevailed on the vacillating Pope to dare all, and to return to Rome. Perhaps one of the greatest gifts that Catherine had was the power to discern the good or strength in an unpromising character and to draw it out. Certainly, it was by some such means that she was instrumental in ending the disgraceful Avignon " Captivity ". The convenient dictum of the Avignonese doctors, " Ubi Papa, ibi Roma ", ceased to have a meaning. Catherine died in 1380, leaving behind her one great mystical classic, the " Divine Dialogue,", in which the soul and the " Eternal God " hold converse. Despite the alleged circumstance of the " Dialogues " that they were dictated to her secretary when she was in ecstasy, they deal largely with a very practical Christianity. They have one characteristic of vision, as apart from ecstasy, that with much that is exquisite and true a certain grotesquerie in the mingling of metaphors is at times apparent. Things are evidently seen *through* each other.

Mysticism, in the next, the fifteenth century, was represented in Italy by Catherine of Genoa, whose life and teaching has been taken for the text of an authoritative analysis of Mysticism by Baron von Hügel.[1] Her genius has a certain connective link with the Franciscan ideals, through the influence exercised upon her in early life by Jacopone da Todi, and she had all Francis' tender sympathy with animals and flowers. " She was most compassionate towards all creatures ; so that, if an animal were killed or a tree cut down, she could hardly bear to see them lose that being which God has given them ".[2] In her too there was the most vivid realization of the two sides of the God-ward life—the *unio mystica*, and the practical service of those around her. Herself of noble birth, she was married to a

---

[1] *The Mystical Element of Religion*, 2 vols.
[2] Von Hügel: quoted from the " *Vita*," vol. 1, p. 163.

man of high position, but, at the time of the marriage, of worthless character, Giuliano Adorno. For five years, neglected by her husband, she lived a dreary and loveless life, but the experience was preparative to a vast change. Driven in on herself, and disillusioned as to the pleasures of a worldly round of ostentation and gaiety with which she had never been enamoured, her thoughts turned more and more towards God. Her actual conversion has, in one particular, a singular resemblance to that of Julian of Norwich. She prayed, under the condition of God's Will, for a three months' illness, and this came to pass, though, as it would seem, in the shape of mental rather than of physical affliction. But already her husband's fortune had failed him, and though the accounts of their worldly misfortunes are, as is the case with other events in Catherine's life, rather conflicting, Giuliano, also now a converted man, and his wife moved into a little artisan dwelling in the poorer quarter of the town, close to the great Hospital of the Pammatone, founded by Bartolommeo Bosco, a Genoese merchant prince, fifty years previously. Here, in visiting and tending the sick in the 130 beds of the Hospital, in looking after the wants of 100 foundling girls, also trained in the Institution, and in ministering to the sick and the poor of the squalid neighbourhood, Giuliano and Catherine lived out their useful and devoted years. He became a Tertiary of the Franciscan Order ; but it is remarkable that Catherine, with all her early drawing to the life of a religious, never took any vows herself. Of the practical and ever increasing usefulness of her life there can be no doubt whatsoever, nor of its attractive capacity for warm friendships. Yet all this was accompanied for years, as Baron von Hügel carefully describes, by the most singular psychopathic states. One of the most distinctive marks of her spiritual life was a longing desire for the Holy Communion—she seems to have been a daily communicant for nearly the entire period from her conversion in 1474 to her death in 1510—and her communions were followed often by states of complete absorption in prayer lasting for hours, " transparently real and sincere, and. . . so swift and spontaneous as to appear quasi-involuntary ".[1] These absorptions were primarily spiritual, and may be taken as the first decisive appearance in the mystical life of the Prayer of Quiet or of Union. Another distinguishing mark of Catherine's experience was the capacity for prolonged and again quasi-involuntary fasts. In each case, that of the fast or of the absorption, it was the—to her—realized Presence or Will of our Lord that was the impelling force. A third characteristic may also be noted, as it is one that links her thought to that of the great Spanish mystics of the next age. She had a strong psycho-physical smell-and-taste impression, most pleasurable, which was wont to come to her in connexion with her reception of the Eucharist. " Having on one occasion received Holy Communion, so much odour and sweetness came to her, that she seemed to be in Paradise. Whence, feeling this, she straightway turned towards her Love and said : ' O Love, dost Thou perhaps intend to draw me to Thyself with these savours ? I want them not, since I want nothing but Thee alone, and all of Thee '. Here, then, she turns away from and transcends, precisely as St. John of the Cross was soon to insist so strongly that we should do, the sensible and immediate, and reaches on to the spiritual, ultimate, and personal ".[2]

[1] See Von Hügel : *The Mystical Element in Religion*, vol. i. pp. 227–229.

[2] Von Hügel, *ib.* p. 180, who quotes from the " *Vita e Dottrina* " by Marabotto and Vernazza.

CHAPTER IX

Spanish and French Mystics

THE coming of the Reformation brought about nothing
less than a revolution in the spiritual world. Just
as the Renaissance, with its influx of new light and knowledge in every department of Art, Science, and Letters,
changed for ever the outlook on intellectual and material
processes, radically, but with such abruptness that even
now we, who have dwelt for more than three centuries in
the midst of " new heavens and a new earth ", still think
familiarly in the terms of that old cosmos of the medieval
conception, so the Reformation, child of the Renaissance,
wrought its own abiding changes in the sphere of religious
thought. Not the least striking of these changes was witnessed in the realm of Mysticism which itself, as we have
seen, contributed not a little by way of preparation to the
tremendous crisis in faith and spiritual " customary law "
which was finally precipitated by other and rougher means
in the sixteenth century. Putting it broadly, the results
of the Reformation on Mysticism were twofold.

(1) In the first place, as the whole of the Western religious world was split up into two camps, one owning obedience to the Papacy, the other withholding it, so it was with
Mysticism. Henceforth we have two schools of mystics,
and the distinction between them does not merely lie in
the fact that the one retained the old allegiance, while the
other dispensed with it. Each retained, and each dis-

pensed with a great deal besides.   It will have been noticed
that later medieval Mysticism a good deal resembled the
gradual building up of—say—English case law.   Nearly
every mystic had his scheme of the inner life, and nearly
every mystic, whilst true to the general laws of the *Scala
Perfectionis* laid down by his predecessors, added something
of his own, drawn from his particular experience.   Certain
features, not to recapitulate overmuch, had become common
and recognized principles.   In one form or another we find
the three stages of Ascent everywhere, *Purgatio, Illuminatio,
Contemplatio :* from Pseudo-Dionysius onwards the *Via
Negativa* is, if not always absolutely enjoined, still nearly
always traceable in the background of mystic thought :
while other ideas indigenous to the mystical mind are those
of the Divine Darkness, and of the possibility or actuality
of the Ecstasy as the culmination of the *Unio Mystica* on
earth.   This tendency to formulate, to make diagrams
of the most intimate and veiled pathways and shrines of
the spirit, was accentuated by the Scholastics, who incor-
porated the mystical experience within the body of recognized and official theology, and was, of course, in large
measure the outcome of the legalizing, system-loving spirit
of the Latin Church.   Now the outstanding difference after
the Reformation between the schools of Mysticism which
adhered to the Latin obedience, and those mystics who no
longer recognized it, was just this, that the former preserved and even accentuated the idea of the scheme, within
whose bounds their mystical faculty was to work itself out,
while with the latter all notion of a plan, a ladder, a scale
of progress suddenly disappeared.   The record of their
mystical life becomes the record of pure, simple feeling, of
intimate communion and touch with the Eternal Life.   In
England this was especially noticeable, and the new freedom vented itself in a new capacity of intellect, a facility
for suggestive and pregnant expression.   To a great degree,

and perhaps increasingly as time went on, Mysticism found its votaries and prophets among the poets.

(2) On the other hand, as was said, the older Mysticism outlined, schemed, circumscribed, continued its course, also in its own province most fruitful and always, to a certain class of mind, peculiarly helpful, in allegiance to the Latin Church. But more. After the first shock of the Reformation had passed, the great need of the Roman Catholic Church was internal reform and reconstruction, if ever it were to regain possession or partial possession of the European heritage which it had so nearly lost. So we find, not unexpectedly, the great Catholic mystics of the sixteenth century—what is known as the Spanish school—busily engaged, sometimes against enormous odds, in producing order out of chaos, a kind of military and chivalrous obedience to rules that should dominate body, intellect, conscience and heart alike, instead of the worldly and luxurious *laissez-faire* that numbed the Church of their day. Take Ignatius Loyola, or St. Teresa, or John of the Cross, all are of the same type as of the same nationality, "outwardly cumbered with much serving, observant of an infinitude of tiresome details, composing rules, setting up foundations, neglecting no aspect of their business which could conduce to its practical success, yet 'altogether dwelling in God in restful fruition'".[1] All three were distinctively Spanish in mind and mood, yet the work of the first changed the face of half Europe once again and, more than any other agency, brought about—by strenuous work opposed to work, skilled knowledge to knowledge, and a burning inner devotion,—what is known as the Counter-Reformation in Germany, Bohemia, and Austria; while the words and character of St. Teresa became a classical and secular influence for the whole Church of Christ. It is of her and of her disciple, St. John of the Cross, that we should here take

[1] E. Underhill: *Mysticism*, p. 523.

some account, partly for the reasons we have noticed, and
partly as a matter of due sequence, because Spanish Mysticism, though so far-reaching in its after influence, was really
a late flowering, out of due time, of medieval Mysticism.

St. Teresa was born at Avila in 1515, just two years
before Martin Luther, who once, at any rate, when stirred
to wrath by the untrammelled excesses of Carlstadt's
mysticism, sought to dispose of the whole mystical foundation by declaring, " Human nature could not survive the
least syllable of the Divine utterance.   God addresses man
through men, because we could not endure His speaking
to us without medium ".   Teresa would have been more in
agreement with her great contemporary when he wrote his
golden sentence, " Tenta ergo ut ne Jesum quidem audias
gloriosum, nisi videris prius crucifixum ".[1]   There was,
after all, something in common between those two ardent
natures, both born reformers ; for there was always a man-
like quality in Teresa, partly, no doubt, an inheritance from
a long line of noble Castilian ancestors, which came out in
such exhortations to the nuns of her reformed Carmelite
foundation as, " I would have you, my daughters, to be
brave and valiant men ", and her descriptions of some raptures as " raptures of Feminine Weakness ".

The life of St. Teresa, which, Dr. Inge says curiously,
" is more interesting than her teaching ",[2] will always, of
course, affect differently constituted minds in different
ways.   Those who wish it concisely and vividly told, but
with a distempered malice rare even in his singular work,
will find it, with accompanying discussions, in Vaughan's

[1] " Strive that thou learn not of even Jesus Himself as glorified,
unless first thou hast known Him as crucified ".

[2] Inge : *Christian Mysticism*, p. 218.   Cf. E. Underhill's exhaustive work on Mysticism, in which quotations from St. Teresa's works
and allusions to her teaching outnumber the references to any other
individual mystic.

" Hours with the Mystics ".[1]   We read there of her childlike
enthusiasm when a girl to set out by herself for Africa to
convert the Moors ; of her early visions and raptures, of
her subservience to her confessors, her meticulous self-
analysis in her autobiography, the ready and incessant use
made of her as its tool by the Roman Church in the work of
setting up far and wide her reformed " discalced " Carmelite
houses.   We are told of her, it is true, as the great exponent
and expert with regard to the Prayer of Quiet, but we are
bidden in an aside to note how the Church of Rome could
commend and beautify such " quietistic " mystics as were
thoroughly obedient to its system of the confessional and
the Sacraments, whilst for such, later, as Molinos or Madame
Guyon, who showed themselves at all restive to its control,
it had nothing but cold disapproval or direct repression.
Now there is some truth in all this.   Teresa was for years
a visionary, and not all her visions were of equal validity.
She was certainly one of the agents in the great reform movement that took place within the Roman Church, and her
mysticism was a mysticism within stricter bounds than
those permitted to pre-Reformation mystics.   The confessional acquired vastly increased scope and authority in the
management of the individual life owing to the rise of the
Jesuit Order.   Teresa herself chose Jesuit direction in the
later years of her life, and with many souls, though emphatically not with hers, such direction tended towards
a self-analysis at once morbid and profitless.   Again, St.
Teresa learned the element of the Prayer of Quiet from her
first director, the Franciscan mystic, St. Peter of Alcantara,
and it is in regard to the development and definition of
this " orison " that her teaching as a mystic is profoundly
important.   As for the distinction that her Church made
between Quietist mystics of seemingly closely resembling
types, some credit must be given to the discernment of a

[1] *Op. cit.* bk. ix. chs. 1 and 2.

Church which had inherited and exercised for so many centuries precisely the qualities of discrimination peculiar to a statesmanship that can gauge and measure what in human belief is safe or unsafe to the body politic ; and some allowance made for the additional caution exercised by that Church after experiencing the tremendous shock and upheaval of the Reformation crisis.

Later and more sympathetic accounts than Vaughan's have made us familiar with the real Santa Teresa whose warm and vigorous personality, humorous common sense —she could not bear solemnity and sanctimoniousness— practical usefulness—" she was an admirable housewife and declared that she found her God very easily amongst the pots and pans " [1]—and gifts as organiser and reformer made her so great a power in her generation ; the Teresa, again, whose burning love for her Lord compelled the enthusiastic admiration of our English poet, Crashaw, and profoundly modulated his own spiritual life. Her actual life may be divided into three periods, the first, one of Vision ; the second, of her Quietistic experience, and teaching ; the third, arising from the second, of her immense and practical activities. The first may be dismissed in a very few words, though it is interesting to note that it was prefaced by a conversion which occurred through her reading in the Confessions of St. Augustine how he heard the voice, " Tolle, lege." " When I read," she says, " how he heard the voice in the garden, it was just as if the Lord called me ". This shews how imitatively impressionable her mind was, though there can be no doubt as to the sincerity with which she recalled the many visions that followed, especially since, like Joseph with his brethren, she found herself an object of suspicion and dislike owing to these special privileges. The visions were not ecstasies ; she heard " locutions ", she saw " the sacred Humanity ". But, as many

[1] G. Cunninghame Graham : *Santa Teresa*, vol. i. p. 299.

of the mystics have taught, such phenomena in the spiritual life, if actual (and at times Teresa was in doubt of her own experiences) are only vouchsafed to beginners.

The middle part of her life was that during which her doctrines of Quietism and of the modes of Prayer connected therewith were fully developed. We are introduced to the subject by an allegory. " Our soul ", says Teresa, " is like a garden, rough and unfruitful, out of which God plucks the weeds, and plants flowers, which we have to water by prayer. There are four ways of doing this—First, by drawing the water from a well ; this is the earliest and most laborious process. Secondly, by a water-wheel which has its rim hung round with little buckets. Third, by causing a stream to flow through it. Fourth, by rain from heaven ". The first is ordinary prayer. The second is the prayer of Quiet, " when the soul understands that God is so near to her that she need not talk to Him ". " In this state ", both Vaughan and Dr. Inge comment in almost identical phrase, " the Will is absorbed, but the Understanding and Memory may still be active ". It is curious to note that Vaughan insists that Teresa was " utterly ignorant of the past career of Mystical Theology, hears, indeed, of a time-honoured division of the Mystical process into Purgative, Illuminative and Unitive ; but . . . does not adopt the scheme. . . . The philosophic element is absent altogether from her mysticism ".[1] This is something of an exaggeration. Dr. Inge justly points out that by her mention of the Will, the Understanding, and the Memory, Teresa makes these the three faculties of the soul, and so shews herself perfectly aware of the scholastic philosophy.[2] Moreover,

---

[1] Vaughan, *op. cit.* bk. ix. ch. 2 ; cf. Inge, p. 221.
[2] Fr. Zimmerman, however, in his Prefatory Essay to " *The Ascent of Mount Carmel* " by St. John of the Cross, attributes Teresa's correctness in these matters to her habit of referring to her director and other theologians for enlightenment, pp. 8, 9.

the three stages of the Mystic life appear pretty plainly, if not in set terms, in her experiences. To return: the third stage is the Prayer of Union, or Contemplation, " a sleep of the faculties, which are not entirely suspended, nor yet do they understand how they work ". God becomes as it were the Gardener of the soul, and works through its faculties, using them; this state is distinguished by the peculiar infallible certainty of something communicated or received, which we have noted as one of the mystical marks. There is a fourth state still, which was wholly indescribable—another mystical " note ". All that she could say was: " The Lord said these words to me; The soul unmakes herself to bring herself closer to Me. It is no more she that lives, but I ". Either of these last states might be described as the Ecstasy or Rapture, and it is somewhat difficult to distinguish between them. But St. Teresa felt the distinction evidently, and laboured to express it. But what is above all things noticeable in the last three states of " orison " is the continuous growth throughout of surrender, passivity, motionlessness. In Teresa's case it had even physical as well as psychical effects. The great school of Quietism had been inaugurated, and Teresa was certainly its chief instructress, however much she may have imbibed from Peter of Alcantara, or Francis of Osuna. The following quotations from her own description of the spiritual experience referred to will explain better than anything else the new principle. " In this state there is no sense of anything; only fruition, without understanding what that may be, the fruition of which is granted. It is understood that the fruition is of a certain good, containing in itself all good together at once; but this good is not comprehended. . . . But this state of complete absorption, together with the utter rest of the imagination . . . lasts only for a short time; though the faculties do not so completely recover themselves as not to be for some hours afterwards in some

disorder. . . . It cannot be more clearly described, because what then takes place is so obscure. All I am able to say is, that the soul is represented as being close to God; and that there abides a conviction thereof so certain and strong that it cannot possibly help believing so. All the faculties fail now, and are suspended in such a way that . . . their operations cannot be traced. The will must be fully occupied in loving, but it understands not how it loves; the understanding, if it understands, does not understand how it understands." Again, " the soul is entirely asleep as regards herself and earthly things. During the short time the union lasts she is, as it were, deprived of all feeling, and, though she wishes it, can think of nothing . . . she is, as it were, absolutely dead to the world, the better to live in God ".[1]

Clearly, we are not far from St. John of the Cross and his Dark Night of the Soul. Not to be repelled by all this, we have to remember that it possesses all the marks of a veritable psychological experience, all the notes of a true mystical experience, and that its results were not nullity, or lazy absorption in self, but a peculiarly active period of practical and lasting work for the Church.

This in part took the form of carefully noting down her experiences, which she did in three works, her " Life ", the " Way of Perfection ", and the " Interior Castle ". In part, again, it resulted in her founding a small convent where the ancient Carmelite rule might be observed in all its pristine strictness. The General of the Order approved and also commissioned her to found two houses of Reformed or " Discalced "[2] Friars as well. At this time she first met John de Yepes.

John, unlike herself, was born of poor parentage. He

[1] Quoted from E. Underhill: *Mysticism*, p. 425.
[2] " Discalced " signifies the return from the shoe to the ancient sandal, a change symbolical of much more.

was in his twenty-sixth year when, in 1567, he encountered
St. Teresa.   Dissatisfied with the many mitigations of the
Carmelite rule which he had followed since he was twenty-
one, he was on the very point of exchanging this Order for
the Carthusian, when the great opportunity of his life came.
Instead of leaving his Order, he found himself urged by
Teresa, and commissioned by the Papal Nuncio, to reform
it.   John was a person, " small in body, but great in soul ",
and " distinguished by surpassing austerity and zeal ".[1]
The Reform spread rapidly : under the fostering care of
Teresa and of John, who became her confessor, convents
of the Reformed rule sprang up everywhere.   Too fast, in
fact.   The best monks in other houses naturally left them
for the new and stricter foundations.   Superiors became first
disheartened and annoyed, then openly hostile, and in the
midst of the work, in 1575, the Nuncio, its great protector,
died, leaving in possession of the field a General of the Order
whose regulations he had several times overruled.   John
was at Avila and was suddenly arrested by the Calced
Carmelites, and hurried off as a rebel to the Order to a dark
and stifling jail at Toledo.   There he underwent a martyr-
dom of cruel treatment for more than eight months.   It
would seem almost impossible that men pledged to the
religious life could have found it in them to treat a fellow-
friar, however interfering and contumacious they probably
thought him, with such studied cruelty as was visited on
poor John of the Cross from day to day.[2]   Finally, he
effected his escape, and the tide of ecclesiastical opinion
turned slowly in his favour.   He busied himself in his work

[1] Thus Vaughan : *op. cit.* bk. ix. ch. 3, who manifests a sincere
admiration for John of the Cross.   Elsewhere he says, " The mysticism of John takes the very highest ground. . . . He pursues [his goal]
unfaltering, with a holy ardour. . . . He displayed in suffering
and in action a self-sacrificing heroism which could only spring from
a devout and a profound conviction ".

[2] David Lewis : *Life of St. John of the Cross*, pp. 79–101.

as a reformer till the end, and that work was constantly chequered by opposition and by increasing bodily debility. At the very end, he was taken during his last sickness to a convent whose prior was in enmity to him, and took care to show it, an enmity in no way reciprocated by St. John, whose spiritual record bears an exquisite resemblance to the character of his Lord in his steady forgiveness of every personal injury and slight. A great part of his life was passed under the shadow of misunderstanding and the menace or reality of personal violence, but if ever a man took to heart the words of Christ with regard to voluntary cross-bearing, it was St. John, and it is as St. John of the Cross, consequently, that his name and fame have come down to us.

Is it any wonder that something of the darkness and dereliction of the cell of Toledo, the cell in which he composed his world-famous spiritual elegy, "The Song of the Obscure Night", should appear in his work? Yet to St. John it was still, despite suffering and sighing, his "happy lot". "Oh! guiding night!" he cries, "Oh! night more lovely than the dawn! Oh! night that hast united the Lover with His loved!" What, then, is St. John's doctrine of the "Night of the soul"?

Let us take his own words. "The journey of the soul to the Divine Union is called night for three reasons. The first is derived from the point from which the soul sets out, the privation of the desire of all pleasure in all the things of this world, by detachment therefrom. This is as night for every desire and sense of man. The second, from the road by which it travels; that is faith, for faith is obscure, like night, to the understanding. The third, from the goal to which it tends, God, incomprehensible and infinite, who is in this life as night to the soul".[1] The only sensible

[1] *The Ascent of Mount Carmel*, transl. by David Lewis, p. 11.

desire which God permits is that of obedience to Him and carrying the Cross. In explaining this first night of the senses, John gives way to the crudest Acosmism. God resembles no created thing, therefore we must empty our minds of all created things, if we would walk in the Divine Light. This is the negative road pursued to the utmost. The second night, that is, of Faith, is the darkest of the three. Faith is compared to midnight. It is like the sun, which " blinds the eyes and robs them of the vision which it gives, because its own light is out of proportion with, and stronger than, our power of sight ".[1] We have to believe what we are told, as a blind man receives news of colour. Reason and memory are annihilated by this second Night, and even the search for sweetness in communion with God is forbidden as " spiritual gluttony ". We must seek for bitterness in Him, give ourselves up to suffer. We cannot deny to all this an extraordinary spiritual heroism or stoicism. St. John at least never falters, but pushes his ideas to their extreme logical limit, such as no saint before or after him has ever attempted. The third and last Night is that of the Will, in which " the soul sinks into a holy inertia and oblivion, in which the flight of time is unfelt, and the mind is unconscious of all particular thoughts ".[2] Were this third Night St. John's goal, there would be nothing for it but to condemn it, as a form of Eastern Nihilism. But it is only the final stage on the road to the union with that " sweetest love of God, too little known ", " the going forth in perfect liberty to the fruition of the union with the Beloved ".[3] All through this third night gleams from the Dayspring near at hand visit the soul.

St. John's heroism of heart and singleness of purpose

---

[1] *The Ascent of Mount Carmel*, transl. by David Lewis, pp. 66, 67.
[2] Inge : *op. cit.*, p. 227.
[3] *Ascent of Mount Carmel*, p. 62.

have called out praise from many little in sympathy with his method, but much in sympathy with its aim, the possession of the Pearl of great price, Christ. For His sake St. John thought no experience, inner or outer, too hard. Be it remembered, too, for it is important, that St. John's following of the negative road of Dionysius and the Neo-Platonists was undertaken in an entirely different spirit from theirs. The Neo-Platonists wanted a reconciliation of philosophy and religion ; they sought to define by endless abstractions the Being of God ; their intellect was ever to the forefront. No such reconciliation ever entered St. John's head, his experiment was purely psychological : he wanted Christ, and his literal interpretation of certain Gospel sayings was his way—the particular way suggested to him individually—of reaching " the Beloved ". He " left all ", and followed Him. Who shall say that John of the Cross was wrong ? We may grant that terrible bodily sufferings may have had their effect on his thoughts ; and we must always remind ourselves that no individual mystical experience has an exact and perfect validity for any one else. This said, it is possible to learn lessons of self-sacrifice and Christian resolution tempered like steel from this strange Spanish saint.

As an interlude, we may glance North of the Pyrenees to the gracious and winning figure of St. Francis de Sales (1567–1622). Vaughan says in his peculiar way that " de Sales was to John, as a mystic, what Henry IV was to Philip as a Catholic king ". There is this much of truth about such a remark that, while we find Quietism in St. Francis' works, it is mixed with maxims of a more practical tendency, and that the harsh and dark lines of Spanish Mysticism are softened and adapted to the needs of the well-to-do and rather fashionable pietism to which he ministered. Take the instance of Contemplation. There is no Dark Night, there are no rigours of actual Rapture such as St. Teresa described ;

there is what Francis names " indistinct contemplation "
instead.   " Oh ! que bien-heureux sont ceux qui . . .
reduisans tous leurs regards en une seule veue et toutes
leurs pensées en une seule conclusion, arrestant leur esprit
en l'unité de la contemplation . . . prononçant secrette-
ment en leur âme, par une admiration permanente, ces
paroles amoureuses : Oh ! bonté ! bonté ! bonté ! tousjours
ancienne et tousjours nouvelle ! " [1]

Far more in the direct succession to St. John was Miguel
de Molinos (1640–97), a devout Spanish priest.[2]   He arrived
in Rome about 1670, and became a great favourite with
Pope Innocent XI, who lodged him in the Vatican.   In 1675,
he published his famous " Spiritual Guide ", in which the
practice of devotion is divided into two parts—Meditation,
for beginners, and the interior way of Contemplation, resulting in complete union with God.   Self-will must be annihilated, and an undisturbed passivity of soul encouraged,
till, " sinking and losing ourselves in the immeasurable sea
of God's goodness ", grace is supernaturally infused into this
passivity of being.   He speaks much of the prayer of silence,
of which there are three kinds, the silence from words, the
silence from desires, and the silence from thought.   It is
impossible not to see that there is danger in all this, despite
much beautiful and permanently valuable teaching.   The
danger may be illustrated by two of the condemned propositions : " Oportet hominem suas potentias annihilare ",[3] and,
" velle operari active est Deum offendere ".[4]   Suspicion
rests however upon the authenticity of some of the con-

---

[1] *Traité de l'Amour de Dieu*, liv. vi. chap. v.

[2] Molinos is particularly well known to English readers through
the medium of " John Inglesant ", where Mr. Shorthouse gives a
vivid and accurate account of his arrest and condemnation, ante-
dating these, however, for the purpose of the story, by about thirty
years.

[3] " It is necessary that man annihilate his own capacities ".

[4] " To will to be actively at work is an offence to God ".

demned articles, since Molinos was accused of encouraging shameful vices, which, in a man of his high character, was impossible.   But the Jesuits and their pupil, Louis XIV, were thoroughly aroused by teaching which minimized the importance of the ministrations and offices of the Church ; in 1685 Molinos was condemned and imprisoned for life ; in 1687, two hundred of his followers were arrested, and the persecution of Quietist opinions spread to France.

It was to Madame Guyon, a French lady of position who was suffering from the mortifications of ill-health and an unhappy married life, and was endeavouring in vain to find religious consolation, that an old Franciscan friar uttered the memorable words, " Madame, you are disappointed and perplexed because you seek without what you have within. Accustom yourself to seek God in your heart, and you will find Him ".   All through her life she was to prove the truth of this counsel.   Her beauty was shattered by the small-pox ; her work at Gex amongst the young, the poor, and the sick was destroyed by suspicions of her orthodoxy ; her books, " The Torrents " and the " Short Method of Prayer ", were burned in the market-place at Thonon.   There followed a brief summer-time of repose and Court favour at Paris ; a select group of Quietists gathered round her, and Madame de Maintenon showed her favour and introduced her to her splendid institution at St. Cyr, where she made the acquaintance and friendship of Archbishop Fénélon.   Then came the storm of condemnation of Quietist opinions, which, starting with the condemnation of Molinos, spread to France. Bossuet was charged to examine Madame Guyon, an examination which he conducted with singular severity and fanaticism while she lay ill at Meaux.   He obtained, of course, her submission, and gave her a certificate of orthodoxy, but when she retired from Meaux to Paris he chose to interpret her journey as a suspicious flight, and secured her arrest and incarceration for four years in the Bastille.   After her liberation in 1702 she went to spend the remainder of her days at Blois.

ᣟ Meanwhile, Bossuet had attacked not only the doctrines, but the character of Madame Guyon in ten books, entitled " Instructions on the State of Prayer ", to which he required the Archbishop of Cambrai's express printed approval. This Fénélon could not give, since he regarded the book as a mere travesty of Madame Guyon's opinions. In self-defence, he published a mystical book of his own, which he called " Maxims of the Saints ", and which gave rise to furious and lengthy controversy. At the instance of Louis XIV, the Pope, Innocent XII, at length reluctantly gave consent to the censure of twenty-three propositions extracted from the book, though the censure did not extend to the explanations which Fénélon rendered of the book. It is now time to see what particular phase of Quietism it was which excited the French controversy. It centred in what was known as the doctrine of Disinterested Love, and this doctrine was common to the writings alike of Madame Guyon and of Fénélon.

Madame Guyon's mysticism, which resembled that of St. Teresa in its experience of the Ecstasy, but was much more emotional and devoid of self-control, may be represented by three verses from her poem, " The Acquiescence of Pure Love ", translated by Cowper, and often enough quoted :—

Love, if Thy destined sacrifice am I,
  Come, slay Thy victim, and prepare Thy fires ;
Plunged in Thy depths of mercy let me die,
  The death which every soul that loves desires ! . . .

To me 'tis equal, whether Love ordain
  My life or death, appoint me pain or ease,
My soul perceives no real ill in pain ;
  In ease or health no real good she sees. . . .

That we should bear the cross is Thy command,
  Die to the world, and live to self no more ;

Suffer unmoved beneath the rudest hand,
   As pleased when shipwrecked as when safe on shore.

This absolute renunciation of the ordinary ties and preferences of the self for the sake of the Highest Love was with Madame Guyon, as with others of the period, part of an overmastering and deeply interesting impulse which swept over Europe in the latter part of the seventeenth century. Antoinette Bourignan (1616–1680) in Flanders was an even more thorough-going, certainly more violent and less loveable, empiricist of Madame Guyon's kind. The possession of a single penny, she found, kept her from full communion with her God, and she therefore renounced everything. Yet the fact remains that, as with John of the Cross, so with Madame Guyon, and the rather unamiable Madame Bourignan, this absolute self-abandonment proved, as the Gospel always declared it would prove, an unquestionable and mighty power. We have seen the work accomplished, in the face of all opposition, by the Spanish mystics ; crowds gathered around Molinos ; Madame Bourignan, with her forgetfulness of all things, and her inner communion with Another,[1] founded a sect with large ramifications ; Madame Guyon was the centre of a wide and devoted circle of learners in Paris. We shall see later the influence of this doctrine in England.

With regard to Fénélon, he was drawn into the controversy by the high-handed action of Bossuet, who marred a great career and character by his Court complacency on this occasion, rather than involved in it as an experimental mystic. Bossuet knew little or nothing about the mysticism which he was attacking, although mystical expressions

---

[1] See A. R. McEwen : *Antoinette Bourignan, Quietist.* " When I am recollected in my solitude in a forgetfulness of all things, then my spirit communicates with Another Spirit and they entertain one another as two friends who converse about serious matters ". p. 109.

appear in his works, as they would in the works of any Catholic theologian ; and Fénélon came forward, a champion of the oppressed, to explain theologically the teaching of Disinterested Love, and also of the Prayer of Pure Contemplation.   There are, he says, five kinds of love to God :   (1) Servile love, which looks for reward : (2) a higher kind of servility, which seeks the comfort of God's love in return for its own : (3) the love of hope, which looks for eternal welfare : (4) Interested love, in which selfish motives are still present, and (5) Disinterested love, which loves God for Himself only, careless of what soul or body may suffer, here or even hereafter.   Now even Chrysostom and Clement are found suggesting that if souls in this last state were to find themselves in hell by God's Will, they would not love Him less.   The flaw here would seem to lie in the coarse conception of hell as a definite " locus " rather than as a privation of God ; and love to God cannot exist without God as its real Energy.   Fénélon was emphatic on our need to the last of co-operation with God :   we must not be merely as strings of the plectrum on which the breath of the Spirit sweeps or as wax for His impress, notwithstanding the mysterious ache of the soul—surely a psychological fact— for this state of passivity.   We should not " hate ourselves ; we should be in charity with ourselves as with others ". " Vocal prayer, for Christ practised it, cannot be useless to contemplatives " ; and again, in a beautiful sentence, " we pray as much as we desire ; and we desire as much as we love ". We can never get beyond Christ ; we can never possess God in His absolute simplicity.   Still, Fénélon declared that the state of " pure love ", although rare, although intermittent, has been possible to the saints ; and though he asserts, in his " Explanations of the ' Maxims of the Saints ' ", sent to the Pope, that Hope must always abide, his assertion scarcely defends him from keeping the name of that virtue, but doing away, at least potentially, with its reality.   In any case, his

very guarded Explanations did not save him from the accusation of "indifference to salvation", the "abolishment of
the love of gratitude", and a tendency to look on the contemplation of Christ's Humanity as a fall from the heights of
pure contemplation.   The truth was that on Fénélon's
head, and in Fénélon's day, fell much of the condemnation
which the extreme teaching of many mystics, hitherto recognized or at least not denied by the Church, had been long
heaping up for itself.   "The action between God and man
must be reciprocal", as Dr. Inge has said; pure love would lead
to the destruction of love, for love requires two living factors
and "the person who has attained a 'holy indifference',
who has passed wholly out of self, is as incapable of love as
of any other emotion".[1]   It is the attempt "to wind ourselves too high for mortal man".   It was more than unfortunate, too, that the whole controversy in France and in the
Papal Court should have become tinged and warped, and
its issue prejudged, by motives of high ecclesiastical policy,
the Jesuits alarming themselves for the authority of the
Church and recognizing in Mysticism a power making for
independence and freedom, and the French King, under
their influence, bringing the whole tyrannous force of a
bigoted old age to bear on the Pope in order to secure the
condemnation, at every cost, of Quietism and the Quietists.

[1] Inge: *Christian Mysticism*, p. 241.

CHAPTER X

Post-Reformation Mysticism in England

BROWNE AND TRAHERNE

HITHERTO, the path which Mysticism traced out for itself has been pursued of set purpose within the limits of the Roman Catholic obedience.[1] It is necessary now to retrace our steps considerably, and to take up the thread of the story once more at the period in England immediately succeeding the Reformation. The reason for this division of the subject will be at once apparent. England produced during the seventeenth century a remarkable succession of mystical writers, men of fine, if sometimes wayward genius, at least half of them poets, who thus inaugurated that close connexion between English poetry and English Mysticism which became a fact almost without exception in the nineteenth century. The school of English Mysticism in the seventeenth century suffered division again within itself, owing to the fact that the full results of the Reformation had still to work themselves out, and would finally leave the national religious thought parted in two camps, Churchmanship and Puritanism, each with its own peculiar gifts of apprehension and expression of the Divine. Between the two camps, and in spirit owning full allegiance to neither, stand the Cambridge Platonists, whose

[1] Madame Bourignan was excepted, on account of her adhesion to the doctrine of Disinterested Love.

gospel of light and quietness of spirit comes as a keen refreshment amid the incessant jangles of a distracted time. In one respect, however, all schools of Post-Reformation English Mysticism are alike distinguished from mystics before the Reformation and of the Roman Church afterwards. The scheme of the mystics' progress, worked out so often and with ever-increasing philosophical and psychological subtlety, disappears. The simple, broad outlines of Purgation, Illumination, and Contemplation may be at the back of some mystical minds, and the terms are, more or less loosely, used ; but the *Scala Perfectionis* is never insisted on as an indispensable framework of the spiritual life. Instead, we get feeling, experience, ever fresh, and noted down with all conceivable delicacy and power. The mystical touch, that curious ineffable Somewhat which differentiates the mystic from the simply spiritual man, is none the less there ; it appears in paradox, or in a singular felicity of epigrammatic expression, in which heart and brain are equally at work, or again, it comes out in some phrase to which only the initiated can really respond. " Cor ad cor loquitur ".

But English Mysticism of the seventeenth century owed so much of its peculiar expression to the circumstances of the times that it is needful to make a short digression in order to understand of what sort was that English world to whose oversight, in 1603, the ill-fated Stuart dynasty came.

" The spacious times of great Elizabeth " were over ; the " bright occidental star " had set ; the day had dawned of " new faces, other minds ". The difference indeed between the atmosphere of the reigns of Elizabeth and James I was so emphatic that it set it mark even outwardly on the attire and fashions of men ; so quickly the stiff ruff became the falling collar ; the close-brushed hair, the loose locks ; the high small hat, the graceful *sombrero*. It was a world which intended, for some time at least, and it hoped for a long time, to take its ease, to eat, drink, and be merry on the much treasure heaped up. For, in truth, it was a rich world, in things material and intellectual.

(1) The great material prosperity of the times arose from several causes. Chief of these, of course, was the opening up of a New World east and west by the great explorers of the sixteenth century. In the wake of the explorers went the soldiers and the traders. New trade-markets and new trade-routes were being discovered and utilized in all directions. Virginia in America, Archangel in Russia, and the coasts of far-off Hindustan are three names that suggest a little of the vast change in progress. The East India Company was founded in 1600. Of course there were rivals in the field. The Dutch succeeded in clearing their English rivals out of the Spice Islands in 1623—the beginning of a century-long race between the two peoples for Colonial Empire. With the other great colonial world-power England's struggle was far more profitable than any peace could have been. For Spain—" martyr to her Catholicity "—was declining fast, and all through the later years of Elizabeth English seamen snatched her treasure-ships, appropriated bits of her New World possessions here and there, and generally diverted a large part of her yearly colonial revenue into the London Exchequer. It was a buccaneering process, but extraordinarily prosperous. Another cause of wealth was the long internal peace of England, which meant growth and free exchange in internal trade ; coal was got from the Tyne-pits, and iron from Sussex and Kent, there were the hardware manufacturers in Warwick, Stafford, and Worcester, and the weaving industry of East Anglia, where had settled the Flemish and Dutch weavers who had fled from the persecutions of Alva's troopers. And lastly, a great deal of the ancient wealth of the Church, its abbeys, its monasteries and their lands, had passed permanently into private hands which would keep what they had got.

All this material well-being was reflected in the outward appearance of things. Men built great houses in town and country, and expended much taste in their architecture. Very noticeable in the late Elizabethan and Jacobean manor-houses is the absence of all defensive building. Peace, men thought, had come to stay. Vast gardens in the Italian style were laid out round the houses, which were destined as, and often became, little courts for the cultivation of an artistic and comely life. Such were Lady Bedford's house at Twickenham, Lord Falkland's house at Great Tew, Lord Worcester's at Raglan, and Lord Winchester's at Basing. The lesser houses of the period, too, with their well-finished stone mullions and picturesque gables and porches, show the same general standard of well-being and of good taste. One curious evidence of prosperity was the commonness of the use of silver for drinking-vessels and ornaments in the England before the Civil Wars. In fact, for a widespread prosperity, it would be hard to find a comparison with the era of the first James. Even the days of Charles I's personal government (1630–41) were exceedingly prosperous. The Puritans really rebelled on principle only.

(2) With the material prosperity went a vast intellectual expansion and well-being. The Renaissance, a century before, had unrolled before men's minds the forgotten wealth of the classics : the discoveries of Copernicus, revolution-izing all former astronomical ideas, the voyages of Colum-bus, Cabot, Amerigo, and other daring explorers upsetting all former geographical notions, had literally brought around men a new heaven and a new earth. The progress of science began, or rather started afresh, after centuries of uneasy slumber ; we can hardly conceive the whirl of excitement, of novelty, of adventure in which the minds of the thinkers of the sixteenth and seventeenth centuries habitually moved. To-day, though scarcely yet wholly familiarized with the facts of what was then the New Astronomy, we know them

for facts. Then they had only just broken on the wondering intelligence of men. Every way the earth's horizon had rolled back, and the skies had, as it were, given way and let the startled gaze go through to the infinite space in which the insignificant ball of the earth was poised and rolled. At the same time ancient philosophies—the vast thought-systems of a world without Christianity—were coming to their own again.

(3) From all this there could be but one result, a freedom of thought hitherto unknown. All the old ties and sanctions were suddenly loosed and dissolved. The Church's teaching about earth and sun had been proved mistaken; the Church's half-suspicions of Nature and her beauty and order gave way to a boundless scientific curiosity and a daring imaginative appreciation. At the same time the great political movement of the Reformation shattered the outward unity and authority of the Church. The medieval ideal, the medieval conception of the Papacy as arbiter of the world, the medieval conception of the almost absolute dominance of the spiritual over the temporal, broke up into confusion, never completely to reassert themselves again.

(4) Three forces were at work, however, to keep the best minds of the seventeenth century—at any rate in England—true to Divine things, anxious for Divine guidance.

(a) A feeling of Disillusionment that was very widely spread. The first excitement aud glory of the Renaissance had passed away, and the new heaven and the new earth had not brought all that they had promised to bring. The wisdom and the splendour, the luxuries and the prosperity of the New Age had produced an aftermath of grossness, of greed and of cruelty, that drove many to recoil from a world so outwardly glorious and yet so terribly vile. So we shall find once more the turning within for the true and lasting wealth, a retirement from Courts and affairs, from power and place, to quiet communings apart with Nature and the world of Faith, as with Herbert, the Ferrars, Henry More and William Penn.

(b) A curious pre-occupation with Death. This appears up and down nearly all the writings of the poets and mystics, and is legibly inscribed on the tombs and monuments of the period. We have the skulls and crossbones, the full-length skeletons, the inverted torches and broken columns, all the grim outward imagery of dissolution, carried sometimes to an excess such as that of Dean Donne's weird monument in St. Paul's. The truth was that the exact and detailed certainties of the medieval Church with regard to the hereafter had suffered the blight of distrust and scepticism which had befallen its other authoritative doctrines. Men no longer had the life beyond the tomb pictured before their eyes in clear and immortal colours, and as that light failed, the tomb itself, and all its accessories, rose up before them dark and enigmatic as ever. It is the clear approach to God, the laying hold of Him in some new and direct fashion, that alone will conquer this fear.

(c) Lastly, the very increase of learning that brought the pagan classics brought also the re-opening in their fullness and their original meaning, of the Holy Scriptures, and the great spiritual movement of the Reformation. The place that the English Bible held in the hearts of the seventeenth-century mystics cannot be exaggerated. It coloured their thoughts and moulded their speech, and that increasingly as the century went on.

If we were to search for a man and a mystic symptomatic of his age in exactly the qualities of mind just enumerated, we should find such a one in Sir Thomas Browne, the physician of Norwich. Not the deepest or most eloquent or most spiritual of seventeenth-century writers,—although many of his thoughts were profound and spiritual and all were eloquently expressed—we have in him a learned man, full of a great curiosity and wondering delight in life, and quite as great a curiosity about death, restless in speculation, yet of a steady devoutness, tinged with the light and fire of mystical apprehension.

His life, as we glance at it, looks uneventful enough, but to Browne at thirty years old " it is a Miracle, which to relate were not a History, but a piece of Poetry, and would sound like a Fable ". The miracle to us is its quietude and sweetness through such troublous days, for Browne was representative of his time in this too that he lived over nearly the whole of the century, being born in 1605, the year of Gunpowder Plot, and dying in 1682 within three years of James II's critical reign. His father was a man of wealth, who died in his boyhood. He had also a beautiful and holy mind, if we may judge from a lovely little story told of Thomas Browne's infancy. " His father used to uncover his breast when he was asleep, and kiss it in prayers over him, that the Holy Ghost would take possession there ". The youth that followed this carefully tended boyhood was that of the well-to-do young man of the age. He went to Oxford in 1626 and then travelled, making the Grand Tour in France and Italy. He meant to be a physician, and so attended classes at the Medical Schools of Padua and Montpellier. Leyden gave him his M.D. in 1633, Oxford the same degree four years later. In 1637, he settled at Norwich, where he remained for the rest of his long life, " much resorted to for his skill in physic ".

He was known throughout his life as a good Church of England man, " attended the public service very constantly, never missed the Sacrament in his parish ; read the best English sermons he could hear of, with liberal applause ; delighted not in controversies ". During the Civil Wars he was studying flowers and stars, and while others were throwing up ramparts and field works, he was digging up and improving the Norwich drains. He heartily rejoiced at the Restoration, and was glad to see the Anglican service coming to its own again in the Norwich Churches. On Coronation Day, he walked up and down the streets, exchanging congratulations "civil and debonair". Thenceforth his life, peaceful and beloved, pursued a yet happier, calmer course. He brought up a large family, and his two boys, Edward and "honest Tom," did him credit. One event only broke the even tenour of their father's life. In 1671, Charles II visited Norwich and wished to knight the Mayor. The Mayor, with rare and charming generosity of soul, besought the King to bestow the honour instead on the famous doctor of Norwich, and this was done.

Now why should Sir Thomas Browne regard this even, tranquil, ordinary life as a thing of wonder, or miracle? "Of these wonders", says Samuel Johnson, who wrote his biography, ". . . his life offers no appearance". But, as Browne himself observes, "we carry with us the wonders that we seek without us", and if we turn to his books, we find at once that the inner soul of this prosperous, kindly citizen of the world was a storehouse of beautiful imaginings and strange experience.

During his life he wrote five books, the famous " Religio Medici " first, when he was a young man of about thirty. This saw the light anonymously in 1642 and in a corrupt form, the MS. having been handed a good deal about, until it came under the eyes of that singular and rather kindred spirit, Sir Kenelm Digby. Digby was a Roman Catholic, and saw fit to make some "Animadversions" on the book, which really attracted him immensely, and so Browne brought out a correct edition under his own name. At other intervals in his life there came " The Garden of Cyrus ", a fanciful attempt to trace a mysterious persistence of the number five through creation (the least effective of his writings) ; " The Discourse of Vulgar Errors ", a good example of the workings of the enquiring, scientific mind at its outset, then " Christian Morals ", a book much admired by Johnson, who edited it, and lastly, the famous " Urn Burial ", a treatise on various rites of burial, occasioned by his digging up some old funeral urns in his garden. This very aptly illustrates the trait in seventeenth century thought that we noted—its somewhat grim pre-occupation with death.

Let us take up the " Religio Medici " and listen while Sir Thomas Browne discourses to us. It is the creed of his own mind and spiritual life—the creed, as he thinks, of the scientific man, who can be a terrible sceptic at times. But in reality Faith always has the last word with him, so much so that Walter Pater denies that Browne ever doubted at all, and says that, as a consequence, the " Religio " is far more bracing to Piety than to Faith.[1] He is a Christian, but because that name is somewhat general, " to be particular, I am of that Reformed new-cast religion, wherein I dislike nothing but the name ". But he is broad-minded, and, like many of his thoughtful contemporaries, whose grand-fathers could remember the roods in their churches, and the chanting of the Mass in the Oxford chapels, he has a rather tender feeling for the older obedience. Holy Water and Crucifix do not " abuse (his) devotion ", nay, at the latter sight, " I can dispense with my hat, but seldom with the thought or memory of my Saviour ". He will not own the nativity of his religion to Henry VIII, but he insists on being at least polite to the Pope, " to whom, as a temporal Prince, we owe the duty of good language ". Of his baptism, he beautifully says; " from this do I compute or calculate my Nativity, not reckoning those *horae combustae* and odd days, or esteeming myself anything, before I was my Saviour's and enrolled in the register of Christ ". Now more deeply of his inner life: " I love ", he cries, " to lose myself in a Mystery, to pursue my Reason to an O Altitudo ! 'Tis my solitary recreation to pose my apprehension with these involved *Ænigmas* and riddles of the Trinity, with Incarna-

[1] W. Pater: *Appreciations. Sir Thomas Browne.*

tion and Resurrection . . . I desire to exercise my faith in
the difficultest point, for to credit ordinary and visible
objects is not faith, but persuasion . . . I would not have
been of those Israelites who pass'd the Red Sea, nor one of
Christ's patients on whom He wrought His wonders : then
had my faith been thrust upon me, nor should I enjoy the
greater blessing promised to all that believe, and saw not ".
Again, he practises self-recollection,—" in my retired and
solitary imagination I remember I am not alone, and therefore forget not to contemplate Him and His attributes Who
is ever with me, especially those two mighty ones, His Wisdom and Eternity ",[1] and in this connexion he quaintly
adds, " who can speak of Eternity without a Solecism, and
think thereof without an Exstasie ?   Time we may comprehend ; 'tis but five days older than ourselves ".   His
thoughts on Prayer are beautiful and unselfish, and extend
wistfully beyond what was thought right in his day.   Just as
" I cannot contentedly frame a prayer for myself in particular, without a catalogue for my friends ", nor " go to cure the
bodie of my patient, but I forget my profession and call
unto God for His soul ", so, " I could scarce contain my
Prayers for a friend at the ringing of a Bell, or behold his
corps without an orison for his soul.   'Twas a good way,
methought, to be remembered by posterity, and far more
noble than a History ".   But he puts this last opinion on a
level with one he once conceived as to the soul's dying with
the body, and being miraculously raised together with it at the
last Day ; and to this he exquisitely adds, " So that I might
enjoy my Saviour at the last, I could with patience be nothing

---

[1] Cf. his most mystical sentence, " If any have been so happy
as truly to understand Christian annihilation . . . the kiss of the
spouse, gustation of God, and ingression into the Divine shadow,
they have already had a handsome anticipation of heaven ".   Had
Browne, one wonders, come across the writings of the Spanish
Mystics ?

almost unto Eternity ". This brings us to his thoughts and love of God. " All that is truly amiable is God ", he says, and he loves God with all his might. " Dispose of me ", he prays, " according to the wisdom of Thy pleasure ; Thy will be done, even in mine own undoing." This is the true mystic's prayer. He sees the mystery of God reflected in the three-fold mystery of self ; but, most and clearest, he sees God in the world of Nature. " There are two books from which I cull my Divinitie ; besides that written one of God, another of His servant Nature, that universal and public Manuscript, that lies expansed under the eyes of all ; those that never saw Him in the one have discovered Him in the other ". He does not " disdain to suck Divinitie from the flowers of Nature ", and truly, for Browne, the spirit of the Lord broods over the face of all things. " This is that irradiation that dispels the mists of hell, . . . and preserves the region of the mind in serenity. Whosoever feels not the warm gale and gentle irradiation of this Spirit, (tho' I feel his pulse,) I dare not say he lives ; for truly, without this, to me there is no heat under the tropic, nor any light, tho' I dwelt in the body of the sun." Finally, in one perfect phrase, " Nature is the Art of God ", as elsewhere he quotes, " Lux umbra Dei ".

In his thoughts on the " music of the sphears " he anticipates Addison ; indeed, " there is a music wherever there is a harmony, order, or proportion ". He has, too, some profound and characteristic things to say of that inward harmony which is the love of soul to soul. " Conceive light invisible, and that is a spirit ", he cries, and then, " United souls are not satisfied with embraces, but desire to be truly each other, which being impossible, their desires are infinite ". The man who thus ponders is, all the while, the humblest of mortals. " Defenda me, Dios, de me ", is the first prayer of " his retired imaginations ", and " to bring up the Rere in Heaven " his utmost ambition. No doubt it was with

senses thus cleared of wilful sin and vanity that he could see
so well the music and glory of God in Nature.

Browne, like his contemporaries, was a good deal engrossed,
though not morbidly, with thoughts of Death and the hereafter.   Sleep is so like death to him that he " dare not trust
it without prayer and an half adieu to the world " ; but
he is not afraid of it, any more than " a well-resolved Christian " should be.   What is it to die ?   Why, " to cease to
breathe, to take a farewell of the elements, to be a kind of
nothing for a moment, to be within one Instant of a Spirit ".
As to what comes after death, he believes of course in
both Heaven and Hell, but thinks not overmuch about the
latter—" I can hardly think there was ever any scared into
Heaven ; they go the fairest way to Heaven that would
serve God without a hell ".   His view of Heaven is deeply
spiritual : " the necessary mansions of our restored selves
are those two contrary and incompatible places that we call
Heaven and Hell. . . When the soul hath the full measure
and complement of happiness ; when the boundless appe-
tite of that spirit remains completely satisfied, that it can
neither desire addition or alteration, that, I think, is truly
Heaven, and this can only be in the enjoyment of that
essence, whose infinite goodness is able to terminate the
desires of itself, and the insatiable wishes of ours ; wherever
God will thus manifest Himself, there is Heaven, though
within the circle of this sensible world.   Thus the soul of
man may be in Heaven anywhere ".

We have lingered a little over Sir Thomas Browne, because his mysticism is typical of a new world of thought
and emotion.   Quaint he certainly was—" coint " in the old
French sense of " adorned "—his mysticism was adorned
with all the curious ornaments of his own predilection, some
of them archaic, some provincial, a few even grotesque, but
they were set to beautify a very rich and inviting house of
thought.   Even if it is true, as Pater said, that " to Browne

the whole world was a museum ; all the grace and beauty it
has being of a somewhat mortified kind ", yet " over it all
was the perpetual flicker of a surviving spiritual fire, one
day to reassert itself ". As he himself put it, " All life, all
actions have their spring in the Resurrection."

It will not be out of place here to mention another lumin-
ary of seventeenth century Mysticism, who in some respects
—his joy in Nature, for example—resembles Sir Thomas
Browne, but whose light has only recently reached us. Mr.
Bertram Dobell was the astronomer to whose patience and
discrimination the discovery of the new star was due.[1]
Traherne, a divine of little interest before, has now an abiding
interest for all lovers of poetry and, still more, of magnificent
English prose, for his prose is better than his poetry. Of his
life little is known. An Oxford scholar, he became chaplain
in the household of the Sir Orlando Bridgeman, Keeper of
the Privy Seal under Charles II, and died in 1674, probably
in middle age, but the date of his birth is uncertain, most
likely about 1636. His chief memorials are his Poems and
the " Centuries of Meditations ", that is, meditations
arranged in groups of hundreds. There are four complete
centuries, and the beginnings of another.

---

[1] The story of the discovery of Traherne's writings (see *Poetical
Works of Thomas Traherne*. Introduction by Bertram Dobell) is
curious. A friend of Mr. Dobell's found the MS. of Traherne's
Poems and Meditations in the rubbish-box of a book-stall in
the Charing Cross Road. He bought them for a few pence, and
soon recognized their worth without, however, the faintest clue
as to their authorship. Dr. Grosart, a critic, took an interest in
the investigation and finally ascribed the authorship of the poems
to Vaughan. He was just about to publish an edition of Vaughan,
with Traherne's poems added, when he died, and the Traherne MS.
passed, after a little, into Mr. Dobell's hands, who, after a long
series of inquiries, identified poems and prose alike as the work
of Traherne, who hitherto had only been known for a few books
on theology of no great mark. In one of these, however, a poem
in the newly discovered collection was found, and this formed one
of the chief links of identification.

In mind and mood Traherne shares in part the spirit of the early Caroline poets, in part that of the Cambridge Platonists. His Christianity is as ardent as theirs, and there is no mist of Pantheism in the extraordinary felicity and splendour of his view of Nature. In one respect he resembles Vaughan, and, later, Wordsworth. He looked on childhood, and back at his own childhood, as being a time in which hints and flashes of heaven and of God were all around him before the world closed in. His childhood was set like a little spit of land amidst " murmurs and scents of the infinite sea ". His account of his child-thoughts is one of the most rare and fascinating pages of autobiography anywhere to be found.[1]

He begins his book by a wise saying, " As nothing is more easy than to think, so nothing is more difficult than to think well ". He is going to devote his life to God, therefore to think well is to serve God in His interior court, and the love of God is realized and made our own by meditation. So he comes at once to his great joyous theme—not in the least " mortified "—that the world as God made it is very good, and that God is to be discovered in it. " Everything is ours that serves us in its place. The Sun serves us as much as is possible, and more than we could imagine. The Clouds and Stars minister unto us, the World surrounds us with beauty."[2] Yet we can never enjoy the World aright till we see how " a sand exhibiteth the wisdom and power of God ",[3] for " some things are little on the outside, and rough and common, but I remember the time when the dust of the streets were as pleasing as gold to my infant eyes, and now they are more precious to the eye of reason ". Two qualities, he thinks, are needful to a real enjoyment of the riches of Nature, the recognition whence they came, and the unselfish

[1] *Centuries of Meditations*, pp. 156–179 *passim*.
[2] *Centuries of Meditations*, i. 14.
[3] *Ibid.* i. 27.   [4] *Ibid.* i. 25.

sharing of them with others. Thus, " pigs eat acorns, but neither consider the sun that gave them life, nor the influence of the heavens by which they were nourished, nor the very root of the trees from whence they came. This being the work of Angels, who in a wide and clear light see even the sea that gave them moisture, and feed upon that acorn spiritually while they know the ends for which it was created ".[1] In fact, to consider any good gift is " to drink it spiritually ; to rejoice in its diffusion is to be of a public mind ".[2] Then he turns to the thought of God's generosity in desiring that we should share and enjoy all this. " God did infinitely for us when He made us to want like Gods, that like Gods we might be satisfied. . . Want in God is treasure to us. For had there been no need He would not have created the world. . . . But He wanted Angels and Men, Images, Companions ; and those He had from all eternity ".[3] Then he turns this thought round on ourselves : " You must want like a God that you may be satisfied like God. . . Wants are the bands and cements between God and ourselves. Had we not wanted we could never have been obliged. Our own wants are treasures. And if want be a treasure, sure everything is so ".[4] So he comes to the love of God, the love of which he wonderfully says that it " never ceases but in endless things ". He goes through all the world finding beauty and gifts, till he is brought up at that which " the throne of delights, the centre of Eternity, the Tree of life ", and that is the Saviour's Cross. " God ", he exclaims, " never showed Himself more a God than when He appeared man ; never gained more glory than when He lost all glory ; was never more sensible of a sad estate, than when He was bereaved of all sense ".[5] He recognizes the majesty and the power of this Dying in the lives of men.[6]

[1] *Centuries of Meditations,* i. 26.
[2] *Ibid.* i. 27. [3] *Ibid.* i. 1, 42. [4] *Ibid.* i. 44, 51.
[5] *Ibid.* i. 90. [6] *Ibid.* Cf. i. 60, 61.

Perhaps one may add one or two epigrammatic sayings of this remarkable man, sayings that throw a sudden ray of light on a dark place, like a sunbeam falling into a shuttered room. "I have found that things unknown have a secret influence on the soul, and, like the centre of the earth unseen, violently attract us". "Love has a marvellous property of feeling in another. It can enjoy in another, as well as enjoy him". "All transient things are permanent in God". "It is the glory of God to give all things in the best of all possible manners". "It is consonant with God's nature that the best things should be the most common". "It is some part of Felicity that we must seek her".

With suchlike arresting thoughts Traherne's "Meditations" are sown. They put the earth and its wonders before us in a new and entrancing fashion; there is no one in the whole range of mystics who looks on Nature just as Traherne does; we take a fresh breath, rub our eyes, and get our gratitude newly back again, as if indeed we were abroad with him on some sunlit down, seeing with him God's grace in every "spire of grass" and in His "orient and immortal wheat".

CHAPTER XI

Post-Reformation Mysticism in England

THE CAROLINE POETS AND THE CAMBRIDGE PLATONISTS

BROWNE and Traherne introduce us very fitly to the group of poet-mystics who conferred a peculiar glory on the English Church of the early Seventeenth century. Browne's gift was " one for the emotions and the imagination ; he felt the wonder of the world, he widened the bounds of charity ; his divinity is composed of these two elements—wonder and love ".[1] All this is true of Traherne while, perhaps more than Browne, he recognized a Divine order under the scheme of Nature, and drew more resolutely in contemplation near to the Cross. Wonder and love ; the reading of Nature and of earthly ordinances—those of the Church for example—as parables and shadows of the Divine ; a very definite feeling of the Cross as the centre round which life groups itself ; these may be taken as the messages to the world uttered by Donne, Vaughan, Crashaw, Herbert, and the companion of the two latter, who, though not himself a poet, made his life and the lives of those around him a poem, Nicholas Ferrar. If it be said that the name of mystic more truly belongs to Donne, Vaughan, and Crashaw than to Herbert and Ferrar, that is true : but Bemerton and Little Gidding have left a fragrance which is unmistakably

---

[1] Prof. Dowden : *Puritan and Anglican.* p. 68.

that of the Saviour's mystical utterance, " He that loseth his life for my sake, the same shall find it ".

John Donne, who, for curious and intricate felicity of thought, most of all the group, resembled Sir Thomas Browne, was born in 1573.[1] He was brought up by an uncle, an accomplished Jesuit priest, who sent him to Oxford, where he formed a life-long friendship with Sir Henry Wotton, Then, after the usual travel abroad of a young man of fashion, he entered himself at Lincoln's Inn and became known as a shining member of the most witty coterie of the age, the coterie of the Mermaid Tavern. In this select circle sat, caroused, and conversed Inigo Jones, John Selden, Ben Jonson, Michael Drayton, and no doubt the great and mysterious Shakespeare himself. Among these, the youthful Donne was known as " a laureate wit ; it was impossible that a vulgar soul should dwell in such promising features", which shews that he possessed a handsome person as well as a fine mind. He had at this time no other thought than that of a secular career ; he volunteered for the great expedition to Cadiz in 1596, and afterwards became secretary in the Lord Keeper's household. At that time he began to throw off a quantity of verse, sonnets, lyrics, love-songs, elegies, which were handed about amongst his friends in manuscript. The next event in his life was a run-away marriage with the daughter of the house in which he was secretary, and this led to a short imprisonment in the Fleet at the hands of the irate father, and a long set-back in the hopes of worldly success.

By this time he had run through his fortune, but by no means his friendships. Donne always had a genius for

---

[1] It is interesting that he could trace descent through a series of Roman Catholic relatives, all of whom had suffered for their faith, to the family of Sir Thomas More. His great grandmother was the Margaret Griggs, whom readers of Miss Manning's charming " *Household of Sir Thomas More* " will remember.

friendship, and his letters to his various friends form part of the literary legacy of his life. One of his friends was the Countess of Bedford, who held a kind of court of letters at her great house at Twickenham; another a Sir Henry Goodere, who had grown rich on confiscated Church land; a third was Bishop Andrewes. A great depression and disillusionment took hold of Donne at this period; he had read hard and made the knowledge and wisdom of the world his own; he was a fashionable poet and even a Court favourite, for he often sat at the Royal table amongst a group that was called "the King's living library". But his writings at the time shew increasing disgust with what life has brought him, and by degrees this turned to a new interest in religion and holy things. King James was a shrewd judge of character, and early marked out Donne as a man who ought to be a priest. Both the first two Stuarts were keenly anxious to recruit the ranks of the Anglican clergy with men of character and learning. James was sure that Donne had the vocation, and told him so three times, adding at last that if he remained a layman he must give up all hope of preferment. At length, in 1615, Donne yielded and was ordained, and a year after was made one of the Royal chaplains: and five years later James, in his own peculiar way, appointed him to the Deanery of St. Paul's.[1] After the custom of the age, he held three livings besides, Sevenoaks, Blunham, and St. Dunstan's in the West. In this last-named City parish dwelt the draper and angler, Isaak Walton, who became the Dean's devoted disciple and friend and gave us Donne's biography among the other exquisite little "Lives" with which he enriched English literature. Donne came to the front at once as a great preacher; to him we owe the

---

[1] "Dr. Donne", said James, "knowing you love London, I do therefore make you Dean of St. Paul's; and, when I have dined, then do you take your beloved dish home to your study, say grace there to yourself, and much good may it do you".

first missionary sermon ever delivered in England, preached
before the Virginia Company of Adventurers—bishops, peers,
clergy, soldiers, and traders—amongst whom sat Nicholas
Ferrar; and every year after his Ordination saw a growth
in holiness and in insight into Divine things. Of his preaching Walton tells us quaintly that he was " like an angel from
a cloud, but in none; carrying some, as St. Paul was, to
Heaven in holy raptures, and enticing others by a sacred art
and courtship to amend their lives ". While another, perhaps rather unregenerate, hearer, wrote this rapturous
couplet on the effect of his words:

> " Corrupted Nature sorrow'd that she stood
>   So near the danger of becoming good ".

The death of wife and children, causing him a grief from
whose melancholy he never fully recovered, was followed
by a visit to Germany as Chaplain to the English Embassy,
which seriously enfeebled his health. During his last illness,
he composed some remarkable Devotions, and also, seemingly, his celebrated " Hymn to God the Father ", perhaps,
in its strange mingling of humility and daring, the most
characteristic of all his religious pieces. Walton hints that
the Hymn was written while its author's thoughts dwelt
sadly on " those pieces that had been loosely—God knows,
too loosely—scattered in his youth ", and which he wished
" had been abortive, or so short-lived that his own eyes had
witnessed their funeral ".

Two other characteristic acts he performed in his last
days. One was the preparation of memorial gifts to his
friends, bloodstones, set in gold, and engraved with the
figure of Christ crucified, not to a Cross, but to an Anchor—
George Herbert was the recipient of one of these : the other
act was the ordering of his own monument. A painter was
sent for who was required to draw a picture of Donne in his
winding-sheet, standing on a funeral urn. The Dean him-

self was the actual model, and the monument, the only vestige of the old Cathedral which escaped the Great Fire, is still to be seen in St. Paul's.

In earlier manhood Donne, as it has been said, was " a son of the Renaissance, belated, born out of his time ". There was the eager zest for life and all that it held, something rich and sumptuous, occasionally even unscrupulous, in his diction, corresponding to those portraits of him in his prime, with bright eyes and curled hair and beard. Later, all this was subdued to the faith of a humble Christian, but the best of it was transformed, not utterly stifled.

What we notice about Donne as a whole is his keen individualism. His poetry was a revolt from the Elizabethan school of poetry. That magnificent poetry has been compared to music in the sense that it is universal in range ; the thought and emotion of any great intellect or fancy. Shakespeare, for example, has so general a genius that it is impossible, though always tempting, to guess at his religion, occupation, tastes or hobbies. But Donne speaks for himself alone, and of experiences that could not happen to any mind but his. So his ideas are often so strange as to give a sense of shock, and the very words seem hewn out one by one. Here is a verse on love :—

> " Twice or thrice have I loved thee
> Before I knew thy face or name ;
> So in a voice, so in a shapeless flame
> Angels affect us oft, and worshipp'd be ".

Donne will, in fact, reason upon everything, earthly love and heavenly as well, and for this cause his poetry does not at all lend itself to brief quotation. Long poems like " The Progress of the Soul ", and " the Anatomy of the World " must be read through and studied, and that with care lest stray trivial-seeming lines escape the attention, and a treasure be missed, lines like, " I must confess it could not choose but be Profane to think thee anything but thee ", or (on death) " when bodies to their graves souls from their graves remove ". Donne " liked a craggy subject to break his mind upon " ; he had the courage to state his experience, he loved and was loved with a rare devotion, and his love to God was of the same intensity. He would often say in a kind of sacred ecstasy—" Blessed be God that He is God, only and divinely like Himself ".

Henry Vaughan was born at Newton St. Bridget in Wales in 1621. He always added the odd word " Silurist " to his signature of his poems ; and this is supposed to mean that he laid emphasis on the claim of his family to be *par excellence* the Vaughans of Wales, living as they did in the South-Eastern part of the principality, where once the British tribe of the Silures had dwelt. All that we know of his life is that he went to Oxford, and then, as old Anthony à Wood says, " the Civil War beginning, he was sent for home to the horror of all good men, and followed the pleasant paths of poetry, became noted for his ingenuity, and published several specimens thereof. He became a physician, and was esteemed by scholars as an ingenious person, but proud and humorous ". In his poems he at first imitated Donne, a bad model for a young poet, because of Donne's lack of form. In 1631, Herbert's " Temple " came into his hands and altered his whole literary life. In the preface to " Silex Scintillans ", his best known book, he speaks of the " blessed man George Herbert, whose holy life and verse gained many pious converts, of whom I am least ".

It is as a mystic even more than as a poet that Vaughan is famous. His poetry is full of the quaint conceits and ornaments of the period. But even they point out Vaughan's great gift. He loved and interpreted Nature better than any poet of his day. To take a few instances. On Dawn he has,

> " The whole creation shakes off night,
> And for thy shadow looks the light ;

> Stars now vanish without number :
> Sleepie planets set and slumber.
> The pursie clouds disband and scatter ;
> *All expect some sudden matter* " :

and this single line, " I see a Rose bud in the far **East**".
This of the night sky, " Stars nod and sleep, and through
the dark air spin a fiery thread ": of a cornfield, " the
purling corn ", alluding to its rustle in the breeze : of the
Earth at spring-time, that she " purples every grove with
roses ", are examples of the charming conceits in which his
poetry is rich.

But these would not make the poet a mystic. Vaughan
sees Nature all shot through with intimations of God, which
in his thought take again and again the form of light. He
is a very apostle of light, white light [1] too. He sees this
mortal life as a half-lit space between two worlds of light,
We, exile-like for the time being, travel from one to the
other. Hence, like Traherne, he looks back longingly to
his childhood—" my striving eye dazzles at it, as at Eternity "—and forward with a sort of nostalgia to the light
that is coming. Even the Judgement Day is to him a " day
of life, of light, of love ". " I saw eternity ", he sings, in
an immortal passage,

> " I saw eternity the other night
> Like a great Ring of pure and endless light.
>   All calm, as it was bright ;
> And round beneath it, Time, in hours, days, years,
>   Driv'n by the spheres
> Like a vast shadow mov'd, in which the world
> And all her train were hurl'd, ".

As life goes on and grows more lonely, the nostalgia
is increased by the ache of human loss till he breaks
out :—

---

[1] " White " is a favourite word of Vaughan's : cf. " the white
designs which children drive ", " Welcome, white day ", " the old,
white Prophets ", " His white and holy train ", " the white-winged
Reapers ", " Dear Saint, more white than day ", etc.

" They are all gone into the world of light !
    And I alone sit lingering here ! "
" I see them walking in an air of glory
    Whose light doth trample on my days ".

He has, too, the mystic's thought of God : " There is in
God, some say, a deep but dazzling darkness ",—the darkness which is excess of light.

Meanwhile, the light breaks through in shafts and beams
to comfort the exile's path, best provided for by the disciplined expectation of " inward quietness and clearness ".
It comes to the observant soul through many chinks and
reflected from many mirrors in Nature, but man, if we may
take the hint of Vaughan's own title-page, may be also a
light-bearer, *silex scintillans*,—a flint stone, perhaps, but
a flint stone on fire and sparkling.

Readers of " John Inglesant " will remember how,
amongst the visitors to Little Gidding in Shorthouse's
vivid description of that wonderful religious household,
was a Mr. Richard Crashaw, " the poet of Peterhouse, who
afterwards went over to the Papists and died Canon of
Loretto ", and how, walking in the garden, he " spoke of
the beauty of a retired religious life, saying that here and
at Little St. Marie's Church, near to Peterhouse, he had
passed the most blissful moments of his life, watching at
midnight in prayer and meditation ". Like most of the
personal touches in that remarkable book, this is exactly
accurate, and, brief as it is, represents almost all that we
know of Crashaw. He was born in 1616, was educated at
the Charterhouse and at Pembroke Hall, Cambridge, became a Fellow of Peterhouse, and, in company with sixty-
five other Cambridge Fellows, suffered expulsion in 1644
for a refusal to sign the Solemn League and Covenant. He
was received into the Roman Church, and died in 1650.
His mysticism was of the warmly coloured, picturesque,
Latin type ; his favourite subjects were the life and suffer-

ings of the Saviour, the glories of the Blessed Virgin, and the praise of St. Teresa, for whom he felt an overwhelming admiration and reverence. As we compare Vaughan and Crashaw, we are irresistibly reminded of Shelley's lines :

> " Life like a dome of many-coloured glass
> Stains the white radiance of eternity ".

Vaughan seems to live in and for glimpses of that white radiance : he dislikes the commingling of it with earthly hues. But Crashaw brings us inside the " dome of many-coloured glass ", and the white light, to some almost intolerable, is broken up into a myriad tints and glories, and, it must be added, spangles. As a poet, Crashaw was far more of a craftsman, and had a far juster ear for music, than either Donne or Vaughan ; when he is really touched, he can touch others ; he had truly seen his own vision and heard in the Holy Mount " the sound of words ". But his delight in his art runs away with him, at times, until the art becomes artificiality : he places his gems of thought amid rows of decorative glass beads, and seems really to leave the task of discrimination to his reader without any idea that all is not of the same value. If St. Teresa, the soul of common sense and humour, had ever read his poems addressed to her, she would probably have loved them and laughed at them at the same time. Was there ever such ode as that in which he first speaks of her, with its magnificent beginning, " Love, thou art absolute, sole lord of life and death ", its description of the mystical Rapture (which yet follows close on the intolerable " conceit " of the seraphim who " turn love's soldiers " to " exercise their archery " upon the saint), and its beautiful close in which he depicts her in heaven ? But if we would see Crashaw at his best—and a poet should be judged thus—we can always turn to his lovely Hymn of the Nativity, his version of the 23rd Psalm, and the contrasts of terror and tenderness in his " Dies Irae ".

> " O, that Trump ! whose blast shall run
> An even round with th' circling sun,
> And urge the murmuring graves to bring
> Pale mankind forth to meet his King.
>
> *   *   *   *   *
>
> " Dear, remember in that day
> Who was the cause Thou cam'st this way ;
> Thy sheep was strayed, and Thou wouldst be
> Even lost Thyself in seeking me ".

Meanwhile Nicholas Ferrar, the host of Crashaw in many a quiet Sunday's " retreat ", ruled over the holy household at Little Gidding, that household (unique in religious history as an instance of an entire family quitting the world for the " quiet life ") which was surely in the poet's thought when he sketched his " Description of a Religious House " ; and George Herbert, the friend of Donne and the inspirer of Vaughan, exchanging the life of the successful courtier for that of the humble parish priest of Bemerton, was, through three brief years, making exquisite proof of his ministry as the Church's servant and poet. It was in the life of ordered service that the Ferrars and Herbert alike found their sure experience of God, and through it that they drew many to a like ideal of self-renunciation and charity. It was in such a round of service—that of " the priest to the temple "—that Herbert felt the near Presence of his Saviour and sang it to such measures that his poems,—with Keble's " Christian Year "—serve, and will always serve, to indicate and recall to men's minds the peculiar ideals and attractiveness of the English Church, its gravity, its mild rule, its sober beauty, its temperate delight in Nature and in Reason as intermediaries for communion with God. Of these ideals the Ferrars and George Herbert were prophets, and the latter, indeed, with his high gifts as a religious poet—imagination, and a curious felicity of diction set off by a touching homeliness—an especially persuasive one. The Great Rebellion broke rudely in upon a movement towards a retired and holy life of which there are many indications, a movement which was gathering real and vital force. Perhaps the true ideal of the Church of England was never nearer realization than on the eve of the Civil War, which temporarily destroyed so much that belonged to its deepest, if hidden, life, but was just in the delicate stage of formation. It is true, however, that some power was needed to reinforce in the Church the strength of the devout life as manifested by the beautiful, but exotic, rule of Little Gidding, and the sweet and serious, but not very robust, discipline outlined by George Herbert. This strength was afforded by the school of thinkers whom we come next to consider, and whose clearness of outlook and depth of spirituality were found not only proof against the distractions of the Commonwealth period, but have left a lasting legacy to the Church of "light and life and love".

II

The "Cambridge Platonists", as this school of thinkers and group of delightful men is usually termed, won their title by their combination of a real Christian faith with a reverent following after the teaching of Plato and his great disciple, the mystic Plotinus. But in no extravagant sense. They saw, as Plato saw, the world as the mirror of Deity, the reflection of the Ideal; they sought after God, as Plotinus sought, by the way of meditation from which the expectation of Immediacy of contact was not absent; but they gloried in the fullest use of all human faculties, and not in their denial. For them no *Via Negativa*; rather, they insisted on the employment of the Reason, as the Divine prerogative of man, and claimed for Religion the whole field of the intellectual life, just as Herbert claimed music and poetry, and Cromwell politics and war, and Sir Thomas Browne science and letters. They believed that there can be no ultimate contradiction between philosophy or science and the Christian Faith, and so they succeeded, through dark and troublous times, in keeping a bright future before their eyes—they were splendid optimists. " Reason ", they taught, " doth depend upon self-improvement by meditation, consideration, and prayer and the like ". " Then also it is the Divine governor of men's life ; it is a light flowing from the Fountain and Father of lights ". Benjamin Whichcote, one of their number, exclaims, " It ill becomes us to make our intellectual faculties Gibeonites ", and John Smith, another of the group, finely adds, " That which enables us to know aright the things of God must be a living principle of holiness within us. Some men have too bad hearts to have good heads. He that will find truth must seek it with a free judgment and a sanctified mind ". Like Browne, these men and their companions contrived to live through all the worries and plagues of the Civil War in strangely peaceful and undisturbed fashion, radiating little circles of tranquil light around them. In an age of hot-headedness they won by their balanced judgement and persistent charity the name of " Latitudinarians ". Of such breadth of mind as theirs, the more the better !

Benjamin Whichcote, whom we may take as the first example of the group, entered Emmanuel College in 1626. Both Universities must have been wonderful places to know just before the Civil War. The brilliant Court of Charles I. stayed again and again at Oxford, and the King and Queen, with Laud and Sanderson, Falkland, Hales, and Chillingworth might have been seen walking in the Grove of Trinity or in Christ Church meadows ; while at Cambridge in a single day one could have met Milton and Thomas Fuller,

George Herbert, Crashaw, and Jeremy Taylor. Amid such company Whichcote moved, and in 1630 became Tutor in his College. Bishop Burnet tells us that Whichcote " set his students much on reading the ancient philosophers, chiefly Plato, Tully, and Plotin, and on considering the Christian religion as a doctrine sent by God both to elevate and sweeten human nature ". In addition to being " a wise and kind instructor ", he became noted as a preacher, and for twenty years gave the Sunday afternoon lectures in Trinity College Chapel to throngs of delighted hearers. When the Civil War came, Cambridge was filled with Puritan troopers, for the Eastern Counties were mostly hot for the Parliament'; but Whichcote remained undisturbed and imperturbable. Indeed, he was made Provost of King's in 1644 when Dr. Collins was turned out for Royalism, and it is good to find him insisting that his predecessor should receive half the stipend throughout his lifetime. Not only did Whichcote refuse himself to take the Solemn League and Covenant, but he got most of the Fellows of King's excused also. He must have been a man of winning temperament and of strong character, for he was so respected as to become Vice-Chancellor under the new régime, and was consulted by Cromwell on the question of granting toleration to the Jews. After the Restoration, ejected in turn from his Provostship, he became first a country and then a City rector, and of his parochial ministry we are told that he preached constantly, looked after the children's education (often at his own expense), relieved distress, and made up quarrels among his neighbours. One instance of his charity we know—he left provision for relief to poor housekeepers disabled by age or sickness.

His sermons were often prefaced by this prayer : " Oh ! naturalize us to heaven ! May we bear the image of Christ's resurrection by spirituality and heavenly-mindedness. O Lord, communicate Thy light to our minds, Thy life to our souls. . . . Go over the workmanship of Thy creation in us again . . ." Religion in his view is natural and vital to man, and can never be disallied from truth : " We are as capable of religion as we are of reason ". " Religion is the first sense of man's soul, the temper of his mind, the pulse of his heart ". Again : " the mind makes no more resistance to truth than the air does to light ", and, taking the conception higher, " The soul of man to God is as the flower to the sun ; it opens at its approach and shuts when it withdraws ". He talks of Redemption thus : " It is a Divine nature in us, a Divine assistance over us " ; and, at a time when the total depravity of human nature was roundly asserted, he points to a higher thought of man's potentialities : " There is nothing in the world hath more of God in it than man hath ", and again, " Have a reverence to thyself, for God is in thee ". For Conscience he has a beautiful and characteristic term, " the home-God ". But why ? Because of his view of the salvation which Christ brought. To the hard legal views of the age, wherein Christ's righteousness is, as something external to man, imputed to man almost artificially, Whichcote opposed the belief in an actual vital at-one-ment wrought within the soul. " We come at that which Christ hath done for us with God by what He hath done for us within us ". " They deceive themselves who think of reconciliation with God by means of a Saviour acting upon God in their behalf, and not also working in them to make them God-like ". " Heaven is first a temper, then a place ". With this belief—as old as Christian Mysticism—in the inward immanent Christ, he built up his wonderful breadth of charity. " Men's apprehensions ", he cries, " can be no more alike than their faces are set in one mould ", but he is a friend to all who manifest the Christ-life.

There is a well-known passage in " John Inglesant " in which the hero, visiting " Lady Cardiff " at " Oulton ",

comes across Dr. Henry More, the Cambridge Platonist.[1]
The passage is worth quoting, inasmuch as the words put into
More's mouth are his own, culled from various sources,
and sum up very aptly this remarkable man's attitude towards Nature and towards God. " One fine and warm
day in the early spring, Inglesant and the Doctor were walking in the garden at the side of the house bordering the
chase and park. . . . The Doctor began, as upon a favourite theme, to speak of his great sense of the power and benefit of the fresh air. ' I would always ', he said, ' be *sub
dio* if it were possible. . . . I can read, discourse, and
think nowhere as well as in some arbour, where the cool
air rustles through the moving leaves ; and what a rapture of mind does such a scene as this always inspire within
me ! To a free and divine spirit how lovely, how magnificent is this state for the soul of man to be in, when, the
life of God inactuating her, she travels through heaven
and earth, and unites with, and after a sort feels herself, the
life and soul of the whole world, even as God ! This indeed
is to become Deiform—not by imagination, but by union
of life. God doth not ride me whither I know not : but
discourseth with me as a friend, and speaks to me in such
a dialect as I understand fully—namely, the outward world
of His creatures, so that I am in fact " Incola coeli in terra ",
an inhabitant of Paradise and heaven upon earth ; and I
may soberly confess that sometimes, walking abroad after
my studies, I have been almost mad with pleasure—the
effect of Nature upon my soul having been inexpressibly
ravishing. . . . No ! I am not out of my wits, as some
fondly interpret me, in this divine freedom, but the love
of God compelleth me ' ".[2] Here of course we get very

[1] Inglesant is of course an imaginary personage, but the description of the household at " Oulton ", with its strange assemblage of
mystics and charlatans, is true to life of Lady Conway's establish-
ment at Ragley, More's constant resort.

[2] Shorthouse : *John Inglesant*, ch. xvii.

near the Mystical doctrine of centuries back,—deification, and the Ecstasy.

The man who at times spoke words like these lived all his life in a great calm. His environment, whether of men or affairs, mattered little to him, so long as he possessed the unfailing joys of Nature and of the inner life. He did not care to adjust himself to outward changes in Church and State ; like Whichcote, he simply ignored them. As a little boy at Eton, he had worried himself about the mysteries of necessity and free-will, and the problem of hell, making up his mind at last, as he mused in the playground " with a musical and melancholic murmur ", that if he were predestined to Hell, he would behave himself as well as possible there, " being persuaded that if I thus demeaned myself, God would not keep me long in that place ". This persuasion of the Divine justice and goodness remained with him all his life, and the influence of the little " *Theologia Germanica* " quickened it to a steady and burning love of God.

In 1631 More entered Christ's College, a tall, thin youth of " rapt expression ", and made friends with Whichcote and his circle. He took orders, but would seldom preach, and refused all advancement, declining in turn as the years went on the Mastership of his College, two Deaneries, and two Bishoprics. He believed he could do the Church greater service in a private station ; and a host of pupils and friends gathered round him by whom he seems to have been regarded as a kind of oracle. His character, in truth, showed a rare combination of intellectuality and saintliness, mystical insight, and a charming sanity and courtliness of manners. He died in 1687.

One or two sentences from his writings will serve to indicate some main trends of his thought. " The soul of man is a little medal of God ". " The oracle of God is not to be heard save in His holy temple, that is, in a good and

M.C.   P holy man, sanctified in spirit, soul and body ". " If we would teach others, we must adapt ourselves in part to their capacity, for he that will lend his hand unto another fallen into a ditch, must himself, though not fall, yet stoop and incline his body ",—excellent charity and common sense. He is sharply opposed to two tendencies in Mysticism, that of the *Via Negativa* of approach to God,[1] and that of making little of the external facts of the Gospel and the historical Christ ; with the latter mistake he charges the Quakers.   The resistance to these two inclinations, common to so many mystics, in one who undoubtedly possessed the capacity for the true mystical ecstasy, is remarkable. Of all the Platonist group he evinced most clearly the combination of psychic with spiritual powers. Like Thoreau, he possessed, for example, an extraordinary power of attracting animals, playing often with birds, which would sit singing on his fist, and even, we are told, with snakes.

John Smith, whom we will take as our last example of the Platonist school, was born in 1618 of aged parents who had been long childless, and was therefore compared by Bishop Patrick to John the Baptist. There is little to tell of his life ; he entered at Cambridge in 1636, and became the associate of Whichcote and More ; and, after a brief career of intense study and keen evangelical fervour, he died at the early age of thirty-four. His short life and his sermons, however, left a deep and abiding impression, which may be compared to that of Hurrell Froude in the Oxford Movement, though Smith's was by far the more gracious and disciplined nature of the two.

In the mid-seventeenth century when men were splitting

---

[1] " The waste, silent solitude " found by those who " make their whole nature desolate of all animal figurations whatever " has, he thinks, nothing Divine about it ; it really proceeds from " the stillness and fixedness of melancholy " of their own oppressed animal nature.

hairs about predestination and the scheme of salvation, imputed righteousness and the like, Smith dealt with themes such as these : God in His world—Divine Immanence ; God in man—the kinship of the Divine and the Human ; God in Christ—the Incarnation ; God in Himself—the "Altogether Lovely". A few extracts from his discourse will illustrate the tone of his teaching, and its epigrammatic force.

"The world is in God, rather than God in the world". "He could not write His image so that it could be read, save only in rational natures. Whenever we look upon our own souls in a right manner, we shall find an Urim and Thummim there". "Faith is that which unites man more and more to the centre of life and love". "The foundation of heaven and hell is laid in men's own souls". "The Gospel . . . is that whereby God comes to dwell in us, and we in Him". "Religion is life and spirit, which, flowing out from the source of all life, returns to Him again as into its original, carrying the souls of good men up with it". "It is only life which can fully converse with life". He has a sound and beautiful bit of teaching on the subject of the mystical Ecstasy. "Who can tell the delights of these mysterious converses with the Deity, when reason is turned into sense, and faith becomes vision ? . . . By the Platonists' leave, this light and knowledge (that of the ' contemplative man ') peculiarly belongs to the true and sober Christian. This life is nothing else but an infant-Christ formed in the soul. But we must not mistake ; this knowledge is here but in its infancy".

"He lived", said Bishop Patrick, who preached his funeral sermon, "by faith in the Son of God"; and this faith was "of a kind to draw down heaven into the heart. He lived in a continual sweet enjoyment of God". This may be said of his school in general. The Cambridge Platonists were believers in the doctrine of the Inner Light, which was to attain so well-marked a place in English religious thought under the influence and teaching of George Fox and his followers. But they identified it, in Dean Inge's words, " with the purified reason ". Through this medium they beheld and loved the world in its order and beauty ; by this means they followed after and felt the Divine warmth and guidance in their lives. With them, as Mr. A. E. George beautifully puts it, " the tree of knowledge grows beside the tree of life ".[1]

[1] E. A. George : *Men of Latitude in the Seventeenth Century,* p. 102. Mr. George's book contains admirable sketches of Whichcote, More, and Smith, as well as of Sir Thomas Browne and others, and I should like to express my indebtedness to his pages, as to those of Dr. Inge, for several of the quotations from the writings of the Cambridge Platonists given above.

CHAPTER XII

Puritan Mystics—Bunyan and Fox

WHAT the Cambridge Platonists sought and found in their own serene and reflective fashion was the theme and goal of numberless perplexed souls—and sects—in their troublous times. The temporary breakdown of the English Church system, with its quieting and consoling influence—a break-down perhaps bound to come as the result of the disruptive tendencies of two opposed schools of thought struggling for mastery within the Church, but certainly hastened by the arbitrary rigour of Laud's enforcement of the " beauty of holiness ", the fine watchword of a mind at once thoroughly devout and thoroughly Erastian—this break-down left the Commonwealth period the confused scene of all sorts of attempts, individual and organized, to realize the kingdom of God upon earth.[1] The absence of any system of Church government having a moral sanction in the consciences of people—for Presbyterianism was an exotic, and an exotic transplanted from an unfriendly soil—allowed full scope for the most diverse religious experiments, some of them affecting not only the inner life, but the fabric of society and of the family. A

---

[1] Thus, even of William Dell, one of Cromwell's army chaplains, and a man of real truth and insight, Baxter could write, that " he took Reason, Sound Doctrine, Order, and Concord, to be intolerable maladies of Church and State, because they were the greatest strangers to his mind ".

number of strange religious communities sprang up, such as the Ranters, Seekers, and Muggletonians, the Family of Love, the Levellers, and Diggers, amongst the last of which Gerrard Winstanley deserves more than a passing word. Meanwhile, certain older bodies such as the Baptists and Independents went on their appointed way, and last, but not least, the Quakers, summing up into a focus all the vague and diffused teaching as to the Inner Light, had their momentous beginning under the leadership of George Fox. It is with the individual, rather than with any society, however, that Mysticism has its business, and therefore we shall do well to select and examine certain well-marked characters and lives, and to consider them as representative of what was best in the spiritual thought and teaching—a confused medley, at first glance,—of the period. That it was, at any rate, a time of "Sturm und Drang" for the soul is evident; the painful, often blundering, search after what was true and real and would bear the stress of life was going on on every hand; conventions had broken down, and in numberless cases the soul felt itself nakedly face to face with its Maker.

This is, as Professor Gardiner has said, the essence of Puritanism; and in that sense we can take John Bunyan as a type of the Puritan mystic. But in truth the title, if it tempt us to limit the power and range of Bunyan's religious genius, is a little misleading. Bunyan's theology was certainly Puritan, but his soul was much larger than his theology. There is nothing distinctively Puritan in his wise, warm-hearted outlook on human life, and he was, it may be remembered, brought up as a faithful son of the Church of England. No one loved bell-ringing more than he; no one, to start with, enjoyed more unreservedly the observance of King James' "Book of Sports"—witness the "tip-cat" on Sundays—none, by his own statement, felt a more affectionate reverence for the parson and clerk, or believed more firmly in their well-nigh supernatural virtues. He tells us he was much attracted and wrought upon by the Church service and the vesture of the minister ; and though he drifted away from all this, and his after days of hardship and captivity must have made him look with changed eyes upon the Church of England, yet traces of it all·were left with him. The cheerfulness, the homely loving-kindness, the recognition of the place in religion of mirth and of all human affections, which shine out so notably in the Second Part of the " Pilgrim's Progress ", are not in the least characteristic of the customary Puritan standpoint of·his age. Who is it who has remarked that the bell-ringing which Bunyan denied himself in Elstow steeple is heard by Christian again·and again from within the Holy City, as he nears the welcome of its shining walls ?

But all this came later. What entitled Bunyan to the name of mystic, and without doubt gave him his power and certainty in dealing with the secrets of character and the mysteries of human souls—so that he came to be known in after life as " Bishop " Bunyan—was his own tremendous spiritual struggle, his own anguish of heart and hardly-won peace. By these Bunyan makes his appeal to all who awake to the reality of these three vast factors in the drama of the spiritual life, God, Evil, and the solitary human soul.

There are, then, two periods in Bunyan's life, each represented by a great book.. There is the period of crisis, of struggle, of conversion, and its story is told in that marvellous autobiography, " Grace Abounding ". And there is the period of fruitful toil and experience, the period too of his imprisonment, of which the outward and visible sign is the " Pilgrim's Progress ".

Let us note before we go further, what was the influence that above all others came into Bunyan's life and thought, and gave him his vehicle of expression. Bunyan's lan-

guage, so vigorous, so terse, so pathetic, is the language of
the English Bible; Bunyan's thought is the thought of a
man who, like all his contemporaries, took the Bible literally. No criticism vexed them; no gloss, save indeed the
gloss of Calvinism, disturbed them; every word meant
just what it said, every word smote with a vivid freshness
on the eyes of the age that had just discovered the Book,
and every word—this most important of all—was literally
and actually inspired, written by the finger of God Himself.
It was the Bible that again and again intervened to stir up,
terrify, or comfort Bunyan in his time of tribulation. He
had one friend, good Mr. Gifford, the minister of Bedford,
who helped him as Hopeful or Faithful helped Christian,
along the way of life, and his portrait is painted for us in
the Interpreter's House in the picture of " a very grave
person " with " eyes lifted up to heaven, the law of truth
written upon his lips ", which " stood as if it pleaded with
men ". But he is only authorized to be a guide of souls
because " the best of books is in his hand ". One of Bunyan's clearest achievements was to bring the Bible into
homely and graphic play with all the circumstances—hopes,
fears, and joys of everyday life. He simply wove it into the
texture of English thought and imagination.

John Bunyan was born in 1628, the son of a travelling
tinker at Elstow, a mile from Bedford. His cottage, which
still stands by the roadside, is a poor little hovel, but the
poverty of the parents did not prevent their boy from having
a good education at the Bedford Free Grammar School.
During his boyhood he frequently rambled about with his
father over the countryside, and many wayside sights and
prospects printed themselves on his mind, to be afterwards
reproduced in his great allegory. The sloughs of the miry
tracks, the steep hill, the valley meadows, the dark corners where footpads might lurk, the fairs like that of Bedford itself, the pleasant country houses, even, maybe, at

that time, a wayside Cross or two, all these he took notice of ; it is a fascinating speculation whether, with his father, he may not have visited Little Gidding, and from his memories of the household and its ways, have sketched the House Beautiful.[1] Bunyan enlisted for a soldier in early manhood and it is odd that we do not know on which side in the Civil War he fought. But the soldier characters of Christian and of Greatheart, as well as the heroes in Emmanuel's army in the " Holy War ", may, more likely than not, have been sketched from the Captains and Corporals of Cromwell's Ironsides. It was after his return from the wars and his settling down to a married life with a wife who brought him for all dowry two pious books—the " Plain Man's Pathway to Heaven " and the " Practice of Piety " —that Bunyan's initial struggles began, the struggles that we can trace in the " Grace Abounding ".

It was a critical time for this great soul, with its keen but as yet undisciplined imagination. Professor Dowden reminds us how St. Teresa could say, " With the aid of discipline and Divine grace, twelve months hence I shall be able to do things that are now impossible ", and how this quiet certitude was a thing unknown in Bunyan's early experience. The contrast is indeed violent ; " if the most striking characteristic of ' Grace Abounding ' is its vivid realization of the unseen, hardly less impressive is the sense it leaves with us of the difficulty and uncertainty of the

[1] For Gidding was at no great distance, and the coincidences of account are at least striking enough to save the idea from mere fancifulness. Thus the maidens of the House Beautiful with their names remind one of the names of Virtues assumed by the Ferrar ladies ; the study in the House Beautiful, of the Concordance Room at Gidding ; while in the Second Part of the " Pilgrim's Progress " there is the catechizing of the children, the playing of the " virginals ", the cure of Matthew's illness, to recall the catechizing of the " Psalm-children ", the constant use of the organs, and the work of the dispensary carried on at Gidding.

writer's progress ".[1]   Here we see very impressively the lack to Bunyan of some great instructional system such as was behind Saint Teresa.   She was taught what seasons of aridity meant, and how to persevere through them ; what was real temptation and what more nearly approached morbid hallucination.   Bunyan was alone, or nearly alone : no such help was his.   The promptings of his troubled conscience and the whispers of inward temptation became to him, in some moods, like actual sounds and voices, and were taken by him as such.   One Sunday, in the middle of a game of " cat ", such a voice darted into his soul: " Wilt thou leave thy sins and go to heaven or have thy sins and go to hell ? "   A little after, while ringing the bells in Elstow tower, there came the thought, " What if the bells should fall upon thee ? " and then, " What if the steeple should fall ? "   He dared not stay, nor ring among the ringers any more, though he would go and lean against the door-post, and listen longingly to the chimes. Sometimes the words would sound behind him as he walked, " Satan hath desired to have thee ", and he would turn his head to see the speaker.   He compared his soul to a child smuggled away by a gypsy under her apron.   " Kick sometimes I did, and also shriek and cry, and yet I was as bound in my temptation as the child in the apron ".   He felt himself to have sinned against the Holy Ghost, or to be impelled at other times towards that unknown sin.   At times the Tempter would taunt him by pointing to a bush or a tree, and whisper, " Pray to these ".   Then arose the inner urging, as it seemed to him, to " sell Christ ".   We do not know precisely what meaning he attached to this temptation, but " Sell Him, sell Him, sell Him ", used to echo through his heart, and to this he would respond, " I will not, I will not, for ten thousands of worlds ".   Truly

---

[1] Dowden : *Puritan and Anglican*, pp. 241-2.

his burden—the burden of Christian—was very heavy; truly he, if any one, was plunged into the Slough of Despond, "whither the scum and filth that attend conviction of sin doth continually run", and no good friend Help was able to assist him out. What are we to think of all this? So far as we can gather, his worst offences were swearing, and playing games on Sunday. But that there was a real and terrific struggle in his soul is a fact too certain to be put aside; it was exceptional in depth and fierceness, and seemingly disproportionate to its occasion, but ought it to be slighted for the latter reason? Two of Bunyan's biographers have sought to do so; to persuade us that Bunyan's burden was not so very big after all, and that really a good deal of needless fuss was made over it. But it is possible that Macaulay and Froude were not the best or most sympathetic judges of a condition such as Bunyan's. If Bunyan's mind was ever in danger of losing its balance, it was the extremity of his inner anguish—a real anguish— that caused his trouble; for we may very well recall two facts about him. It was a mind singularly strong, shrewd, and humorous that was visited with this awful storm of spiritual anxiety. No touch of exaggeration or insanity ever marred Bunyan's after-life of steady usefulness. Then, surely, what cured him was an actual conversion, a spiritual healing—not a dose of "practical common sense", or a return to his former normality. No Worldly Wiseman could have explained his state, or helped him, nor could Mr. Civility have done him the slightest good. Mount Sinai, with its flashes and thunderings, was too close. His deliverance from temptations and trials, which, faint and spectral to a Macaulay, were to Bunyan more actual and painful than the pangs of a mortal disease, took place thus. The first ray of hope dawned on him from hearing two or three poor women at Bedford, sitting in the sun, discourse to one another of the new birth and the things of God.

Bunyan's own heart began to shake, he tells us, and now the very Bible whose denunciations and severity had increased for a time his trouble, shone out to his soul in utterances that gave him accesses of joy and peace. From cover to cover it was to him the authentic Voice of God, so that when a verse like, " Did ever any trust in God and was confounded ? " met him, he was comforted and encouraged to hope. Then a text from a sermon he heard from the Song of Solomon, " thou art fair, thou art my love ", sang itself in his heart, till " I thought I could have spoken of His love and of His mercy to the very crows that sat upon the ploughed lands before me ". There came into his hands an old ragged copy of Luther's " Epistle to the Galatians ", and this, he records, " is fit for a wounded conscience ". Then, finally, to quote his own words, " suddenly this sentence fell upon my soul, ' Thy righteousness is in heaven ', and methought withal I saw with the eyes of my soul Jesus Christ at God's right hand. There, I say, was my righteousness ; so that wherever I was, or whatever I was a-doing, God could not say of me, ' He wants my righteousness ', for that was just before Him ". Was not this, after all, Bunyan's experience of the deliverance from self which is the secret of all spiritual and eternal life, and was it very different from Augustine sitting in his garden, listening to the " Tolle, lege ", and opening his New Testament at the words, " Put ye on the Lord Jesus Christ " ?

The man who passed through this soul-shaking experience was one whose faith was henceforth firm as a rock ; and we shall have much mistaken Bunyan if we put him down as a mere enthusiast. As soon as his inward crisis was over and peace had come to him, all the strong, sensible gifts of his nature, as well as those exquisite ones of imagination and poetry, came into full and beneficent employment. The face of his portraits is that of the sturdy

Englishman of the Midlands, of a person who knows and observes the world with kindly and very definite insight. He has humour to help him as well. Moreover, as his life proved, he kept always true to the light of conscience. His visions and voices, even at their keenest pitch, were always referred to the judgement of conscience and Scripture. He was never in danger, as were some of his contemporaries, of trifling with the moral law.

His importance, as a mystic, is revealed by the " Grace Abounding ", just as his marvellous insight into human nature and his immortal poetry of soul have their expression in the " Pilgrim's Progress ". But allegory, however perfect, has no essential connexion with Mysticism, and we must deny ourselves, in consequence, any exploration of the treasures of the " Dream ". The experience of the " Grace Abounding " has been noticed in some detail because it was and is representative of a certain troubled and critical way by which souls are led to the freedom of the City of God. Not so many perhaps, as the older-fashioned Evangelicals believed, who took it almost as a standard process of the inner deliverance. But it is typical, nevertheless, of a vast and valid experience, that of Conversion, which is, in its measure, true in all ages of the Church.

We can now turn, by way of contrast, to another experience and another man, products also in chief of the rich soil and keen religious air of the Commonwealth period.

" An institution ", says Emerson, " is the lengthened shadow of a man, as Quakerism of George Fox ". And as the founder of Quakerism, Fox's name has come down in history. Yet anything further from his thoughts and desires than to start a new sect could not possibly be named. It was the bearer of a world-wide message that he believed himself to be, the re-discoverer of a forgotten but essential realm of Christian thought and experience ; and to a certain

extent he was right. The causes for which Quakerism
fought through very dark times—liberty, equality of opportunity, education, toleration—have become watchwords,
almost platitudes, of the whole Christian world. It is the
glory of the Society of Friends that its influence has been
at work behind nearly all the great social reforms of the
last hundred years. On behalf of Prison Reform and the
Abolition of Slavery the Friends were foremost, in the
cause of Peace and of healing the effects of War they have
been equally and constantly zealous, and in our own day
their efforts in the care and education of working men and
women and in such movements as that of the Adult Schools
are well known. These things are scarcely a coincidence,
and they are indeed high praise. They give a strongly
Catholic character to a Society which outwardly discards
Catholic signs and symbols ; they stamp as one of the most
beneficent of social forces a conviction and a creed that
lay the strongest possible stress on the guidance of the inner
individual light. Mysticism, not for the first time, proves
itself a direct agent for the most practical issues of life.

In George Fox we have the mystic who is seer and prophet. Again and again, in veritable powers as well as in
resemblance of methods, he reminds us of some of the old
Jewish prophets. He wandered about as they did ; he
had his visions and revelations as they had ; he was impelled, as they were impelled, to interrupt the complacent
beliefs and worship of his age, and to suffer, as they suffered,
the penalties of captivity and outlawry. And, like them,
he left a deep impression for righteousness, and he awoke
again in the minds of men belief in " the living God ", the
indwelling Christ, the real kingdom of the Holy Ghost.

In many ways Fox sought, unconsciously to himself, to
recover and restate old Catholic truths. For his revolt,
the revolt that sometimes betrayed him into harsh and very
Old Testament language concerning his opponents, was

not a revolt against the English Church. It was not by the spirit of Andrewes and Laud that he was provoked. His soul was incensed by Presbyterian hardness and formalism rather than by high sacramental doctrine, by Calvin's " Institutes " rather than by Hooker's " Ecclesiastical Polity ". He raged against the immense and windy sermons of the day, against the sermon-like prayers, against the Calvinistic tenet that a large portion of mankind was created for endless misery ; he waxed hot against the superstitious reverence for every letter of Holy Writ, even in its English translation, and against the determination to keep the Lord's Day as if it was the Jewish Sabbath unrevised by Christ. In short, he stood for the vital breath of the Word of God, and for the old Christian liberty of mind and heart, which had been nearly forgotten in that era of confident theological systems. " The Light that lighteth every man " and is " the Life of men ", this was Fox's principle and watchword.

His life, from his birth in the last year of James I, till his death just after the dawn of that Toleration in 1688 for which he had fought his good fight, was one long record of struggle and of suffering, first inward, then outward. In Fenny Drayton Church as a child, his eyes must often have rested on the beautiful motto of the Purefoy family, " Pure foy ma joye ", and it may perhaps have entered into the inmost woof of his thoughts.[1] He had a high character, as a boy, for truth : " if George says, ' Verily ', there is no altering him ", and " when boys and rude people would laugh at me, I let them alone, and went my way ". So his Journal tells us ; and this, through life, was his imperturbable habit. A word must be said about the " Journal ", from which most of the material for lives of George

[1] At least, so Professor Hodgkin in his excellent memoir, *George Fox*, very happily conjectures, p. 11.

Fox is taken. It is a curious and exact revelation of a soul, often self-conscious, always set without reservation on the one path it had chosen, but revealing, as few personal documents have done, the heights and depths of the spirit of man. That striking phrase of Cromwell's, "The dark lantern of the spirit", would be no inapt motto for the "Journal". In it we learn of his first strivings after truth, and the results, sometimes quaint indeed, of his visits to neighbouring "priests" for counsel and help. One of such advisers used what Fox had said to him for his next Sunday's sermon; another was angry because his questioner trod by mistake on his flower-beds; a third told him to smoke and sing psalms; a fourth thought he needed physic; yet another gossipped of him among his servants and neighbours. All through we try to find the nature of Fox's inner trouble. Of what burden was he seeking to be rid? We cannot help comparing his beginnings with Bunyan's. Both became masters of the spiritual life; and both took a steadfast course through Vanity Fair; and yet how different were their initial trials. There is no load of unforgiven sin with Fox, no agony of self-loathing. Fox's anxiety was rather about the sin of the world, and an inward struggle to get at a clearer notion of God's will and the meaning of the Christian Faith. When he was twenty-two, his troubles began to grow lighter, and he records what he calls "openings", such as that "being bred at Oxford or Cambridge was not enough to qualify men to be ministers of Christ", and that "God . . . did not dwell in temples made with hands". Each of these "openings" sounds to us a commonplace; neither was so in Fox's day, and there is in them an interesting intimation of the coming tenets of the community of Friends. At last there came the great turning-point of his life. He has tried all men, and found comfort from none: "when all my hopes in them and in all men were gone, so that I had nothing out-

wardly to help me, nor could I tell what to do; then, oh!
then I heard a voice which said, 'There is One, even Christ
Jesus, that can speak to thy condition', and when I heard
it, my heart did leap for joy. (He) opened the door of Light
and Life to me". It is curious and significant that this
crisis and "locution" should have been almost immediately followed by an "opening" that all Christians,
Protestant and Papist alike, were believers, and, if so, born
of God, and passed from death unto life. This was an enlightenment so much before its times that it brought him
and his followers often into the strange suspicion that they
were Roman Catholics in disguise; and, years after, William
Penn found it quite possible to be on good terms with James
II, and was indeed a favourite at his court. All these early
struggles of Fox resulted in a wonderful thought of his
Journal: "I saw the infinite Love of God. I saw also,
that there was an ocean of darkness and death; but an
infinite ocean of light and love, which flowed over the ocean
of darkness".

On the external circumstances of Fox's ministry up and
down the country, on his frequent sufferings and imprison-
ments and those of his followers—a terrible page in the
annals of religious persecution—we need not dwell. Bad
under the Commonwealth, those sufferings were intensified
tenfold in the period of the later Stuarts. Nor need we
tell again the charming romance of Swarthmoor Hall, his
courtship and marriage of Margaret Fell, which lingers like
a ray of sunlight over the "militant Quaker's" stormy
life. Some details of the man's own character and person
are, however, interesting, as shewing that he possessed in
no common degree gifts of the psychic order to which
reference has already been made, as accompanying often
the mystical sense. We come often upon records of a
"power" being felt while he was by, of hostile crowds
being tamed, of judges owning to a feeling of awe and be-

coming suddenly courteous and even deferential to their strange prisoner. He would do the bravest and apparently most foolhardy things; once, for instance, he turns into the roaring bar of a public-house and exhorts the barful of tippling squires and stable-men, leaving them silenced and in a kind of fear: in his prisons he would work upon the hearts of his jailers and fellow-prisoners; once the sheriff who arrested him was so impressed that the next day he was fain to go out into the streets and start preaching himself; in another case the jailer, like him of Philippi, and all his house, were converted. Of course, he was often terribly ill-treated and knocked about, yet in the midst of one of these riots, at Lancaster, as he was being led, handcuffed, through the midst of a raging mob—"the spirits of the people being mightily up "—he gazed earnestly upon them, and a great shout arose, "Look at his eyes! look at his eyes!" These are strong hints of something magnetic and compelling in the man's glance and presence, stronger than his personal grace and strength—for he had both—would account for. Perhaps the greatest proof we have of this is in the influence he exerted over the tremendous personality of Cromwell on the one or two occasions when they met. At their first interview Cromwell left him with tears in his eyes; and it will be remembered that it was Fox who, a few days before the Protector's end, met him riding into Hampton Court at the head of his guards, and felt " a waft of death go forth against him ". A man with the faculty of such presentiments would be capable of evoking awe.

But now, what were Fox's doctrines, that gave him no rest till they were proclaimed, and were his legacy to the Society [1] he formed?

---

[1] The Society of Friends gained the more familiar, and not now misliked, name of " Quakers " from Mr. Justice Bennett of Derby,

First, the Doctrine of the Inner Light. Christ not only died for all, but, according to Fox, "enlightened all men and women with His divine and saving light", and "none could be a true believer but who also believed in it". But particular stress must be laid on his claim to insight into truth by Christ's "immediate spirit and power" which also gave him revelations as to special duties and missions, intimations always implicitly obeyed. Dr. Hodgkin remarks that "though the ' Inward Light ' is the main article of Fox's preachings, many other things, the disuse of sacraments, the abandonment of a liturgy, silent worship, unpaid ministry, are all in his mind necessary consequences of that doctrine ".[1]

The second crucial part of Fox's teaching was his insistence on personal holiness, as against the Calvinism of the day which always had a tendency to slide into Antinomianism, and also against the Arminian school which, although it produced saintly men, yet exacted little by way of necessity. It is easy to see how these two great doctrines of the Inner Light and Christian holiness, so congenial to the spirit of Mysticism, if exaggerated as—not Fox himself, but—some of the first Quakers exaggerated them, might lead to the errors of a belief in personal Inspiration and of Perfectionism. It was not, however, for supposed errors such as these that the Society of Friends suffered its first and fiercest trials. The immediate causes of conflict with the authorities were their refusal of military service, which brought them into suspicion of disloyalty to whatever régime was in power, their refusal to take the oath in courts

who tried some of its members, and affixed this title to them " because they bade him tremble at the word of the Lord ".

[1] Hodgkin, *George Fox*, p. 30. It may be remarked, however, that silent worship was in part the outcome of an innocent attempt, during the later Caroline persecution, to evade the penalties of the Conventicle Act attached to preaching and public prayer.

of law, in an age when, witness the Test Act, the oath was accounted of extraordinary importance, and the refusal of the ordinary deference of the doffing of the hat. But the great Quaker principles remained undimmed when the clouds of misunderstanding engendered partly by their undue stress on lesser external points and partly by the acrimonious intolerance of the times had passed away; and these principles constituted a vital reinforcement to the light of religion, sometimes low-burning enough in the England of the seventeenth and eighteenth centuries.

Before closing this chapter, it is necessary to add one or two words on a few other exponents of the vast mystical movement which swayed men's minds in the mid-seventeenth century, and produced in every body and sect those " Seekers " whom Cromwell once so highly praised, and who in some ways were analogous in principle, though not in point of organization, to the " Friends of God " of an earlier date.[1] Gerrard Winstanley, who took so large a share in the strange " Digger " movement of the Commonwealth period, was one of these. His central idea, like Fox's, was that of the Divine Light in the soul; Christ is that Light and Christ's life in the heart is the true Resurrection; he was a Quietist in his recommendation that men " wait with a quiet silence upon the Lord till He break forth within their hearts ", but he was no Quietist in the sense that he in any way discounted activity. " Action ", he says, " is the life of all, and if thou dost no act thou dost nothing ".[2]

---

[1] " There were almost certainly Seekers among all the religious societies of the time ". Rufus Jones, *Studies in Mystical Religion*, p. 452, where also Penn's words are quoted : " as doves without their mates ; seeking their beloved, but could not find Him (as their souls desired to know Him) whom their souls loved above their chiefest joy " (*Preface to Fox's Journal*).

[2] Quoted from L. H. Berens, *The Digger Movement*, pp. 65 and

Another thinker of some note was John Saltmarsh, who became, while rector of Brasted in Kent, a Parliamentary Army Chaplain. His chief book, "Sparkles of Glory", evinces that preoccupation with the idea of God as Light which was perhaps the special contribution to religious thought of his age. Though he knows that " the candle of the Lord cannot shine anywhere with more snuff than in " him, yet " the Lord hath lighted it ". His main teaching is the progressive revelation of God to man : first by external law, ceremony and symbol ; then by the presence in flesh of Immanuel ; lastly (it sounds like an echo of Joachim of Floris) " by the naked unveiling of Himself in Spirit ". The way to see the truth clearly, he teaches, is to live in its power, to have Christ's life in us and so to " incarnate Him over again ". This is another, probably unconscious, repetition of a very old mystical doctrine.

William Dell, at one time Master of Caius College, Cambridge, and afterwards ejected from his Bedfordshire living in 1662, is the last exponent of mystical thought of whom we may take account before passing on to consider the life of the religious genius whose teaching more or less lay behind and influenced all the " prophets " of the Inward Light of this period, not even excepting Fox himself. Dell's career had been a changeful one. He started as a Churchman of such pronounced views as to act for some time as secretary to Archbishop Laud. About the time of the Archbishop's execution, however, he is found preaching in the Parliamentary army, and to his powers of exposition Baxter was singularly uncomplimentary. His mind was, however, then and for some little time after, undergoing a process of change, and soon he, too, is found uttering the message of the indwelling Christ, Word, Light and Life. There is one great insistent note of all true Mysticism which

113. In this interesting account of Winstanley he is credited with supplying a good deal of the motive force behind the founders of Quakerism.

he sounds with power and beauty—the note of an Experience. " Religion ", to be true, " changes the very nature of men. . . finds men birds of prey, and makes them doves ; it finds them flesh, it makes them spirit ; it finds them sin, it makes them righteousness ".

CHAPTER XIII

Behmen and Law

WE must now retrace our steps some little way in point of time in order to consider the life and teaching of the remarkable thinker whose speculations were at the back of very much of the English seventeenth century Mysticism described in the last two chapters. The name of Jacob Böhme (or Behmen, as he is perhaps more commonly called), the self-taught shoemaker of Görlitz, in Lusatia, is one of extraordinary interest. We may premise by saying that without doubt the Cambridge Platonists, as well as men like Winstanley and Fox, were deeply indebted to him. Behmen's expressions, for instance, as to the antithesis of Light and Darkness were reflected over and over again in their writings. But, besides this, Behmen summed up in his system an extraordinary amount of obscure, but, as he developed it, significant teaching which had gone before him, and he left a legacy of pregnant thought which has never since been fully exhausted. His life may be very briefly told. He was born in 1575, and as a boy was sent out to tend the cattle in the fields. Like Blake afterwards, he was a visionary from very early years. He had a good practical schooling, and was then apprenticed to a shoemaker, and it was as a humble shoemaker and glover that he lived his life. In early manhood, he received one day a mysterious warning from a chance customer that he was destined to become great in spiritual things, and

also to suffer persecution. He married in 1594 and had
four children, and in all ways behaved as an admirable husband and father. Like Fox and Bunyan, he had, to begin
with, his period of deep melancholy, but his sorrow was of
the nature of Fox's rather than of Bunyan's, and arose from
the insoluble mystery of life, and the problems of sin and
misery he saw around him. This period was succeeded
by three successive and, as far as it is possible to judge,
authentic Ecstasies, possessing the true notes of mystical
experience. That is to say, there was no organic disturbance, the experiences were transitory, indescribable, and
yet to the utmost degree authoritative, and resulted in a
conviction of the underlying One-ness or harmony of all
things in God. The authoritativeness of his visions induced
Behmen to begin the writing of his books, starting with the
" Aurora ", and numbering thirty in all. Of these, " The
Three Principles ", " The Threefold Life of Man ", " Signatura Rerum ", and " Mysterium Magnum " are the most
famous. But they brought Behmen into life-long trouble.
A nobleman, Carl von Endern, saw the " Aurora " and had
some copies made of it. Unfortunately, Richter, the
Lutheran pastor of Görlitz, a narrow-minded bigot, got
hold of one of these, and not only held up Behmen to scorn
from his pulpit but prevailed on the Town Council to pro-
hibit him from any work but that of " sticking to his last ".
Behmen actually restrained his pen for seven years, but
the inward pressure became too great, and he then dared
all and wrote on till the year of his death, 1624. He was
threatened with death at the stake, and was forced finally
to flee from Görlitz to Dresden, whence he returned only to
die. On the other hand, persecution produced its inevitable
effect of directing attention from far and wide to his teaching. This attention was of the most varied kind. There
were those, then and afterwards, who were frankly and sometimes boisterously impatient with what they read. Henry

More, the Platonist, believed indeed that Behmen's " mind was devoutly united to the Head of the Church, the Crucified Jesus . . . but is to be reckoned in the number of those whose imaginative faculty has the pre-eminence above the rational ".   But Bishop Warburton roundly declared, " Behmen's works would disgrace Bedlam at full moon ", and the saintly John Wesley pronounced them " sublime nonsense, inimitable bombast, fustian not to be paralleled ".   In our own day, Mr. Sharpe concludes that " with true Mysticism (Behmen) has no affinities whatever ".[1]   On the other hand, there is Sir Isaac Newton, shutting himself up for three months to study Behmen ; [2] there is the fact already noticed of his great influence amongst men of saintly thought in England ;   there were his two eminent disciples, Saint Martin in France, and our own William Law, whose mysticism was a devoted advocacy of Behmen's chief principles, while in more modern days Hegel praised him and Franz Baader lectured on him.   The number indeed, of those with whom his is a name familiar and revered is, it may be safely said, steadily increasing.

Why, we may ask, this divergency of opinion ?   Partly it is due to Behmen's actual teaching, and partly to his mode of expressing himself.   To take the latter point first, More was right enough in what he said of Behmen's imagination, and, in Dr. Inge's words, " the scholars who gathered round him supplied him with philosophical terms, which he forthwith either personified—for instance, the word ' Idea ' called forth the image of a beautiful maiden—or used in a sense of his own.   The study of Paracelsus obscured his style still more, filling his treatises with a bewildering mix-

---

[1] A. B. Sharpe, *op. cit.* p. 170.   He praises, however, Behmen's " meditative mind ", " constantly fixed on the idea of God ", and his " many sane and devout reflections ".

[2] Overton : *Life of William Law*, p. 188.

ture of theosophy and chemistry. The result is certainly that much of his work is almost unreadable : the nuggets of gold have to be dug out of a bed of rugged stone ".[1]

But the difficulty about Behmen extends far beyond his use of words, beyond even the fact that his imaginative force caused him to move from a purely subjective type of Mysticism to Symbolism, and a very difficult Symbolism, too. The truth is that the mystical student must always discard a good deal of Behmen, owing to the fact that he offers us by turns true Mysticism and its very questionable by-product, Theosophy. Behmen was a religious genius, but as life went on he took to himself masters whose guidance was sometimes beneficent, and sometimes the reverse. Weigel was one of his masters, and Weigel's teaching of the value of nature-study as part of the self-education of the soul—" you become that which you have learned "—was of the utmost importance. But, as we saw above, Paracelsus was another of his guides, and while to Paracelsus he owed two of the most important of his mystical principles, to him also was due that infusion of Theosophy into Behmen's teaching which alienated and still alienates many of his readers.[2] For Theosophy is the extension or exaggeration of the intuitions of Mysticism concerning the Divine, and their erection into systems possessing no other validity than those of a powerful imagination and the perception of real or supposed analogies between the worlds of nature and of grace, of the outward and the inward. Moreover, in all theosophies as such there is either discordance or a tendency to disregard the *magisterium* of the Church. This was seen markedly, as well as the lack of the mystical

[1] Inge, *op. cit.* p. 278.
[2] Was it with conscious reference to Behmen's connexion with Paracelsus that Wesley used the term " bombast " derived, of course, from the second name of that really remarkable man— Bombastes ?

authoritativeness, that authoritativeness which is identical with the leap of response in the human soul to its message, in the case of the early Gnostics. In the case of Behmen the true mystic and the theosophist are blended, so blended that his doctrine will always possess a power and an appeal which will again be for ever half spoiled by the acquired verbiage and the over-systematizing with which he drapes them.

Let us put on one side, therefore, interesting in some respects as they are, such speculations of Behmen's as his *Quellgeister* or Fountain-spirits, the seven forms of life of the Eternal Nature, or *Mysterium Magnum*, a term derived from Paracelsus.[1] What is interesting about these speculations is that, although theosophy, they are original theosophy. The term *Mysterium Magnum* is borrowed, but not its meaning. Paracelsus understood by it primeval Chaos, out of which he supposed darkness and light, hell and heaven, somehow to have proceeded ; Behmen's *Mysterium Magnum* is rather the Divine Eternal Nature, correspondent to His Will, His inward Being, His Wisdom. Again, the coincidence between Behmen's seven *Quellgeister* and Basilides' seven intellectual and moral impersonations (the first rank of his successive emanations) and Saturninus' seven astral spirits (lowest of his series and bordering on matter) is curious, but it is nothing more than a coincidence. Behmen could have known little, if anything, of the Gnostics, and with him there was no gulf, as with them, to be bridged between the supreme Spirit and Matter. " With him, the thought becomes the act of God. Matter is not a foreign, inert substance . . . the material universe exhibits, incorporate, these very attributes which constitute

---

[1] See Vaughan : *Hours with the Mystics*, bk. viii. ch. 8, for a description of these Qualities, the Astringent, the Expansive, the Bitter, the Qualities of Fire, Love, Sound, and Corporeity, or operative manifestation.

the Divine glory. Nature is not merely of, but out of, God ".[1]

The two great principles of mystical thought, which Behmen emphasized, and of one of which he may be almost called the prophet, belong respectively to the spheres of practical spiritual life and of religious philosophy.

(a) From the very first he was convinced of the doctrine dear to so many mystics, that man himself is the microcosm of the Universe and its processes. This doctrine he pushed to the extent of claiming a sort of personal inspiration for his teaching, much of which was indeed original, but some, especially in later life, tinged, as we have seen, by alien and quite decipherable influences. Thus, " I saw ", he says, " the Being of all Beings, the Byss (Grund) and the Abyss; also, the birth of the Holy Trinity; the origin and primal state of the world and of all creatures. I saw in myself the three worlds—The Divine angelic or para-disiacal world; the dark world, as the original of Nature; . . . and this external visible world, as a substance spoken forth out of the two spiritual worlds. . . . In my inward man I saw it well, . . it opened itself within me, like a growing plant . . . whatsoever I could bring into outward-ness, that I wrote down ".[2] But of inestimable value was the consequent emphasis on the doctrine that the atonement of Christ is no forensic transaction outside us, but a living process within us. We have met with this doctrine before amongst the pre-Reformation German mystics; it was nobly caught up by the older Protestant mystics,[3] of whom

---

[1] Vaughan, *op. cit.* bk. viii. ch. 8. Note.

[2] Vaughan : *op. cit.*, bk. viii. ch. 6.

[3] Notably by Valentine Weigel. " Thou canst have no help ", he says, " from outside. That must come from the Christ within thee. . . . True faith is the life of Christ in us : it is being baptized with Him, suffering, dying, and rising again with Him ". See Inge, *Studies of English Mystics,* p. 140.

Behmen was chief. " If this said sacrifice is to avail for
me ", he writes, " it must be wrought in me. The Father
must beget his Son in my desire of faith, that my faith's
hunger may apprehend Him in His word of promise. Then
I put Him on, in His entire process of justification in my
inward ground . . . I am inwardly dead, and He is my
life ! " In his " Supersensual Life " he counsels " the disciple ", who holds colloquy with " the master ", to turn
away all things that " please and entertain and feed " the
separated will, and so, by way of the Cross, to rediscover
within the true self " what was before nature and creature " ; and much of the doctrine of the Inward Light, dear
to Winstanley and Fox, comes into this discourse.[1]

(b) The other great doctrine of which Behmen was the
modern foster-father amongst mystics is the law of Antithesis as being at the root of all things. He caught up
Heraclitus' dictum, " Strife is the father of everything ",
and echoed it in his, " In Yes and No all things do consist ".
On earth this is evident enough. There could be no knowledge of pleasure without pain, of rest without fatigue, of
heat without cold, of light without darkness. But then
Behmen believed that the spiritual world is the counterpart
of the natural, nay, that it is, as Goethe expressed it, " the
living garment of God ". There is no *Qual* (determination,
quality) without *Quaal* (suffering). Is this law of contrariness then discoverable within the Divine Nature also ?
Behmen boldly answered, Yes. Attraction and Diffusion
are felt everywhere in their ceaseless play, even in the hidden
life of the Godhead. Hence the desire for Self-manifestation
arises in the Abyss of the Pure Will, " in which all things
lie unexpressed ", and which he identified as God the Father.
But nothing can become manifest in the world of existence

[1] The discourse in question has been, with the *Signatura Rerum*,
recently published in Messrs. J. M. Dent's " Everyman's Library ".
Cf. Rufus Jones: *Studies in Mystical Religion*, p. 495.

without contrariness. Hence the Abysmal Will divided
itself, in Its desire for self-expression, and the Godhead
became Darkness. But when the Father begot within
Himself the Son, the Eternal Light, the antithesis of the
Divine Darkness arose. The bond of mutual life between
the Father and the Son is the Holy Spirit, Who is thus
Synthesis, and in Him the archetypes of creation take their
beginning. This tenet of Thesis, Antithesis, and Synthesis
is again exemplified in Body, Soul, and Spirit : and the life
of God Himself is the eternal resolution of darkness into
light, wrath into love, discord into harmony. " Love sub-
mits to the fire of wrath ", is one of Behmen's sayings, " that
it may be a fire of love ".

It is impossible to discuss Behmen's teaching with regard
to the problem of evil without passing the limits we have
set ourselves and trespassing from the sphere of his true
mysticism to that of his theosophy.[1] It must be sufficient
to say that in general his thought is that evil directly arises
whenever any sentient being chooses his own self—the
" centrum naturae "—as his spring of action instead of the
God centre. This, said Behmen, was what Lucifer deliberately did. Thereby the first or dark ternary of *Quellgeister*
—the reader is referred to the note below—became operative
in him, as in all such, unillumined and unmitigated by the

---

[1] This term had a special meaning with Behmen. For in his
speculations the Will in the Godhead conjoined with the Eternal
Wisdom (Theo-Sophia) were Father and Mother of the Divine
creative powers. This Will and this Wisdom become, in Nature,
Force and Space, which beget Motion. Now in Nature are found
the Seven Qualities before mentioned, and the first " ternary " of
these (corresponding to the " salt ", the " sulphur ", and the " mer-
cury " of Paracelsus), is the dark ternary, just as the last three
constitute the bright ternary. Midway is the Quality of Fire, or
the Lightning-flash of the Spirit, which for ever transforms the
dark, or inharmonious qualities, ending their strife, and bringing
light and harmony.

mild Fire of the Word, the fourth Quality. So he became subject to the wrath of God only, that " wrath which has existed from all eternity, though not as wrath, but as fire latent in a tree or stone, until it is aroused ".

It is difficult to compress the system of Behmen or to offer it in any worthy analysis, in a short space. Still harder is it to separate that in his thought which is, and has been proved to be, of permanent worth, from the visions of one who, holy and humble man of heart as he was, certainly used self-hypnotization at times, gazing fixedly, for instance, at the ray of light through a key-hole until he became unconscious of the external world. In spite of such methods, and of some—in the real sense of the phrase—" bombastic " extravagancies, his teaching gives him a place in the great line of German thought which culminated in Schelling and Hegel, and also, since he lays stress on Will as the constitutive principle in the world, makes him a forerunner of Schopenhauer. There is, too, the doctrine of the *unio mystica* which he brings, as St. Paul brought it, into closest touch with his Christology ; and his insistence on the analogy between the visible and invisible world. Then, also, there is his great re-discovery of the law of Antithesis. All these justify his claim to the title of his own time, " the Teutonic philosopher ", and are nothing short of marvellous as emanating from the self-taught Lusatian shoemaker.

His best selective interpreter for English minds is William Law, the Non-juror. Law, until lately, was chiefly known as the author of the " Serious Call to a Devout and Holy Life ", but the revival of interest of late in Mysticism and the mystics have made many aware that this powerful little work with its brilliant character-sketching, the treatise " which was the first occasion of " Samuel Johnson's " thinking in earnest ", and called forth eulogies from such very different judges as John Wesley and Edward Gibbon, is not the sole, or even the chief claim that Law makes on our

attention and admiration. The " Serious Call " was written
during the period when Law was tutor to Edward Gibbon,
father of the historian, with whom, either at Cambridge or
in his house at Putney, a *salon* of religion and letters, he
spent the years between 1727 and 1739. In 1740 he returned
to his birthplace, King's Cliffe, in Northamptonshire, where
he lived with two friends, Mrs. Hutcheson and Miss Hester
Gibbon, who placed themselves under his religious direction,
till his death in 1761, at the age of seventy-five. His peaceful and holy life, and that of his companions, was only
flawed by an absolutely indiscriminate charity. Nine-
tenths of their joint income was devoted to that end, and
all the vagrants of the country-side were attracted to the
unfortunate village of their residence.

It was said that the " Serious Call " is not Law's chief
claim on our attention. For it is in no sense a mystical
work. It is an expansion, witty, and shrewd, and solemn
by turns, and always intensely in earnest, of the warning
of the Lord, " Ye cannot serve God and Mammon ". It
was in another mood that Law wrote his later treatises,
" The Spirit of Love ", " the Spirit of Prayer ", " The Way
to Divine Knowledge ".[1] In the meantime had come the
great crisis of his life, his discovery on a bookstall of some
writings of Behmen. These " spoke to his condition ",
and he became thenceforth, whilst retaining his loyalty to
the system of the English Prayerbook, the eager disciple
of Behmen, and his interpreter to the England of his
day.

It was by use of Behmen's insistence on a redemption in
us if it is to be for us, that Law saw he could counteract
the cold and formal Deism of his day, the Deism which
viewed God as a vast Being distinct from His creation,

---

[1] For a reproduction of these and other of his writings somewhat
abridged, see *The Liberal and Mystical Writings of William Law*,
edited by William Scott Palmer.

vast indeed, yet a Being amongst beings.   His steady teaching of the Immanence of God has two sides to it.

(a) On one side it concerns Nature. " Everything in temporal Nature is descended out of that which is eternal, and stands as a palpable visible outbirth from it " ; yes, but, again, " in Eternal Nature, or the Kingdom of Heaven, materiality stands in life and light ; it is the Light's glorious Body, or that garment wherewith light is clothed ".   And yet again ; " Everything, by its form and condition, speaks so much of God ; and God, in everything, speaks and manifests so much of Himself ".[1]   Bishop Warburton accused Law of discipleship to Spinoza, but Law will have none of that " gross confounding of God and Nature " which he held to be Spinozism.   In other words, he believed in God's Transcendence, as well as His Immanence, and fought Deism and Pantheism alike.

(b) The other significant side of Law's teaching is that which concerns man. " He sees that man . . . is the theatre of real events . . . and in matters of religion only those things which happen *in* a man happen *for* him.   A Christ that is not in him cannot be for him ".[2]   It is interesting to notice the process by which Law arrived at this conclusion. " If Christ was to raise a new life like His own in every man, then every man must have had originally in the inmost spirit of his life a seed of Christ, or Christ as a seed of heaven, lying there in a state of insensibility. . . . The Word of God is the hidden treasure of every human soul, immured under flesh and blood, till as a day-star it arises in our hearts ".[3]   This is the old doctrine of the Synteresis or Divine Spark in the soul, taught by Eckhart and the German medieval mystics.   Therefore, " a bare,

---

[1] *An Appeal to all who Doubt* (*Liberal and Mystical Writings of William Law*), pp. 51, 52.

[2] *Ib.* Preface, p. 5.

[3] Quoted from Inge : *Christian Mysticism*, pp. 282–3.

historical, and superficial faith cannot save the soul ",
there is needed " a real strong hunger which lays hold on
Christ, and causes the arising of a new birth or nature in
the very essence of ' man's being '. An inward Saviour
. . . raising His own Divine birth in the human soul, has
such a fitness in it as must make every sober man with open
arms ready and willing to receive such a salvation ".[1]
Nevertheless, such doctrine must have sounded strange
enough in the " sober " ears of the eighteenth century. In
one point Law appears to depart somewhat from the teaching of his beloved master, Behmen, when he declares there
is no " wrath ", or " dark fire " in the Divine Being, but
only in us, and that " the precious Blood of His Son was
not poured out to pacify Himself, Who in Himself had no
nature towards man but love, but it was poured out to
quench the wrath and fire of the fallen soul ".

Behmen had more disciples than one, in addition to an
indirect and diffused influence which, great even in his own
day, has been steadily growing since. In our own country
William Blake, in Germany, Eckhartshausen, author of
" The Cloud upon the Sanctuary ", in France, the troubled
Transcendentalist, Saint Martin, owned themselves his disciples. A few words in especial must be said about Blake.
We have long passed the time when even such tempered
harshness of criticism as—of all people's—Coventry Patmore's [2] on his art and poetry can pass muster. Blake is
a great deal more to us than a craftsman whose art it is—
to modify a little Fuseli's phrase—" good to steal from ".
He is an acknowledged seer and mystic, born out of due
time, and most oddly and incongruously out of place at the
end of the Georgian era. What was his method, and what
was his message ? These are dangerous questions to answer

[1] William Law : *The Grounds and Reasons of Christian Regenera-
tion.*

[2] Patmore : *Principle in Art, etc.,* xv.

within a few sentences. But if one views a collection of Blake's drawings one gets a certain clue at once. They have, to the first rapid glance, an appearance of straightforward childishness ; they are naïve to a fault in their attempts—which are sometimes, like the poems, of exquisite beauty, and sometimes confess to a curious clumsiness—to express somehow, anyhow, what their creator had in mind. Only he had a great deal in mind, and his medium was inadequate. Mostly we recognize that, nowadays, and we see that Blake's—to the world—weird gift was the gospel quality of childlikeness. Childlike he remained through life ; the abruptness and definiteness of vision and expression of this " God-intoxicated " man were alike those of a child. Everybody knows and can smile over certain anecdotes of the awkward or alarming manifestations of these qualities ; but no one who takes up Blake's poems can fail to be arrested by the loveliness of some of the " Songs of Innocence ", or by such lines in his more tangled poems as,

' O Forgiveness, O Pity and Compassion ! If I were pure I should never
Have known thee ",[1]

which, as Miss Underhill remarks, is the echo of the old Catholic cry, " O felix culpa ! ", or by the lines,

" If God dieth not for man, and giveth not Himself
Eternally for Man, Man could not exist, for Man is Love
As God is Love. Every kindness to another is a little death
In the Divine Image. . . ."[2]

Blake's method then is childlike, from that first tremendous vision of God, which he saw as a child, and told with a child's terrible directness. His message was partly caught from Behmen, and partly from Swedenborg, whom he also studied. It is that of Analogy or Correspondence.

---

[1] *Jerusalem*, lxi. 47. See E. Underhill : *Mysticism*, p. 128.
[2] *Jerusalem*, xcv. 25.

" Correspondence is the central idea of Swedenborg's system. Everything visible has belonging to it an appropriate spiritual reality ".[1] Behmen believed also that this world is a parable of the unseen, and that in certain moments of intuition he could interpret the " Signatura Rerum ". But Swedenborg is on much more matter-of-fact ground. He details actual experiences, journeys, conversations, sights and sounds in the world beyond, in a calm, methodical manner. We are far indeed from a Mysticism which rejected all figures and shapes of the Divine Order and Vision. And while there are beautiful and suggestive thoughts in his system,—such as his exaltation of the Divine Humanity as the pattern of the universe—his is rather a commonplace, homely heaven. But in the Doctrine of Correspondence, common to Behmen and Swedenborg, and of which the New Testament contains hints, there was enough to inspire Blake and other poets after him with some of their noblest thoughts. Tennyson's " Flower in the crannied wall " comes at once of course to mind, but Blake was before him seeing " a world in a grain of sand, and Eternity in an hour ", or remarking sadly, " The tree which moves some to tears of joy is in the Eyes of others only a green thing that stands in the Way ", or finding in the sun no mere yellow disc but a sphere wherein the worship of the threefold " Sanctus " was offered daily in the very sight of the unheeding earth. And all because his " doors of perception are cleansed " so that " everything appeared as it *is*, infinite ".

[1] Vaughan : *Hours with the Mystics*, bk. xii. ch. i. seq.

CHAPTER XIV

Modern Mysticism

IN estimating the mystical elements in religion which
have been at work during the last century, and their
influence in the religious thought of to-day, we shall do
well first to recall the limits of our subject. It is with
Mysticism in] Christianity that we are concerned, and[Mysti-
cism has never been, and is not to-day, confined to Christianity. It has been at the root of any and every religion
worthy of the name, in its original and indefectible " feeling
after God, if haply it may find Him ". In ancient days it
inspired, as we saw, the doctrines of Plotinus and his school,
whose teaching we were bound to examine, because of its
vast influence on the Christian Faith; it made Mohammedanism the amazing force it was; [1] Oriental sects as far
sundered as the Kabbalists and the Sufis; thinkers poles
apart like Philo, Spinoza, and Omar Khayyam responded
to different parts of its message. So, in our own time,
Unitarians such as Longfellow, who has sudden and exquisite touches of mystical thought [2] amidst his throng of
fatally fluent verses; Emerson, with his revival of the old

---

[1] " Mohammed's sense of the ' terror of the Lord ' was so intense
that his hair whitened before its time; yet the Arabs called him
' the lover of his Maker ' ".—*Church Times*, Aug. 18, 1911.

[2] See, e.g., his six noble sonnets on the " Divina Commedia ",
and certain passages of the " Golden Legend ", which in itself is
a curiously vivid " vision " of the Middle Ages, if nothing else.

doctrine of " deification ",[1] and the great mystic, Maeterlinck, who at least stands outside of, or indifferent to,
orthodox Christianity, are examples of the same fact.
Mysticism found for itself in Christianity a field of the
richest and most fruitful soil ; but not its only field.   Never-
theless] to that field we are bound here to confine our
attention.

But again, although Mysticism has been the inspiration
of all that, as religion, bears the intimate tests of life, and
can be truly termed religion, yet, when men have tried to
mould its intuitions into a system, " to crystallize it ", as
the current phrase goes, into a habitual process, the breath
of life departs from it.   " Explain it how we may, there
would seem to be something transient and incapable of
passing into *institutions* in the higher action of God's Spirit
in history ".[2]   It is true that the traditional grades of
mystical ascent—of the Scala Perfectionis—are preserved
within the Roman Catholic Communion, but it is no less
strange than true that just when the mystical scheme had
been satisfactorily settled and its unalterable plan laid down,
the convulsion of the Reformation took place, and once
more freed half the religious minds in Europe from a too
exact observance of this chart of the inward progress, useful as in many respects such a chart will always be.   It is
also true that even in the Roman Communion individual
mystics have felt themselves imperatively freed from a rigid
tracing of the access of their predecessors to the *Unio
Mystica.*

So it has been also with other movements, or with movements within other religious communions.   The past cen-

---

[1] In excess, of course, as in the well-known sentences, " I become
a transparent eye-ball. I am nothing. I see all. The currents
of the universal Being circulate through me. I am part of God ".

[2] Upton and Drummond : *Life and Letters of James Martineau,*
vol. i. p. 431.

tury was prolific of such movements, and without doubt, an element of true Mysticism is discoverable within most of them. There was 'in the English Church that great system of faith and of the inner life known as Evangelicalism. This in its transactional and rather forensic doctrine of the " Scheme of Salvation " through Christ, involving as it did the notion of a God always external although " reconciled ", was antagonistic to Mysticism ; nevertheless it had affinities on one side with Mysticism in its insistence on the surrender of the self into the entire hold and power of Another. It is interesting to trace the development of the Evangelical school of thought to the earlier Evangelicalism of the Wesleys and Whitefield in the eighteenth century, which in turn derived in part from the Pietistic Movement in Germany and notably from the " Unitas Fratrum ", or Moravian Brethren,[1] interesting, not only because the alliance between the Moravian Church and the Evangelicals is still in force, but because Count Zinzendorf and his followers did communicate a feature of inner experience of momentous and winning power, the perpetual soul vision, for it was little less, as all their hymns and ritual testify, of the Crucified Saviour. Between the intensity of gaze on the Lord's Passion of the medieval mystic Julian of Norwich, and of Zinzendorf, Böhler, and Cennick there is little to choose ; and this apprehension of the meaning of the Cross resulted, as in the case of Bunyan, Fox—though to his " condition " Jesus Christ spoke with somewhat different message—and the Wesleys, in a fiery enthusiasm of service. In fact, the " practical mystic ", so far as the impulse to evangelization goes, has been a post-Reformation product

[1] " The part the Moravians played in the Evangelism of England in the eighteenth century has never yet been fully chronicled . . . the actual extent of the work was astonishing . . . a spiritual factor of unmistakable influence and power." Bishop Hassé : *The Moravians*, p. 49.

of spiritual experience. Be it still remembered that the experience in question, though vivid, is partial. It is a crisis, a first step, of infinite importance, but by itself it does not constitute the message of Mysticism. It is worth while to note one or two of its developments however. Later Evangelicalism was much influenced, we might perhaps say, found a revival, through the extraordinary wave of spiritual emotion that swept across the country in the " seventies " of last century through the ministry of Messrs. Moody and Sankey. This movement was remarkable in many ways. It came from America, and is almost directly traceable to the strong awakening to " unseen things above " which the awful realities of life and death brought about in the vast encampments of the Northern and Southern armies during the heroic conflict of the Civil War.[1] The result of the movement was seen chiefly in a quickening of the perception of Christ, not only as Crucified, but as a living, personal Companion and Friend. Once more the " Salve Caput cruentatum ! " of the Crusaders turned to St. Bernard's, " Jesu, dulcis memoria ". A new chapter yet in the history of Evangelicalism opened with the founding of the Keswick Convention, and the dissemination of its distinctive teaching of the indwelling and sanctifying Christ, another instance of how doctrines dear to Mysticism have a way of re-asserting themselves from time to time with inexhaustible vitality. A long-remembered event at one of these Conventions was the visit and preaching of Mr. Andrew Murray, whose spiritual writings, full of the message of the Inward Christ, had for several years exercised a profound influence both in and beyond Evangelical circles.

---

[1] It will be remembered that some of the melodies to the " Revival " hymns of the time were originally battle-songs, or plaintive slave-songs. One is reminded of some words of Mr. Maurice Baring : " War is perhaps to man what motherhood is to woman, a burden, a source of untold suffering, and yet a glory ".

It may be asked whether, in the opposite section of English Church thought, the Oxford Movement was not essentially mystical in its conceptions and aims. At first sight, there is much to favour such a view. The stress laid on symbolism in outward rite and ceremony, the presence of poets such as Keble and Isaac Williams in its ranks, the revival, by scholars like Neale, of the so-called " mystical " method of interpretation of the Older Scriptures, would all seem to urge an affirmative answer. Yet, on a closer survey, the conclusion must be arrived at that the Tractarian Movement was really inimical to the true spirit of Mysticism. A renewal of the desire for outward accessories of worship was partly fostered by the Romanticist and medieval taste engendered by the work of Scott and his school ; the older Tractarians were, personally, by no means addicted to outward ceremonial as such, and the swift growth of this ceremonial, which was due to the later Ritualists, rather than the Tractarians, has been largely of a haphazard nature, and still lacks, in the Church as a whole, that regulating sanction, uniformity, and unvarying significance which alone give to outward symbolism a teaching value. The guiding principle of Tractarians and Ritualists alike has been that of a stern and unquestioning submission of belief, will, and heart to the authoritative decrees of an " Ecclesia docens ". This principle is one by no means favourable to the ἦθος of Mysticism which, in the Universal Church, has always acted as a balancing force to it, and, whilst on its guard against Antinomianism, has instinctively fought for freedom in the things of the spirit. Moreover, the " advanced High Churchmen " (it is impossible to avoid the use of some such phrase) have failed to find their " Ecclesia docens ", at least, in regard to the points of doctrine they hold most dear, and so have fallen back on the Medieval Church for a good part of their moral support, being, so far, worse off than strict Roman Catholics, who have at least a living voice and a present discipline behind them.

John Keble, of course, belongs to a different category. Thoroughly faithful to an interpretation of the Church's rubrics and ordinances which had a tradition, unbroken from the Reformation, to support it, he was a nature-mystic as well. The watchword of all his mysticism is contained in the well-known verse for Septuagesima Sunday :—

> " Two worlds are ours ; 'tis only sin
>   Forbids us to descry
> The mystic heaven and earth within,
>   Plain as the sea and sky " :

and, catching up the pen which had fallen from George Herbert's wasted fingers in Bemerton Parsonage two centuries before, this saintly parish priest traced, like him, lovingly and reverently, for all who would hear, the Divine likeness and Divine truths as they were shadowed forth for him in the fair world around. It would be too much to say that his Mysticism was not " cribb'd, cabin'd, and confined " by the necessities of the doctrinal beliefs to which he felt himself pledged, but if, as surely is the fact, Maeterlinck's saying is true, " Une oeuvre ne vieillit qu'en proportion de son antimysticisme ", then the acceptance and study of Keble's " Christian Year " by religious people of all shades of conviction since his day is some proof of a gift which he shared with Augustine, with à Kempis, and with Bunyan.

Yet we feel that the true touch of mystical teaching has been handed on in England by other agency than that of such organized movements as those just considered, or than even such consecrated powers of vision and expression as those of a Keble. In Keble we miss just what the highest mysticism inevitably gives, if only in flashes. Over his work rests such a level, subdued, afternoon light as invariably illuminates Tissot's scenes of the Christ-life on earth. The intuition from beyond, the sense of a revelation, the moment of ecstasy, or anything approaching it, are wanting. Yet these were by no means lacking to the thought of the last century. Stray instances of the mystical spirit, hints and gleams of some subconscious feeling or experience alien alike from simple imagination and simple spirituality are scattered up and down the writings of the time and proceed from minds of very different temperament. What was it that, more than anything else, inspired and supported such a mood, in which a strange illumination, an expectation, a yearning seemed to seek expression? It was the work of the Poets. The Victorian era was a kind of Golden Age of English poetry, and among the throng of the singers of the age, two or three stand out as not merely poets, but seers, with the burden of a message to the world that was, again and again, a definite and exquisite reiteration of one aspect or another of ancient mystical doctrine. Yet what they attained of vision or experience they reached, as Miss Underhill remarks, not by any exact and conscious pursuit of the mystical way, or ascent of its grades: rather, they seemed to dwell naturally in the stage of Illumination.[1] Nearly every member of the great choir of poets of the nineteenth century contributed to keep alive the mystical spirit in England. One might instance the school of pre-Raphaelite poetry, notably the poems of the Rossettis, as evoking the spirit of the Past—of an imaginative Past, at any rate, which does not die with the passage of history— and opening the soul's casement to " faery lands forlorn ". Or one might dwell on the splendid joy in humanity, and in God in humanity, of thinkers such as Browning and

[1] E. Underhill: *Mysticism*, p. 286. A " purged and heightened consciousness " is not the same thing as the process of the Purgative stage on the *Scala Perfectionis*, as Catholic Mystical Theology understood the term.

Kingsley—it is not necessary to place them in the same poetic category—or again on the sense, a true instinct, of loss, of negation, " of the darkness which lies coiled in the abyss of Deity itself, the eternal Nay, which dwells even in the heart of the everlasting Yea ",[1] which finds expression in the poems of Arnold and Clough ; or yet again on the self-absorption in Nature, the well-nigh pure Pantheism, of T. E. Brown, a poet who yet waits to come fully to his own.   These all reflected certain instinctive yearnings, cravings, or triumphant spiritual discoveries of their times, and they all have touches of that psychic intuition or vision which proclaims the mystic.   There are, however, four poets especially who deserve our attention in this connexion. For one thing, all four were naturally, through and through, mystics of a high order ;   for another, all four gave, with whatever qualifications the critic may discern in their writings, unequivocal outward assent to the Christian Revelation.   These four were Coleridge, Wordsworth, Tennyson, and Coventry Patmore.

(1) S. T. Coleridge, who, as a boy at Christ's Hospital, talked—he was always a marvellous talker—in Charles Lamb's hearing of Plotinus and Iamblichus, and, later, found that Tauler, Fox, Behmen, and Law " contributed to keep alive the heart in the head ", exhibited the philosophical side of Mysticism.   " Every man ", he was wont to say, with no doubt as to his own standpoint, " is born either a Platonist or an Aristotelian ", and he made it his work to spread the principles of transcendentalism in this country.   He discriminated sharply between the pure Reason and the Understanding.   The latter is the lower organ that takes notes of and makes its deductions from facts ; the former is a Divine gift of intuition, whereby we apprehend spiritual truth.   In his doctrine as to Reason,

---

[1] R. H. Coats : *Types of English Piety*, p. 183.

itself a beam of the Uncreated Light, Coleridge showed
affinities to the Cambridge Platonists, and to the earlier
schools which discoursed of the Fünkelein, or Divine Spark
in the soul. In some ways he anticipated certain parts of
the Modernist teaching of to-day, as when he depreciates
the importance of facts as facts, and puts the principles
and truths first which the facts illustrate. Granted, indeed,
some universal and eternal Truth, and there must be facts
in time and space to illustrate it. So he arrived at Christianity. Not that he did not, all his days, subscribe to the
orthodox faith, indeed, his devotion to the Church of England was such that he wished it memorialized on his grave-
stone. But the orthodox faith gradually commended itself
to him because he found that the dogmas of the Trinity, of
the Incarnation, and of the Redemption exactly suited the
needs of human nature and were in correspondence with
the philosophic reason. "Christian evidences" troubled
him not one way or the other. There was indeed a time
when he could exclaim, "The article of faith which is nearest
to my heart—the pure fountain of all my moral and religious feelings and comforts—is the absolute Impersonality
of the Deity";[1] but he advanced from this to a stage in
which (in 1834) he talked of Holy Baptism and the Eucharist
as being—not parts of, but—Christianity itself; yet this
again was probably an outcome of his disregard for the
historic facts behind these Sacraments. Thus far would he
go and no farther. Prayer with him was not a vocal act,
but a "sense of supplication", and his whole heart expresses itself in the lines in "Religious Musings"—

> "From Hope and firmer Faith to perfect Love
> Attracted and absorbed ; and centred there
> God only to behold, and know, and feel,
> Till by exclusive consciousness of God
> All self-annihilated the soul shall make
> God its identity ; God all in all".

[1] *Letters*, December 5, 1803.

(2) Wordsworth's poetry "ˌis ", says Dr. Inge, " the best example in literature of a revelation through impersonal external nature ".[1] Of that revelation at its highest, " the serene and blessed mood ", we have already spoken in introducing the subject of Mysticism. Here we must note that there are two facts in Wordsworth's attitude towards Nature and his own nature which make that experience something far more important than any mere passing rapture of the imagination, caught lightly from some sudden appreciation of beauty and as lightly lost. No ; he alludes to it again and again ; it is with him " the highest bliss that flesh can know ", it is the feeling " that we are greater than we know ", the consciousness of what we really are, " habitually infused through every image and through every thought, and all affections by communion raised from earth to heaven, from human to divine ". But this fine exaltation of spirit was only attained because, to Wordsworth's mind, Nature was neither a sphere, as with the medieval ascetics, somehow inimical, somehow dangerous to the single-hearted searcher after God, nor again, a raree-show of curiosities and enigmas out of which the quaintest conceits and the most far-fetched analogies could be spun. The great reign and persuasion of Natural Law had begun in contemporary thought, and Wordsworth's whole disposition, sane, moderate, contemplative, fitted him to be at first the disciple of this trend of teaching, and then, after overcoming the temptation to yield without reservation to its apparently inexorable logic, to become the prophet of a new Gospel. Nature, to his intention, was the store-house of laws whence we can deduce, not accidental likeness to this or that doctrine of the Faith, but the very truths of God's existence. Wordsworth was always, as his " Ecclesiastical Sonnets " show, a devout Churchman ; but his study of Nature was his true worship and his nearest means

[1] *English Mystics*, p. 185.

of access to God. There, rather than in ceremonial, lay the vital symbolism, the real and enduring analogies to things Divine.

But the contemplation of Nature was not the only important factor in Wordsworth's mysticism. By itself it would never have brought him his rapturous moods. It must be a contemplation interfused with sympathy. The mind that observes must be in tune with what is observed. We spoke of Wordsworth's attitude towards his own nature as well as towards Nature in general. It is a fact of the first import if we would rightly apprehend his powers as poet and mystic alike. In Wordsworth's case, and in the noblest sense, " the eye brought with it what it saw". More nearly than any other modern mystic, Wordsworth passed deliberately through a " Purgative " stage. He beat down with steady purpose his natural passions, and with them ambition, love of money, and any tendencies which he detected towards unquiet of mind, hatred and vengeance. It is this long struggle of self-discipline, the fact that " there is volition and self-government in every line of his poetry ", and that " he contests the ground inch by inch with all despondent and indolent humours, and often, too, with movements of inconsiderate and wasteful joy ",[1] that lead us to consider with homage and awe such experiences as that at Tintern Abbey. Wordsworth's teaching, in fine, is that it is not through Nature alone, or through the soul alone, that God finds His means of speech, but through the union of the disciplined soul with Nature. It was from this contact, calmly, reverently, and persistently achieved, that deeper mystical knowledge came, the discernment of " Being spread, O'er all that moves and all that seemeth still ", the " sense sublime of something . . . interfused, Whose dwelling is the light of setting suns, And the round ocean and the living air, And the blue sky, and

[1] Hutton : *Essays*, p. 81.

in the mind of man ".[1]   It is significant, but to the student of Mysticism not unexpected, that with this sense of a personality pervading all things came an ever deeper realization of the poet's own personality, a " sinking into self from thought to thought ".

(3) The work of Tennyson on Nature—supremely great as Wordsworth's, but on other lines—differs from his in two very definite respects.   For one thing, instead of dealing in generalizations, it is exquisite and minute in observation —more, perhaps, the work of the poet with notebook in hand.   For another thing, if we make a few exceptions such as " The Higher Pantheism ", and " Flower in the Crannied Wall ", Tennyson viewed Nature lovingly, unerringly, but did not draw his essential vision of God thence. He never took into his gaze, as did Wordsworth, the world of Nature as a whole, graciously and blandly.   He felt, for example, antipathies.   A whole catena of quotations could be made, for example, to show that Tennyson had a certain dread of and aversion from the Sea.   It was to him the symbol of Change, of Doubt, of merciless Force, of the inexplicable Wrath that coils beneath or peers out from the fair external shows of Nature.   But it must be remembered that Tennyson's was a soul sensitive to every breath of opinion, to every sound of challenging creeds which filled the troubled air of the nineteenth century.   It was like an aeolian harp in its reception and resonance of these various motions and cries of the spirit.[2]   Therefore, to Tennyson, the problem of the world as a revelation of God

---

[1] *Tintern Abbey*, 95–99.

[2] One may instance " Sir Galahad ", " St. Agnes' Eve ", " The Holy Grail ", as reflecting the pre-Raphaelite inspiration ; " Enoch Arden " as a touch of the humanistic spirit of Browning ; while the general restlessness and doubt of his age are again and again expressed in the poems of one who did not fail, on a direct challenge, to profess his unwavering inner faith as a Christian.

was far more complex than to Wordsworth. He, like Wordsworth, could accept the belief in a law operative and faultlessly operative everywhere, but his heart echoed the distrust of his day ; Was that law always and flawlessly good ? What of Nature " red in tooth and claw " ? Therefore Tennyson widened his outlook infinitely, and, whilst never ceasing to be the keen and lover-like observer of Nature, became, where his revelation of God was concerned, the cosmic poet and seer. Yes ; even seer ; for, to take an example, the Evolutionary teaching of " In Memoriam " preceded the appearance of Darwin's great book by about nine years. It was a special gift of his poetry in fact, to receive, idealize, even at times to anticipate, the truths of modern Science—" De Profundis ", the " In Memoriam ", the " Ancient Sage ", and many others of his later and, unfortunately, less read poems witness to this strange power. His contribution to Mysticism, his claim to be considered a mystic, lies, however, elsewhere. The sense of the vastness of all things, their complexity, their entanglements, their seeming self-contradictions grew on him with the years, but also the conviction of a Purpose, the End " to which the whole creation moves". This Purpose in creation he interpreted in terms of Personality. Not only did he cling unfalteringly, if at times as it were almost breathlessly, to his belief in the indissolubility and identity through all change of human personality,[1] but it was in the deepest realizations of his own personality that there came on him that Trance or Ecstasy which he described thrice—in the " In Memoriam ", in " The Ancient Sage ", his own creed, and in the conversation reported in the " Memoir " by his son. Perhaps the last will serve our purpose best for quotation.[2]

[1] As at the close of his fine poem " *Vastness* ". His belief in immortality, survival of individual identity and memory, was quickened to passion by the loss of his friend Hallam.

[2] *Memoir*, vol. I. p. 320 ; cf. for the experience *In Memoriam*

" (There is) a kind of waking trance I have often had, quite from boyhood, when I have been all alone. This has generally come to me through repeating my own name two or three times to myself silently, till all at once, out of the intensity of the consciousness of individuality, the individual itself seemed to dissolve and fade away into boundless being ; and this not a confused state, but the clearest of the clearest, and the surest of the surest . . . utterly beyond words, where death was an almost laughable impossibility ". It was doubtless the repetition of this experience which communicated to several of Tennyson's later poems that strangely psychic touch which continually seems to report of " a world that is not ours ", and is as repellent to some readers as it is fascinating to others.

Now it is remarkable that, despite his overpowering sense of personality, Tennyson twice hints, in the records of his trance-experience, at a possible loss of individuality which should lead to a fuller state of being. Thus, the words which immediately follow the prose quotation above run, " the loss of personality (if so it were) seeming no extinction, but the only true life " ; and in the " Ancient Sage " he speaks of " loss of self ", and " thro' loss of self, the gain of such large life as match'd with ours were Sun to spark ". The clue to this enigma of loss, which is yet a gain, is supplied by the mysticism of Coventry Patmore.

(4) It is to be feared that Patmore's beautiful poetry, and almost equally beautiful prose still goes half unread, and a great deal more than half unappreciated. Just as there are those who, perhaps influenced by the tradition of Fitzgerald's criticism, lay down their Tennyson at the

---

XCV. where the prelude of the perfect calm noted by Plotinus is fully, and, no doubt, with regard to its import, unconsciously, described. In " The Ancient Sage " we have the same process as is recorded in the " *Memoir* ", until " the mortal limit of the Self was loosed, and past into the Nameless ".

end of the " Idylls ", so there are many who only know,
and think it fashionable to despise, Patmore as the author
of " The Angel in the House ". How even they can miss
the incomparable felicity of diction, and the almost uncanny
psychological power of the Preludes and Epilogues which
break the—let us confess—rather ambling narrative of that
poem, it is difficult to conjecture. Anyhow, Patmore was,
in the earlier part of his life, by deliberate and indomitable
resolve, the lyrist, as everyone knows, of earthly love, the
love that completes itself in nuptial bliss. Even of this
period and of this poem, Mrs. Meynell writes, " This laureate
of the tea-table . . . is in his heart the most arrogant and
visionary of mystics ". But there was much more to come.
Patmore gradually saw in the mysteries of earthly love a
living type and symbol of the Divine Union with the soul.
He interpreted love as " the mystic craving of the great to
become the love-captive of the small, while the small has
a corresponding thirst for the enthralment of the great ".
This metaphor, as Mr. Gosse, his friend and commentator,
explains, " he expanded in a great variety of images and
reflections, where the Deity was represented as masculine
and active, and the human soul as feminine and passive ". [1]
God with him was Thesis, Manhood Antithesis, and the
Neuter " is not the absence of the life of sex, but its fulfil-
ment and power ". It is in the poems of the " Unknown
Eros " and especially in the three Psyche odes that this idea
is worked out, and in them " Patmore's genius may be said
to have culminated. If we wish to study his metaphysical
poetry at its most elaborate height of subtlety and symbol,
we should pass at once to these poems. . . . Their subject
must always remove them from popular approval " (it did,
of course, in Patmore's own day), " but it is to be conceived
that a small circle, of those who comprehend, may con-

[1] Edmund Gosse: *Coventry Patmore,* p. 237.

tinue as time goes on, to contemplate them with an almost idolatrous admiration ". [1]

When Patmore dealt, in this "spirit of profound and daring speculation, with the mysteries of religion ", he was, of course, as he was fond of declaring, only reiterating what several Fathers of the Church had hinted, and certain schools of medieval Mysticism had taught. He was a devout, if at times rather irresponsible, Roman Catholic, had made an exhaustive study of Thomas Aquinas, and found extreme delight in the works of St. John of the Cross. His definition of love, applied to the Divine Love, led him directly to the doctrine of that ineffable Self-limitation of God, in His delight to be with the sons of men, which is expressed by the dogma of the Incarnation. Indeed, Patmore shews the mystical reaction from Wordsworth's craving for the Infinite as the true home of the soul, and Tennyson's oft-repeated and fascinated exultation in the "boundless inward in the atom, boundless outward in the Whole ", by emphasizing in characteristic fashion his recoil from such conceptions of Divine revelation. "'The Infinite !' Word horrible ! at feud with life ", he cries, and declares that "but for compulsion of strong grace, The pebble in the road Would straight explode ". And again, "Ah ! who can express

> How full of bonds and simpleness
> Is God,
> How narrow is He,
> And how the wide, waste field of possibility
> Is only trod
> Straight to His homestead in the human heart ".

To him the human body is the "wall of infinitude ", the "little, sequester'd pleasure house, For God and for His Spouse ".

Nor was such language mere poetic theory. This man,

[1] *Ib.* p. 242.

who went to his yearly Retreats with as much jubilation as schoolboys go for their holidays, and who was at last laid to rest "in the rough habit of the stern Franciscan order", knew in his later years an intimate communion with his God which had in it the mingled sweetness and terror which all saints of the mystical order have known, and of which Francis Thompson hints in his commemorative ode on the poet. Patmore did in fact, in entirety, and in utter submission of his strong will, what the earlier mystics had shrunk from doing, he transferred the love-imagery used in the Holy Scriptures, and written plain before him in the facts of human nuptials, from their application to the love " betwixt Christ and His Church " to a union be-twixt God and the individual soul. In the resolute and entranced energy with which he pursued his tremendous ideal, and in the writings—some of the most daring were destroyed—which he left to commemorate it, he remains one of the greatest of mystics.

Here, perhaps, we may fitly bring to a close our survey of the history of Mysticism within the bounds and sanctions of the Christian Faith. It is not necessary to recapitulate the essentials of what constitutes Mysticism ; that was attempted at the outset, and the subsequent task has been to show how the intense, ever-renewed, never completely satisfied craving of the soul for " God Who is our Home ", though not confined to Christianity, has found, despite its emphasis on Immediacy of communion and its strong indi-vidualistic trend, its happiest and native *terrain* in the Christian Church. Christ and Plotinus really met, though centuries parted their earthly lives ; and whilst history would affirm that the thought of Plotinus left an ineffable imprint on Christian doctrine, yet the apparent victory was only, in the long run, part of that great absorptive faculty which Christianity shews for all that is good, strong, and enduring in outside thought or character. The name of Plotinus, to many a true mystic, has become vague and shadowy, the Name of Christ is a reality. " When one wants most to be mystical, and most to benefit by such a spirit, one would still . . . turn to the simple presentation of it in Galilee ". [1]

It is a truism that Mysticism is in the air at the present day. But it is a Mysticism that mostly does not decisively venture beyond its natural Theism, and remains wavering on the verge of the Illuminative stage. It has glimpses of God and longs for Him. Now God is approached from various accesses, and one of His aspects is Truth. It is characteristic of the vague Mysticism of our time that it connects itself, more often than not, with a keen criticism of Christian dogma, or rather of the historicity of the facts on which certain dogmas are founded. This is at once a warning and an encouragement to the Christian Church. Mysticism, though not all the life of religion, which has many factors and activities incidental to its progress, is of the essence of spiritual vitality. It can be alienated, or ostracized from, or starved out of a Church. It can be warped in its growth. Modernism is seeking to prevent the recurrence of any such catastrophe at the present day by its effort to show that the facts of the Gospel history, while not to be reckoned as of prior importance to the inner and external truths which they illustrate, yet are congruous to them and, in some mysterious way, fit in with the needs of man's nature. If it can accomplish this task, well and good ; but if it makes the one step further in its Christian Pragmatism and hints that the faith in man—his will to believe—engendered the records of the facts, and justified those records as symbols merely, then Modernism will fail to satisfy that thirst for the very truth which makes Mysticism something more than Imagination, and will itself have

[1] Dr. H. P. Waddell : *Thoughts on Modern Mysticism*, p. 241.

to struggle for foothold within the Church which must always shelter and sustain in his spiritual life the " plain man " as such. On the other hand, there is encouragement in the outlook. Such an atmosphere of Mysticism as is around us now prophesies for the Christian Society, if the Church can be patient and wise, learn and receive as well as dictate and dogmatize, a great accession of strength and insight. For Mysticism, with its tradition of quietude, its detachment from the world, its eagerness for " God only " is that quality precisely of which the Catholic Church must always avail itself, and which it has the power and commission to train and discipline. The return which Mysticism has always made is inestimable. It is that holiness, which, to use the words of Lord Morley, " is not the same as duty, still less is it the same as religious belief. It is a name for an inner grace of Nature, an instinct of the soul, by which, though knowing of earthly appetites and worldly passions, the spirit, purifying itself of these, and independent of all reason, argument, and the fierce struggles of the will, dwells in living, patient, and confident communion with the unseen Good ".

BIBLIOGRAPHY

I. The following works are suggested as useful to a general introduction to the study of Mysticism.

Dr. W. R. Inge, Dean of St. Paul's	Christian Mysticism (Bampton Lectures).
	Studies of English Mystics.
Dr. Rufus M. Jones . .	Studies in Mystical Religion.
Prof. E. Lehmann . .	Mysticism in Heathendom and Christendom (translated by G. M. G. Hunt).
R. A. Vaughan . .	Hours with the Mystics.
Baron F. von Hügel. .	The Mystical Element of Religion, 2 vols.
William James. . .	The Varieties of Religious Experience (Gifford Lectures).
Dr. H. B. Workman .	Christian Thought to the Reformation, esp. chs. ii., vi.–ix.
E. Underhill . . .	Mysticism.
A. B. Sharpe . . .	Mysticism : Its True Nature and Value.

Lesser books of a general type are :

W. Major Scott . .	Aspects of Christian Mysticism.
E. C. Gregory . . .	An Introduction to Christian Mysticism.
Dr. W. R. Inge . .	Light, Life and Love. Selections from the German Mystics (Library of Devotion).

II. The books that follow are concerned with individual mystics, or schools of Mysticism. Editions of such classics as readily suggest themselves and are easily procurable, e.g., St. Augustine's " Confessions ", the " Imitatio ", the " Pilgrim's Progress ", Fox's " Diary ", the " Christian Year ", are not included. The same is true as regards works of and on the English poets of the seventeenth to nineteenth centuries, cited in the following pages.

The Alexandrines . .	The Christian Platonists of Alexandria (Bampton Lectures), by Dr. C. Bigg.

Neo-Platonism . . .	Neoplatonism (Chief Ancient Philosophies Series), by Dr. C. Bigg.
Plotinus	Select Works of Plotinus (transl. by Thomas Taylor).
St. Bernard . .	The Life and Times of St. Bernard, by J. Cotter Morison.
St. Francis of Assisi .	The Little Flowers of St. Francis (transl. by T. W. Arnold. Temple Classics).
Theologia Germanica .	Edited by Susanna Winkworth. Preface by C. Kingsley (Golden Treasury Series).
Tauler	History and Life of the Rev. Doctor J. Tauler, with twenty-five of his sermons transl. by Susanna Winkworth. Preface by C. Kingsley.
	The Inner Way, thirty-six sermons (transl. with Introduction by Rev. A. W. Hutton. Library of Devotion).
Thomas à Kempis . .	Thomas à Kempis: His Age and Book, by J. E. G. de Montmorency.
	Thomas à Kempis and the Brothers of the Common Life, by S. Kettlewell.
	Hidden Saints, by G. Harvey Gem.
Richard Rolle of Hampole	Works of Richard Rolle of Hampole and his followers. Edited by C. Horstman, 2 vols. (Library of Early English Writers).
Julian of Norwich . .	Revelations of Divine Love. Edited by Grace Warrack.
Walter Hylton . . .	The Scale of Perfection. Edited, with an Introduction, by Rev. J. B. Dalgairns.
St. Catherine of Siena .	The Dialogue of Catherine of Siena, transl. with an Introduction, by Algar Thorold.
	St. Catherine of Siena, by Edmund Gardner.
	St. Catherine of Siena as seen in her Letters. Edited by Vida Scudder.

Saint Teresa . . . Santa Teresa, by G. Cunninghame Graham, 2 vols.

Life of St. Teresa, written by Herself, transl. by D. Lewis, with Introduction by B. Zimmerman.

The Interior Castle : transl. by the Benedictines of Stanbrook Abbey, with Notes by B. Zimmerman.

St. John of the Cross . Life of St. John of the Cross, by D. Lewis.

The Ascent of Mt. Carmel ;

The Dark Night of the Soul ; both transl. by D. Lewis with Introduction by B. Zimmerman.

M. de Molinos . . . The Spiritual Guide. (Edited with Introduction by C. Lyttelton. Library of Devotion).

St. Francis de Sales . Introduction to the Devout Life (transl. with Notes by Rev. T. Barns. Library of Devotion).

Mme. Bourignan . . Antoinette Bourignan, Quietist, by A. R. MacEwen.

Mme. Guyon . . . Life, Religious Opinions and Experience of Mme. Guyon, by T. C. Upham, with Introduction by W. R. Inge.

A Short and Easy Method of Prayer (Heart and Life Booklets).

Sir T. Browne . . . Religio Medici and Urn Burial (Temple Classics).

T. Traherne . . . Centuries of Meditations. Edited by Bertram Dobell.

John Bunyan . . . Grace Abounding to the Chief of Sinners (R.T.S.).

George Fox . . . George Fox, by T. Hodgkin, D.C.L. (Leaders of Religion).

Cambridge Platonists . Men of Latitude in the Seventeenth Century, by E. A. George.

J. Behmen . . . The Life and Doctrines of Jacob Boehme, by F. Hartmann.

The Signature of All Things with other Writings. Introduction by Clifford Bax (Everyman's Library).

Wm. Law   .   .   .   Law, Nonjuror and Mystic, by Canon J. H. Overton.

The Liberal and Mystical Writings of W. Law. Edited by W. Scott Palmer.

Coventry Patmore   .   .   The Rod, The Root, and the Flower.

One or two notes may be added to the foregoing, and necessarily partial, selection of books. Fr. Sharpe's work on Mysticism contains a translation of the " Mystical Theology " of Dionysius the Areopagite. Baron von Hügel makes St. Catherine of Genoa his text. Professor R. Jones' " Studies " gives an admirable account of the movement of the " Friends of God ", and throws much light on mystical thought of the seventeenth century. Barclay's " Inner Life of the Religious Societies of the Commonwealth " and Mr. L. H. Berens' " The Digger Movement in the Days of the Commonwealth " should be consulted on the same subject. Isaak Walton's exquisite " Lives " are, of course, indispensable to those who would understand the life of the English Church of the period, and Professor Dowden's " Puritan and Anglican " selects for sympathetic criticism what was best and lasting in the religious thought on both sides in the great duel of that century. Miss Stephens' " Quaker Strongholds " is an attractive presentment of the doctrine of the " Inner Light ". With regard to certain subjects more or less connected with Mysticism, Mr. A. E. Waite's works on " The Holy Graal " and " Studies in Mysticism ", though marred by preciosities of style, are well worth examination. The reader anxious for further information is referred to the excellent and well-nigh exhaustive Bibliography appended to Miss Underhill's book, " Mysticism ".

GENERAL INDEX

Abelard, Peter, 103

Affective faculty, The, 110

Albertus Magnus, 104, 107, 109, 111, 119, 123

Alcantara, St Peter of, 163, 166

Alexandria, 53, 62, 63 ; Catechetical School of, 54

Alexandria, St Clement of, 19, 20, 40, 52, 53–58, 62, 79 ; the "Stromateis" and "The Pedagogue", 54 ; his use of Mystery-terms, 55–56 ; his idea of "salvation", 56 ; doctrine of the Apathy, 62, 93

Alexandrianism, 51–60, 61–63 ; its merits and defects, 60

Allegories, Rulman Merswin's, 131 ; John Bunyan's, 7, 219,221

Allegorism, 7, 39, 40, 59, 102, 108, 221 ; compared with Symbolism, 39

Amalric of Bena, 98 note, 104, 107

Amelius, 77

Ammonius Saccas, 63, 65, 77

Analysis, 57

Analogy or Correspondence, Theory of, 243, 244

Anchorites, 145, 146–147

"Ancren Riwle", The, 147

Angela of Foligno, 144

Antithesis, The Law of, 237, 239

Antithesis, and Synthesis, Law of Thesis, 238, 259

Antoine Yvan, 13

Antoinette Bourignan, 175

Apathy, The, 62, 68 and note, 93

Aquinas, St Thomas, 89, 104, 107, 109, 119, 123, 260

Aristotle, first read in the West in Latin translations, 105 note

Arminianism opposed by George Fox, 227

Arnold, Mathew, 46, 252

Ascent, Stages of mystical, 18–20, 84, 135, 140, 160

Asceticism, 16, 18, 127–128

Assisi, St. Francis of, see Francis

Attraction and Diffusion, The Law of, 237–238

Augustine, St., 15, 19, 43, 61, 71, 72, 76, 78–79, 80–87, 93, 119 ; as a psychologist, 81 ; his early Manicheeism and Neo-Platonism, 81–82 ; his conversion, 83 ; his psychic faculty, 83 ; his insistence on Love rather than Knowledge in the approach to God, 84–85 ; Augustine and Monnica, 85–87

"Aurora", The, of Jacob Behmen, 232

Autobiography, Suso's, 127–129

Avignon, Papal Court at, 154, 155 ; St. Catherine of Siena's visit to, 156

"Babylonish Captivity", The, 154–156

269

INDEX OF MYSTICS AND MYSTICAL GROUPS